Connecting

with Parents in the Early Years

Jean Mendoza
Lilian G. Katz
Anne S. Robertson
Dianne Rothenberg

Early Childhood and Parenting (ECAP) Collaborative
College of Education
University of Illinois at Urbana-Champaign

December 2003

Connecting with Parents in the Early Years

by Jean Mendoza, Lilian G. Katz, Anne S. Robertson, & Dianne Rothenberg

Published by:

University of Illinois at Urbana-Champaign
College of Education
Early Childhood and Parenting Collaborative
Children's Research Center
51 Gerty Drive
Champaign, IL 61820-7469

ISBN: 0-9710468-1-6

This literature review has been funded at least in part with Federal funds from the U.S. Department of Education, Office of Educational Research and Improvement, under contract number ED-99-CO-0020. The content of this literature review does not necessarily reflect the views or policies of the U.S. Department of Education, nor does mention of trade names, commercial products, or organizations imply endorsement by the U.S. Government. The literature review was modified for inclusion in this publication to accommodate length and topical considerations.

Contents

Chapter 1: Connecting with Parents: An Introduction .... Page 1

Chapter 2: Overview of School Readiness and Vulnerability in Families .... Page 9

Chapter 3: Overview of Programs Serving Young Children and Their Families .... Page 21

Chapter 4: Communication and the Exchange of Information .... Page 37

Chapter 5: Relationships between Parents and Programs .... Page 55

Chapter 6: Emerging Issues in Connecting with Parents about School Readiness .... Page 75

Chapter 7: Connecting the Threads .... Page 99

Chapter 8: References .... Page 117

Appendix

Relations between Families and Early Childhood Programs .... Page 141
    Douglas R. Powell
    Symposium Response

Respecting the Voices of Parents: How the Spirit of Excellence Parent .... Page 157
Empowerment Project Connects with African American Parents
    Evelyn K. Moore and Oscar A. Barbarin
    Symposium Response

Connecting with Parents: The AVANCE Experience .... Page 171
    Gloria G. Rodriguez
    Symposium Response

Parent Panel .... Page 191

Closing Panel: Key Issues for Early Childhood Programs .... Page 199

Comments on Search Strategies Used .... Page 203

Tentative Topics for Proposed Educational Materials .... Page 205

Symposium Participants .... Page 207

Connecting with Parents:
An Introduction

1

Defining the Topic

Parents and the wide range of people who work with families of young children have much to offer one another as they work toward the goal of ensuring that young children are ready to begin their formal schooling. Effective communication is the key to forging and maintaining relationships in which program staff and parents exchange important information and other resources that may have direct or indirect impact on the young child's school readiness.

Recognizing the importance of strengthening the capacity of early learning programs to communicate with parents, the W.K. Kellogg Foundation sponsored a symposium titled "Connecting with Parents in the Early Years" in the spring of 2003. Meeting at the University of Illinois's Allerton Conference Center, an interdisciplinary group that included parents and representatives from national organizations and early childhood programs, social work, early intervention programs, the media, universities, research institutes, and professional education programs spent three days discussing the challenges to effective communication between parents of young children and the programs that serve them. In preparation for the symposium, we provided a preliminary review of the literature on the topic and gave participants and others the opportunity to give feedback on the review through an electronic discussion list. The literature was discussed more thoroughly at the symposium itself during lively and productive sessions. Building on our initial review and feedback received before, during, and after the symposium, we produced this expanded review of the literature. Its purpose is to highlight and discuss key issues facing those who have an interest in parent-program connections: program administrators, policy makers, government agencies, researchers, and charitable foundations.

The focus in this literature review is on the years from birth to 5, which we also refer to as "the years before school"or, simply, "early childhood." (Although many definitions of early childhood include birth through age 8, our

Our purpose is to provide an interdisciplinary review of the literature related to strengthening the capacities of programs that serve families to communicate with parents of young children, with the goal of promoting children's readiness for school.

1

concern in this publication is with that portion of early childhood before kindergarten begins.) When we use the term "preschool," we mean the years from 3 to 5 specifically. Our purpose is to provide an interdisciplinary review of the literature related to strengthening the capacities of programs that serve families to communicate with parents of young children, with the goal of promoting children's readiness for school.

In addition, we consider what is known about enhancing the capacities of parents to communicate with programs that serve their children, especially those parents whose child-rearing efforts face an array of difficulties that jeopardize their children's readiness for school. Such families have been labeled "at risk" or, sometimes, "needy" or "disadvantaged." None of these terms is fully satisfactory, for a variety of reasons; in this review, we have chosen to use the term "vulnerable." We have also struggled with the concepts of "hard-to-reach" parents and "hard-to-serve" parents. We have chosen to use the phrase "hard-to-serve" parents, in most cases.

In this review, we use the term "resources" when discussing what might be provided by a program or exchanged by parents and program staff. Our concept of "resources" is drawn from several disciplines and includes information, social support, influence, money and material goods, and time.

We use the term "connecting" in the title of this review to emphasize the need for strong and effective two-way links between parents of young children and the staff of programs that serve them.

Basic Assumptions

Three basic assumptions have guided our examination of the relevant literature:

- Parents of young children are to be treated with respect at all times.
- A variety of challenges are likely to be encountered in communication efforts, particularly between program staff and parents who are considered vulnerable and hard to serve.
- Parents and program personnel have the ability to change, to learn from new information, to build on resources, and to make programmatic adjustments to encourage the healthy development of young children.

In many countries, it is both traditional and legal for program personnel to instruct a parent concerning his or her parenting behavior. Our first assumption is based on the American tradition that parents are always the primary clients of an early childhood program, and, thus, all parenting decisions are always theirs (except in cases of legally established parental failure). Although many parents could gain much from early childhood specialists that might strengthen their capacities to achieve their goals for their children, program personnel are ideally to treat parents respectfully in all contexts and on all occasions, including the parents who appear to be the most vulnerable. The fact that program providers may readily accept this assumption in theory does not make it an easy one for them to observe in actual practice. On the contrary, it presents one of the major challenges to building constructive relationships between parents and program personnel.

These challenges are explicit in our second assumption. It is clear from a variety of reports that communication between early childhood program personnel and their parent clients is easier in some cases than in others. Parents of young children are characterized by as wide a range of individual differences as any other social group. Early childhood personnel, too, differ from one another and from parents in multiple ways, including gender, race, income level, education level, sexual identity, experience with young children, culture, native language, and fluency in English. Any of these variables can complicate communication. It should also be kept in mind that *within* these groups, a wide range of individual differences in all matters related to parenting and schooling can be expected. Awareness of, and sensitivity to, these differences have to be strengthened if children are ultimately to benefit from the services rendered.

Our third assumption is that despite variations in parenting and family life, the ability to change is fundamental to the human condition. A continuing evolution of ideas and patterns of behavior within families is inevitable and occurs in part because of the normal development of a young child, as well as the life experiences of all the family members. Within the first 5 years of life, most children experience a variety of environments that may encourage or discourage their normal growth and development. One goal of educators and parents during these formative years is to facilitate and guide the process of development in a direction that will increase the child's readiness for his or her next stage of life. Reaching the goal of school readiness may require that adults adjust to new circumstances, process new information relevant to the child's healthy growth and development, and learn new methods of communication.

With these assumptions in mind, we examine the literature of several fields to find out what can be learned about building effective connections with parents, especially those with whom communication appears to be most difficult and perhaps most urgent.

Scope of the Review

Many points of entry are possible into the topic of connecting with families in the interest of their children's readiness for school. The body of theoretical and empirical literature on connections between parents and education programs is large. The literature could be categorized in terms of *types of programs* (e.g., home visiting, parenting education classes); the *age groups* served; the *content of the programs*; the *media* by which connections to parents are maintained; the *frequency of contact* between program personnel and parents; and so forth. For this review, we have chosen to group the literature into categories covering four programmatic contexts for connecting with parents:

- Programs and services for children experiencing chronic or acute illness, trauma, medical diagnoses of developmental delay or disability, or other special needs.
- Programs and services for children facing environment-related risk factors such as poverty or limited English proficiency.

Parents of young children are characterized by as wide a range of individual differences as any other social group. Early childhood personnel, too, differ from one another and from parents in multiple ways, including gender, race, income level, education level, sexual identity, experience with young children, culture, native language, and fluency in English. Any of these variables can complicate communication.

- Programs primarily serving typically developing children who do not face biological or environmental risks.
- Programs and services for children in elementary and secondary schools.

One body of literature relevant to this review is the theory and research concerning families involved in professional interventions for children who are ill, who have experienced trauma, or who demonstrate developmental delays or have disabilities (e.g., cerebral palsy or Down syndrome) or other diagnosed special needs (e.g., blindness). In such cases, the connections between program staff and parents may affect not just overall development and adaptation to society, but the child's very survival. Hospital staff, home visitors, therapists, and other intervention specialists may all be involved in a more or less comprehensive approach to working with the child. Communication between these personnel and parents may be especially intense, with a tight focus on the child's specific needs and the parents' role in helping the child reach optimal functioning. Many interventions begin during the years from birth to 5, and one frequently held goal is to enable the child to function in whatever classroom will be available and appropriate for him or her when entering school. Having a child with special needs can itself increase a family's vulnerability by adding stressors to the parents' lives. Studies of practices within early intervention programs are thus seen as relevant to the purposes of our review of research on connecting with parents, especially those considered vulnerable, for the purpose of enhancing children's readiness for school.

Another set of studies germane to this literature review concerns programming for children whose development or academic success may be compromised by environmental factors. A variety of family factors and processes have been identified as increasing children's risk for failure. Living in poverty, experiencing welfare dependence, being exposed to domestic violence, having a parent suffering from drug abuse, being placed outside the nuclear family, having a single parent, having a mother who has never married, and having a parent who has not completed high school are all considered sources of potential risk to young children and their families. The notion of risk in children is closely related to the concept of vulnerability in families, which is discussed in more detail in the next chapter. Some programs for these children are oriented toward prevention of future difficulties. Others are intended to compensate for whatever deficits the child may experience because of environmental risk factors in the family. Such programs provide interventions to help children in vulnerable families "catch up" with peers whose development is considered normal and who are likely to be seen as ready for school. Parent and child alike may benefit from services offered by early childhood programming geared toward their needs. Our review examines the theoretical and empirical literature on programs for such children because, although the parents face a variety of stressors that create barriers to optimal involvement in their children's education, this involvement may be critical in enhancing the child's readiness for formal schooling.

A third set of studies relevant to our review examines connections between program staff and parents of young children when the emphasis is on

Many interventions begin during the years from birth to 5, and one frequently held goal is to enable the child to function in whatever classroom will be available and appropriate for him or her when entering school.

typically developing children who are not seen as vulnerable or having special needs. Although this literature is not necessarily directly related to children's readiness for school, it does consider some of the types of connections that are possible between programs and parents of young children.

The literature on parent-school relationships in kindergarten through grade 12 is our fourth source for this literature review. We are aware of potentially important distinctions between the relationships that early childhood program personnel develop with parents of young children and the relationships that elementary school personnel develop with the parents of older children. Children's relative immaturity in the years before school compared with school-age children is likely to be linked to greater intensity in the parent-child relationship, which can, in turn, lead to greater intensity in parent-staff relationships. In addition, programs for preschoolers have historically been less bureaucratic and regulation-bound than schools for older children. Less regulation may provide opportunities for a wider range of connections than may be characteristic of the relationships between parents and educators in K-12 schools. On the other hand, K-12 school regulations and budgets may allow for more comprehensive parent involvement efforts than are possible in many early childhood programs. It seems safe to say that concepts gleaned from the K-12 parent-school literature may further our understanding of the ways programs might connect with parents of younger children to encourage school readiness.

Selection of the Literature

Because the issue of communication with parents of young children is interdisciplinary—affecting not only educators but health care providers, social service providers, information providers, and family support professionals—documents reviewed were selected from seven different databases: ERIC, the largest education database; Social Work Abstracts; CINAHL, a nursing and allied health database; Wilson Social Sciences Abstracts; psycINFO, a database of psychology research; MEDLINE, a medical database; and LISA, a library and information science database. All searches were fine-tuned to focus on issues related to communicating with parents. (See the Appendix for a detailed description of the search strategies used.) In addition, we identified and retrieved other relevant documents cited within selected documents. Suggestions for additional resources were also received from participants in an electronic discussion group related to the symposium and from symposium participants.

We soon found that theory in several fields was useful to our discussion; indeed, some theoretical work became essential for its ability to provide new perspectives on old issues regarding communication between parents of young children and the programs that serve them. Theoretical works were selected based upon their apparent influence in a given field and their potential to contribute to the discussion of program-parent connections.

We also reviewed research reports with attention to the issues of design, reliability, and validity. The current focus within the U.S. Department of

Education on evidence-based education emphasizes the use of empirical research that involves the application of rigorous, systematic, and objective procedures to research questions (Whitehurst, n.d.).

Whitehurst (n.d.) and others have identified "levels of evidence" that practitioners may take into account as they evaluate research upon which to base their own practice, choose curricula, or select educational interventions. These levels, from most rigorous to least rigorous, are as follows:

- *Randomized trials:* Randomized trails randomly assign children to two or more conditions in a study, with before and after (pre- and post-) testing; they are sometimes referred to as the "gold standard" of research. A randomized trial is the only type of research that can show a causal relationship between a variable and a particular outcome.
- *Quasi-experimental studies*, including before and after testing: These studies use nonrandom assignment of children to various conditions for ethical or practical reasons and include pre- and post-testing of all children in the study.
- *Correlational studies with statistical controls:* These studies examine the degree of association between two variables using one randomly selected sample group; although some correlational studies are useful in prediction (i.e., the higher the correlation between two variables, the more accurate the prediction), they cannot be used to infer or determine causal relationships. Statistical techniques are used to measure the association.
- *Correlational studies without statistical controls:* These studies examine the degree of association between two variables but cannot determine causality and do not make use of statistical techniques to measure the association between variables.
- *Case studies:* These studies obtain detailed information about an individual to contribute to an understanding of general principles of behavior; findings from single case studies cannot be generalized to whole populations.

The Department of Education's Institute of Education Sciences recently established the What Works Clearinghouse (WWC) to disseminate evidence about what educational interventions have been scientifically demonstrated to work. According to the criteria and standards to be satisfied by the What Works Clearinghouse, interventions (i.e., a program, product, practice, or policy) must scientifically demonstrate beneficial causal improvements in the outcomes of the interventions studied. Close examination of the WWC criteria suggests that the body of available research relevant to our concern for "connecting with families" would rarely, if ever, meet WWC's stringent standards. Indeed, a number of the available studies focused not on measurable outcomes of interventions but on qualitative aspects of parent-staff interactions. (For the complete text of the WWC criteria and standards, please see What Works Clearinghouse, 2003.)

Throughout our review of the existing research, we paid close attention to those studies that would be considered the most rigorous, based on the criteria defined by Whitehurst and the WWC. However, on the topic of relationships between parents of young children and the programs that serve them, a limited number of studies are available that use experimental, quasi-experimental, or correlational designs. A number of factors may account for the paucity of such research. The complexity of communication processes and the fact that communication permeates every aspect of interaction between parents and program personnel create a considerable number of challenges for those who seek to isolate variables and outcomes in the interest of finding causation. Furthermore, the processes by which change occurs in families are not well understood and appear to be multifaceted and closely interrelated. The relative lack of experimental studies in this area may be related to the difficulty of isolating change-related variables to determine whether (and how) specific program activities or staff behaviors actually help bring about change in parents' approaches to child rearing or preparing a child for school.

Questions soon arose concerning the potential usefulness of studies that did not use experimental design but nonetheless addressed important issues regarding relationships between parents and program staff. The findings of small-scale studies, qualitative studies, case studies, and ethnographies—some carried out over several years—seemed to us to raise issues worth discussing. Among these studies, we chose those that appeared to be conducted according to standards for rigorous qualitative research, including the use of "thick description," focus on clear research issues, and strong authenticity criteria (based on Guba & Lincoln, 1989). Our decision to include these studies is in line with a recent Resolution (January 2003) of the Council of the American Educational Research Association (AERA):

> There are multiple components of quality research, including well specified theory, sound problem formulation, reliance on appropriate research designs and methods, and integrity in the conduct of research and the communication of research findings. A fundamental premise of scientific inquiry is that research questions should guide the selection of inquiry methods. (AERA, 2003)

Thus, we have made the decision to include discussion of some studies that, in our view, contribute to the dialogue in a field in which facts and conclusions based on experimental evidence are exceedingly difficult to obtain or simply not available.

We begin this review with an examination in the second chapter of the concept of school readiness and a discussion of vulnerable families. In the third chapter, we examine programs developed to connect with families, especially vulnerable families, toward the goal of enhancing children's healthy growth and development during the years before school. The fourth chapter provides an overview of key terms and concepts from the literature of communication studies and information science, especially as related to interactions between parents and professionals who work with families of infants and young children. The fifth chapter examines the literature on relationships between parents and the staff of programs serving young children and their families. The sixth chapter discusses four important themes

The complexity of communication processes and the fact that communication permeates every aspect of interaction between parents and program personnel create a considerable number of challenges for those who seek to isolate variables and outcomes in the interest of finding causation.

that emerged as areas of concern regarding connections between parents of young children and the staff of programs that serve them, touching on approaches that appear to hold promise for assisting vulnerable or hard-to-serve families. In the seventh chapter, we consider some ways to ethically increase the validity of research with vulnerable parents and families in hopes that future research will incorporate more characteristics of rigorous research design. We also address the implications of the literature review for future research and development, incorporating input from participants in the Kellogg Symposium on Connecting with Parents in the Early Years.

In sum, this review of research and theory addresses the following questions:

- What is meant by school readiness?
- What are its implications for families considered "vulnerable" or "hard to serve?"
- What can communication and information science studies contribute to our understanding of effective connections between parents of young children and the staff of programs that serve them?
- What do theory and research on parent-program relationships contribute to our understanding of the ways parents and staff might connect around issues of young children's readiness for school?
- What approaches, based on research, appear most likely to assist vulnerable or hard-to-serve families?
- What are some implications for future research and practice?

Overview of School Readiness and Vulnerability in Families

2

The Concept of School Readiness

Children's readiness to participate in formal schooling has long been important to educators, parents, and policy makers in the United States. In recent decades, it has been treated with increasing urgency. Concern over school readiness was a driving force behind Head Start legislation (during the 1960s and 1970s) aimed at providing early education to compensate for the potential negative effects of living in poverty. The late 1980s and early 1990s saw a heightened interest in school readiness at the federal level. Of the education goals specified in the original "Goals 2000: Educate America Act," the first was "By the year 2000, all children in America will start school ready to learn" (National Education Goals Panel, n.d.).

Despite widespread agreement over the importance of school readiness, definitions of the concept of school readiness vary widely. Gredler (1992) points out that some view school readiness in terms of children having reached a particular age; others associate it with growth and maturation; and still others "emphasize the role of the child's experience in becoming able to learn particular tasks or subjects" (p. 7). Graue's (1993) detailed study conducted in three elementary schools suggests how conceptions of school readiness may differ among parents and staff and between schools. The meanings that participants in her study gave to readiness, Graue notes, were "locally developed and used," based not only on perspectives on children's growth and development but also on the perceived "local purpose for the kindergarten, [and] notions for what it means to be a good parent or teacher" (p. 248).

Lewit and Baker (1995) found differences between parents and teachers regarding child characteristics that they believed were important to kindergarten readiness. Analyzing data from two 1993 studies (the National Household Educational Survey [NHES] and the Kindergarten Teacher Survey on

Despite widespread agreement over the importance of school readiness, definitions of the concept of school readiness vary widely.

Student Readiness [KTSSR]), they found that the parents who were surveyed believed that academic competencies were more important to kindergarten readiness than did the teachers surveyed. Teachers tended to rate the following nonacademic child characteristics as "essential" or "very important" criteria of readiness: "physically healthy, rested, well-nourished" (96%); "communicates needs, wants, and thoughts verbally (in child's primary language)" (84%); "enthusiastic and curious in approaching new activities" (76%); "can follow directions" (60%); "is not disruptive of the class" (60%); "is sensitive to other children's feelings" (58%); and "takes turns" (55%). Teachers assigned little importance to competencies that *parents* rated as very important, such as the ability to use a pencil or paintbrush or to know the letters of the alphabet or be able to count to 20 (Lewit & Baker, 1995, p. 133). In sum, the teachers' criteria for "school readiness" emphasized children's behavior rather than their knowledge of the alphabet and numbers.

The National Education Goals Panel (n.d.) asserted that school readiness is a combination of factors related to the condition of the children and the capacities of the receiving schools to address those conditions. The first factor, the condition of the children, encompasses five domains: (1) health and physical development, (2) social and emotional development, (3) approaches to learning, (4) language development and communication, and (5) cognition and general knowledge.

The second factor, the capacities of the receiving schools (Shore, 1998), has been described in a variety of ways. An especially concise description identifies four "cornerstones" of ready schools: (1) staff members' knowledge about growth and development of typically and atypically developing children; (2) staff members' knowledge of the strengths, interests, and needs of each child; (3) staff members' knowledge of the social and cultural contexts in which each child and family lives; and (4) staff members' ability to translate developmental knowledge into developmentally appropriate practice (North Carolina School Improvement Panel, 2000, p. 11).

The view of readiness represented by this two-factor approach would require each school to assess each child extensively and carefully, while ensuring that the receiving staff had deep and wide-ranging knowledge of child development and culture. It would also entail offering resources to parents so that they could better help children gain the skills and knowledge needed for school and collaborate more effectively with the staff of the programs and schools that serve their families.

Despite lack of agreement on the meaning of readiness, Lewit and Baker (1995) suggest that the concept was fully expressed in the Goals 2000 Act as "a standard of physical, intellectual, and social development that enables children to fulfill school requirements and to assimilate a school's curriculum" (p. 129). The Act combined two historically different ideas: readiness to learn and readiness for school; although as Lewit and Baker point out, "being 'ready to learn' something may not, however, guarantee success in school" (p. 129).

Policy, research, and practice have for a number of years proceeded in line with the goal of readiness expressed in the 1994 legislation and the work of the National Education Goals Panel, despite lack of unity on the meaning of readiness. Additional shifts in definitions of school readiness can be expected as the implications of the "No Child Left Behind Act" of 2001 become clearer.

The Parent's Role in School Readiness

The parent is often referred to in such terms as "the child's first teacher" (Educate America Act of 1994) or "the one continuous force in the education of ... children from birth to adulthood" (Berger, 2000, p. 152), and in fact parents are involved in their children's education from birth, to the extent that they dedicate resources to the child in that domain (Grolnick & Slowiaczek, 1994, p. 238).

Research has focused for decades on how and what children learn at home, and on the potential effects of family factors on competencies that children need for successful adaptation to school. In the family context, children may or may not acquire fundamental skills, knowledge, dispositions, and values that are related to what formal schooling requires. The everyday tasks of parenting, adequately accomplished, provide children with several essentials for school readiness and for ongoing daily preparedness for the classroom. (For further discussion, see Connors & Epstein, 1995, p. 447.) Besides supplying nutrition, shelter, clothing, health care, and a safe environment, parents or other primary caregivers usually provide the child's first experiences with language, numeracy, social interaction, and problem solving, which help to build the child's foundation of skills and knowledge that he or she will need for school. (For a comprehensive review of research from the mid- to late 20th century on home influences on children's education, see Ryan & Adams, 1995, pp. 3-6; see also Henderson & Mapp, 2002, for a review of more recent research on the topic.)

Similarly, when young children make the transition from home to programs such as Head Start or other preschool environments, their parents may support the program's goals to a greater or lesser extent in a variety of ways. They can support the program by communicating with staff and other parents; volunteering their time; participating in leadership, decision making, and advocacy; collaborating with community resource providers in support of the program; and providing at home the resources that children need to take part in the program. (For more detailed discussions, see Connors & Epstein, 1995; Epstein, 2001, pp. 407-416; or Powell, 1989, pp. 56-64.)

Possible correlations between families' literacy-related behavior and children's literacy achievement have frequently been the focus of investigation. Contemporary research includes an experiment by Lonigan and Whitehurst (1998) with low-income children in four nonprofit subsidized child care centers. The authors reported finding mixed evidence to support their theory that children's oral language benefits when both their preschool teachers and their parents engage them in dialogic reading (a form of shared

The parent is often referred to in such terms as "the child's first teacher" (Educate America Act of 1994) or "the one continuous force in the education of ... children from birth to adulthood" (Berger, 2000, p. 152), and in fact parents are involved in their children's education from birth, to the extent that they dedicate resources to the child in that domain (Grolnick & Slowiaczek, 1994, p. 238).

reading experience). Sixty-six children participated in all aspects of the study. (For critical responses to this study, see Scher, 1998, and Coe & Shelby, 1998.)

In a longitudinal study, Hart and Risley (1995) used behavioral observations of language experiences of 42 children from three socioeconomic categories: "higher SES," "working class," and families on welfare. They found that, in the course of daily interactions, the children in the families on welfare heard approximately 620 words per hour, while children in working-class families heard 1,250 and the children in the higher SES families heard 2,150 words per hour (p. 132). The investigators also found marked differences in the amount of encouraging and discouraging feedback children received, with those in families on welfare receiving far more discouragement than encouragement, and those from higher SES families having the reverse experience (pp. 198-199). According to the authors, a statistically significant association was found between the amount of talk and either gender or race (p. 61). One implication is that children from homes where they hear fewer words enter school less prepared for literacy activities than do children from homes where they hear more words. The sample size in the Hart and Risley study was small and consisted of European American and African American families. It would be useful to apply such intensive behavioral observation and analysis to other populations: Native American families, Hispanic American families, Asian American families, and families that are functionally bilingual. A more complete picture could then be offered of home influences on early vocabulary growth across cultural groups.

Home-related effects on young children's learning in mathematics have also been reported (e.g., Starkey & Klein, 2000), although mathematics has not been as widely studied as literacy. (For further discussion of Starkey & Klein, 2000, see Chapter 3.) This situation may change in the near future. The National Institute of Child Health and Human Development recently established a program to explore the neurobiological, cognitive, linguistic, sociocultural, and instructional foundations of children's development and learning in mathematics and science (Galley, 2003).

In a recent study of 753 children between the ages of 3 and 5, Yeung and colleagues reported finding that "distinct mediating mechanisms operate on the association between income and different child outcomes" related to their school adjustment (Yeung, Linver, & Brooks-Gunn, 2002, p. 1865). Their report suggests strong support for the idea that family income affects children's cognitive development primarily through its relationship to the home environment in general, especially the provision of stimulating materials and enriching experiences. Their findings concerning children's behavior problems suggest that maternal emotional distress can be the main mediator of income effects on the child's behavior, "…[and] a stimulating home environment was indirectly related to lower behavior problems through its association with lower maternal distress and better parenting practices" (p. 1875). They conclude that family income operates on child outcomes in a variety of ways, so that programs are more likely to improve young children's cognitive achievement if they "aim to provide children with cognitively stimulating materials, increase family literacy, or encourage parental engagement in reading and stimulating outings" than if they focus only on parenting skills (p. 1876).

The idea that compensatory preschool experiences can enhance readiness for school, especially in the domains of language and cognition, has been the assumption behind such programs as Head Start, Even Start, PAT, HIPPY, and Early Head Start. Recent findings in neuroscience regarding brain development from birth to 5 appear to support this assumption. (For further discussion of findings on early brain development and their implications, see Shore, 1997; or Shonkoff & Phillips, 2000, pp. 183-217.) The contemporary research in neuroscience also directs particular attention toward the interrelationship between social-emotional development in the earliest years and subsequent adaptation to school.

Self-Regulation, Social-Emotional Development, and School Readiness

Although a considerable body of research examines the roles that parents have in fostering cognitive capacities and skills associated with school readiness, recent literature related to school readiness has emphasized two other interrelated developmental domains in which it is reasonable to assume that parents or other early caregivers have the major role. These developmental areas are the ability to regulate one's emotions, or *self-regulation* (Blair, 2002; Shonkoff & Phillips, 2000), and the development of *social-emotional competence* (Raver, 2002).

Self-Regulation and School Readiness

The term *self-regulation* is generally defined as the ability to master a wide range of tasks that enable one to adapt to one's environment. In infancy, these tasks include maintaining a normal body temperature, learning to conform to the day-night rhythm of human existence, and soothing oneself once basic needs are met. Later, self-regulation includes "developing the capacity to manage powerful emotions constructively and keep one's attention focused" (Shonkoff & Phillips, 2000, p. 93).

In a review of recent neurobiological research on very early development, Blair (2002) argues that regulation of emotions is a major dimension of school readiness, although the connections between neurological development and school adjustment per se have not yet been studied directly. He points out that self-regulatory skills underlie many behaviors and attributes associated with adjustment to school settings; children who are less distractible and whose levels of emotional intensity tend to be moderate and positive in tone "are rated by their teachers as being more teachable, and [they] achieve at higher levels academically than do children without these characteristics" (p. 112). Blair proposes several components of self-regulation related to school readiness, including (1) effortful control and (2) affective synchrony, which are described below.

Inhibitory or effortful control appears to be a major developmental achievement of the first 5 or 6 years of life (Kochanska, Murray, & Coy,

The term *self-regulation* is generally defined as the ability to master a wide range of tasks that enable one to adapt to one's environment.

1997). (For an extensive listing of similar constructs and related research, see Kochanska, Murray, & Harlan, 2000, pp. 222-223.) One significant aspect of effortful control is the ability to concentrate on completing a task in the face of distractions. Deficits in such strategic thinking abilities, according to Blair, are linked with "poor attributions of the self as learner that recursively affect the perceived utility of strategic thinking" (Blair, 2002, p. 114). In other words, if a child sees herself as not competent at planning or staying focused on a task, she is likely to act in ways that confirm that perception. The subsequent poor results of her task-related behaviors "prove" that her strategic thinking is of little use, in a pattern that feeds on itself. Such negative cycles are unlikely to be broken without outside assistance.

Research suggests that one important precursor of effortful control at 24 months is maternal responsiveness during infancy, which can be assessed by measuring *affective synchrony* of the main caregiver and the infant during very early face-to-face interactions (Blair, 2002, p. 113). If the adult does not *optimally* vary her or his signals to the infant (e.g., makes the same sound or facial expressions for too short or too long a time), the infant turns away and thereby (ideally) *causes* the adult to change her or his behavior. With optimal affective synchrony, the infant and adult can engage in extended sequences of responses to each other.

Such interactions are thought to contribute to building the neural connections between the mid-brain and the prefrontal cortex, which are thought to enable later effortful control and deliberate actions, which are in turn strongly related to school-type tasks and expectations. Children who experience insufficient affective synchrony may not fully develop self-regulation and may be identified as behaviorally *unready* for school (Blair, 2002).

Along similar lines, Harrist (1992) found links between what she refers to as *parent-child synchrony* during the preschool years and how teachers and peers rated children's behavior in kindergarten. She conducted systematic observations of parent-child interactions in the home (*n* = 30) and classified them in terms of their synchrony. *Positively synchronous* interaction was characterized by "reciprocity (or balance), a mutual focus of attention, mutually positive affect, and developmentally appropriate responsiveness on the part of the parent" (p. 3). *Negatively synchronous* interaction was marked by mutual focus of attention, but also by "extended, escalating, negative exchanges or 'coercive bouts'" (p. 3). *Nonsynchronous* interactions lacked reciprocity, and the adult's responses were often developmentally inappropriate. Harrist's data support general trends in the literature on parenting styles to the effect that positively synchronous parent-child interactions are associated with school-related competence and "negatively synchronous and nonsynchronous interactions with incompetence such as aggression and social withdrawal" (p. 12).

Some research has tested interventions designed to improve mother-infant interactions, and two studies have suggested that enhanced video-related interventions may help vulnerable parents increase their affective synchrony with their children. One such study in the Netherlands focused on enhancing maternal responsiveness and infant-mother attachment in 90 transracial adoptive families. Mothers' sensitive responses were found to be enhanced when first-time mothers participated in video-feedback sessions with their babies and used a "personal book" that included tips about sensitive response and a space for the mother's observations (Juffer, Hoksbergen, Riksen-Walraven, & Kohnstamm, 1997).

Similarly, Wendland-Carro and colleagues (1999) studied reciprocal interactions in Brazilian low-income mother-infant dyads. Two groups of low-income mothers received video- and discussion-based information about newborn care. One group ($n = 19$) viewed a video focused on basic care and interaction with infants. The video for the other group ($n = 17$) was enhanced with information about newborn competence, affectionate handling, and other aspects of interacting with infants. One month later, the researchers observed mother-infant dyads of both groups in free play and bathing situations. They reported higher synchronized mother-infant interaction in dyads of mothers who had received the enhanced intervention than in dyads where the video was about basic caretaking.

Social-Emotional Development and School Readiness

Not surprisingly, the body of research related to social adaptation in school shows that children who fail to develop sufficient positive relationships with peers and with their teachers do less well in school than their more emotionally positive peers. Raver (2002), in an extensive review of research in this domain, states, "the bulk of longitudinal evidence for the importance of social and emotional adjustment for children's success in school is convincing and clear" (p. 4).

Children's peer relationships in particular play a central role in promoting or maintaining academic adaptation (i.e., competent participation in the school culture). Rejection by peers makes school an unpleasant venue for a child, whereas peer acceptance serves to reinforce and enhance what the school environment offers (Rubin, Bukowski, & Parker, 1998).

Raver (2002) points out that children's emotional adjustment and academic progress influence each other bi-directionally. Young children who struggle early on with reading, for example, may become increasingly frustrated and either more disruptive or withdrawn, which in turn interferes with their learning in a recursive fashion. As indicated earlier, children caught in negative recursive cycles tend to behave in ways that strengthen negative attributions, and they have difficulty breaking out of these cycles without outside help. According to Raver (2002), two decades of research have established that

> aggressive young children who are rejected by their classmates in their first years of schooling are at grave risk for lower academic achievement, greater likelihood of grade retention (being "held back"), greater likelihood of dropping out of school, and greater risk of delinquency and of committing criminal juvenile offenses in adolescence. (pp. 4-5)

Not surprisingly, the body of research related to social adaptation in school shows that children who fail to develop sufficient positive relationships with peers and with their teachers do less well in school than their more emotionally positive peers.

Research suggests that children who have problems in their social relationships may be helped by interventions that involve family members and others who work with them. For example, Webster-Stratton's evaluations of a comprehensive training program for children with conduct disorders and their parents indicate that children as young as 3 who meet the diagnostic criteria for "conduct problems" (high rates of aggression, noncompliance, and defiance) can benefit from an intensive intervention that includes parents, teachers, and the children (Webster-Stratton, 2000, p. 1; see also Webster-Stratton, 1997; Baydar, Reid, & Webster-Stratton, 2003; Reid, Webster-Stratton, & Beauchaine, 2001). The program, which uses videotapes and discussion, gives parents information about appropriate play and involvement, encouragement, nonviolent discipline techniques, and problem-solving strategies. Teacher training includes classroom management skills and suggestions for promoting parent involvement. Children's training includes videos and discussion of social skills, problem solving, and appropriate classroom behavior (p. 3). About two-thirds of participants in the programs studied showed significant improvements, which were maintained after completing the program, as assessed by teacher and parent reports (Webster-Stratton, 1997, p. 157).

Some short-term, low-cost programs designed to support children's social-emotional competence are available and seem to be promising, although Raver (2002) asserts that such interventions are unlikely to be effective for children who "face the greatest emotional hurdles" (p. 3). As she points out, children who have severe emotional problems may live in families facing a host of other difficulties, and "policies aimed at young children's emotional adjustment and school readiness may need to be cohesive and comprehensive if we expect to have a measurable, positive impact on increasing children's chances for school success" (p. 3).

The foundation for the development of physical, cognitive, and social and emotional competence is built during the infant, toddler, and preschool years, and is clearly a major factor in school readiness. In particular, the interrelationship of poverty, family stress, and child social-emotional development presents a central challenge to efforts to improve readiness for school. Given the key role that families play in the early development of competence in these domains, it is vital to consider the impact of family stress on the interactions between parent and child.

Vulnerability in Parents and Families

According to Bronfenbrenner's bioecological paradigm (1995, 1998), a child grows and develops within interconnected contexts, including family, community, and culture:

> Especially in its early phases, and to a great extent throughout the life course, human development takes place through processes of progressively more complex reciprocal interaction between an active, evolving biopsychological human organism and the persons, objects, and symbols in its immediate environment. (Bronfenbrenner, 1995, p. 620)

The foundation for the development of physical, cognitive, and social and emotional competence is built during the infant, toddler, and preschool years, and is clearly a major factor in school readiness. In particular, the interrelationship of poverty, family stress, and child social-emotional development presents a central challenge to efforts to improve readiness for school.

A child's immediate environment may or may not foster optimal growth and development. Some families and some communities have scarce resources, resulting in reduced opportunities for the interactions that children need. "Multiple low family resources" are characteristic of persistent poverty associated with cumulative risks to a child's development (Brooks-Gunn, 1995, p. 481), including the risk of being unready to begin school.

Increasingly, the term "vulnerable" is used to refer to those individuals or families affected by a range of stressors—financial hardship, unemployment, disability (physical, cognitive, or emotional), mental health issues, disruption of the family through death or divorce, a variety of emotional and psychological difficulties, or harmful situations such as war or natural disaster—any of which may impinge upon their ability to effectively manage their lives. Vulnerability occurs when a cluster of these challenges overpowers the available resources, potentially undermining the family's and, ultimately, the child's healthy development.

The concept of vulnerability differs in significant ways from such concepts as "at risk," "needy," or "disadvantaged." All children are potentially vulnerable to negative outcomes because of age and inexperience (W.K. Kellogg Foundation, 2002), and any parent may feel vulnerable and in need of help at times. The focus on need, risk, and disadvantage is an aspect of a "deficit" model that researchers, policy makers, and practitioners have often used when discussing parents, children, and families under extreme stress. The presence of multiple stressors certainly increases the risk of harm for individuals and families, who might well be in need of some assistance. However, too much emphasis on deficits overlooks protective factors and processes in the child, parent, or community that may counteract risks (Masten, 1997, in a review of the literature; Grotberg, 1997; Brooks-Gunn, 1995, in a discussion of research on family resources) and help children grow into competent, contributing adults.

Werner (1993) raised awareness of the importance of protective factors through a longitudinal study of 698 children on the island of Kauai. Data were collected on children at the age of 1 and then again at ages 2, 10, 18, and 32. (Follow-up data in adulthood were collected on 505 of the 698 individuals.) About one-third of the children were initially identified as being vulnerable because they were exposed to a variety of risk factors, including poverty, chronic family discord, and parental psychopathology (p. 504). Werner (1993) found as the study progressed that some of these children benefited from protective factors—within themselves, their families, and their communities—that seemed to buffer the risks that confronted them in ways that contributed to their healthy development.

This human capacity to "prevent, minimize, or overcome the damaging effects of adversity" is the identifying characteristic of *resilience* (Grotberg, 1997). To focus on resilience or strengths in research or practice does not imply that risk factors or trauma have no effect. As Masten (1997) notes, "resilience does not mean 'invulnerable' or 'unscathed!'" It does suggest,

> Increasingly, the term "vulnerable" is used to refer to those individuals or families affected by a range of stressors—financial hardship, unemployment, disability (physical, cognitive, or emotional), mental health issues, disruption of the family through death or divorce, a variety of emotional and psychological difficulties, or harmful situations such as war or natural disaster—any of which may impinge upon their ability to effectively manage their lives. Vulnerability occurs when a cluster of these challenges overpowers the available resources, potentially undermining the family's and, ultimately, the child's healthy development.

however, that vulnerability and resilience in families and children may vary based on the presence or absence of protective factors.

Included in the category of vulnerable parents are adults with primary caretaking responsibilities in a variety of family constellations. Two-parent families may experience vulnerability, but families may be more vulnerable to stress if they are headed by single parents, by grandparents, or by other relatives who have primary responsibility for children. Living in rural or urban areas with high concentrations of poverty or high crime rates may also contribute to vulnerability, and families may be more vulnerable if they have limited access to traditional community supports such as health care, education, transportation, or other resources. Children in vulnerable families are at greater risk than others for poor academic and social outcomes, including school failure, delinquency, drug abuse, and other risk behaviors. On the other hand, some children who are in families considered vulnerable have in their environments more of the "self-righting" protective factors noted by Werner that contribute to resilience in families and children.

The International Resilience Project, a consortium of researchers and practitioners, identifies four categories of characteristics found in resilient children: (1) external supports and resources, (2) internal supports, (3) personal strengths, and (4) social interpersonal skills (Grotberg, 1997). It seems reasonable to assume that resilient parents and families would share similar characteristics. Research and theory have identified a number of protective or resilience-promoting factors or features that contribute to the presence of these categories of resilience in a child. These include parental encouragement of autonomy (Grotberg, 1997); a trusting relationship between child and parent or other adult (Grotberg, 1997; Garbarino, 1992); a family network of socially supportive relationships, including alternative caregivers (see, e.g., Werner & Smith, 1992, pp. 56-57; McCubbin, McCubbin, & Thompson, 1993, p. 172); internal locus of control (see, e.g., Werner & Smith, 1992, p. 177); the ability to self-regulate (see, e.g., Brody, Dorsey, Forehand, & Armistead, 2002); and "faith that life makes sense, that odds could be overcome" (Werner & Smith, 1992, p. 177; Werner, 1993, p. 512), including, for some, a "belief in God" (Grotberg, 1997). Besides these psychosocial factors, biological underpinnings of resilience associated with the central nervous system and the neuro-endocrine system have been examined. (For a detailed review of the literature on biological contributors to resilience, see Curtis & Cicchetti, 2003.)

Providing resources to the most vulnerable families is urgent, particularly in the years before children begin school. A wide range of programs are meant to enhance the resilience of vulnerable families by providing social support, information, and other resources that may ameliorate the stresses that parents experience. Among their protective factors, some parents possess the willingness and ability to connect with programs that address at least some of their stressors, although they may continue to face hardships. In contrast, educators and service providers experience difficulty in recruiting some parents to take part in programs that might directly or indirectly benefit

Among their protective factors, some parents possess the willingness and ability to connect with programs that address at least some of their stressors, although they may continue to face hardships. In contrast, educators and service providers experience difficulty in recruiting some parents to take part in programs that might directly or indirectly benefit their children. Other parents may start out in a program but drop out, or they may participate so minimally that it is questionable whether their children gain the intended benefits. These "hard-to-reach" or "hard-to-serve" parents represent a major challenge to educators and service providers who work with families of young children.

their children. Other parents may start out in a program but drop out, or they may participate so minimally that it is questionable whether their children gain the intended benefits. These "hard-to-reach" or "hard-to-serve" parents represent a major challenge to educators and service providers who work with families of young children.

By definition, such parents are isolated from schools and other agencies that might provide information and other supportive resources. They may be unaware of how to gain access to traditional channels and tools for obtaining information and services that could reduce the impact of stressors in their lives. They may not have the skills or the means necessary to find and use what help is available. In some cases, it may appear that they prefer not to be "reached," even when it seems clear to staff that the resources offered are likely to support the family's strengths and foster resilience. Some authors refer to such parents as "resistant" (see, e.g., Gallagher, Fialka, Rhodes, & Arceneaux, 2002) or "reluctant" (see, e.g., Davies, 1997). Others argue that such labels fix blame on individuals, when in fact attention ought to focus on the barriers that interfere with their participation and on how program staff can work toward reducing the effects of those barriers (see, e.g., Christenson & Sheridan, 2001, pp. 74-75).

The complex and interrelated factors that may challenge the efforts of program staff to connect effectively with parents will be discussed in greater detail in coming chapters.

Overview of Programs Serving Young Children and Their Families

3

Introduction

Over the past century, a variety of programs have been developed that work with parents toward the goal of enhancing their children's growth and development. Beginning with the parent cooperatives of the early 1900s, this chapter provides an overview of the more prominent initiatives for which research has documented the attributes and effects of the program.

Parent Cooperatives

Parent-cooperative nursery schools, first introduced in Chicago in 1916, are preschools, usually serving children from 3 to 5 years old, owned, governed, and partially staffed by the children's parents. During the early years of the parent-cooperative nursery school movement, parents were typically expected to assist the teacher in the classroom at least once per week. The teachers were usually fully qualified professionals in nursery education and often in parent education, and they were expected to share their expertise about children's development and parenting with the parents on a regular basis. In addition, parents were usually expected to participate in frequent meetings in which decisions about the governance and financial aspects of the cooperative were made and other relevant business conducted.

The number of parent cooperatives has diminished as mothers' participation in the workforce has increased. Informal reports of historical trends and descriptive accounts of particular issues dealt with by cooperatives give some of the flavor of these particular institutions. Hewes (1995) points out that during the early years of the cooperative nursery schools, fathers contributed mainly through construction and repair work on the facilities. However, participation of fathers in the classroom has increased since the 1960s.

The number of parent cooperatives has diminished as mothers' participation in the workforce has increased.

Lakey (1997) describes in some detail how a serious conflict was addressed among parents in one cooperative preschool concerning how children should be introduced to homosexual family patterns and learn tolerance toward differences. Lakey's detailed account of how the conflict arose, how it was addressed, and how it was ultimately resolved gives a sense of the powerful role that each family can have in the operation of a cooperative preschool.

Dunlap (1997) explored what she called "family empowerment" as one of the important effects of cooperative preschool education for a group of low-income parents. Defining empowerment as "a process of adult development that enables people to discover, develop, and use the power within themselves…[and]…helping people help themselves" (p. 502), Dunlap describes an exploratory study of very young low-income parents' participation in cooperative preschool education. Instead of using a traditional didactic approach to educating parents by an expert, in this case, the parents' participation twice monthly in their child's classroom provided opportunities for them to try out new skills and strategies for interacting with their own and others' young children. Those parents who stayed with the program reported feeling new confidence in their abilities to participate in such a program—abilities many claimed they had not realized beforehand that they had. However, no examination was conducted of the parents who dropped out of the empowerment program. These "drop-outs" were most likely the most vulnerable parents involved in the program, although no data confirming such an assumption were reported.

Many cooperative preschools in operation today are supported for employees by businesses that provide the space and arrange for the employed parents to participate regularly in their children's preschool classes. Other cooperatives located in the larger community encourage parents to pay substitutes to take their places in the classroom if they cannot participate in their children's daily programs because of employment or other circumstances (Coontz, in press). Cooperative preschools may be one solution to the problem of providing affordable high-quality preschool experiences, but the expectations for parental involvement in the classroom, in the management of the physical facilities, and in the governance of the cooperative constitute a heavy and time-consuming load of responsibilities, making it unlikely that vulnerable and hard-to-reach parents will participate.

Head Start

From its inception nearly 40 years ago, Project Head Start has had a major commitment to community action and the involvement of parents in all aspects of the program (Zigler & Anderson, 1979). One purpose of the training guides for communicating with parents issued by the Head Start Bureau (1996) is to "build partnerships with families" (p. ix). The guides include suggestions for developing effective communication with families, tips on how to speak to and to listen to parents respectfully, examples of handouts that can be used for communication, and many other practical strategies for building strong connections with families.

Cooperative preschools may be one solution to the problem of providing affordable high-quality preschool experiences, but the expectations for parental involvement in the classroom, in the management of the physical facilities, and in the governance of the cooperative constitute a heavy and time-consuming load of responsibilities, making it unlikely that vulnerable and hard-to-reach parents will participate.

The Family Partnership Agreement (FPA) is one example of the suggested ways that Head Start staff can engage parents in ongoing individualized dialogue about family strengths and the goals that parents wish to achieve while involved in Head Start. In the FPA process, the parent is viewed as "the senior partner" (Head Start Bureau, 1998, p. 18). FPA activities may vary from center to center and may include identifying challenges that the parent faces, discussing resources that might help the parent reach specified goals, and creating a family storybook (pp. 21-22).

Studies of many aspects of parental involvement in Head Start and its effects have been reported, although few are sufficiently well designed to yield reliable findings. Furthermore, it is useful to keep in mind that Head Start programs operate in divergent contexts in all of the 50 states and U.S. territories, and the effects of various elements can be expected to vary widely.

Reports of the Head Start Family and Child Experiences Survey (FACES) (Zill et al., 2003), a longitudinal study of 3,200 children and families in 40 programs, indicate that the programs' provisions for parent involvement and education are notable. Most parents reported participating in home visits, parent-teacher conferences, and observing in the classroom. In addition, more than half of the parents had volunteered in the classroom, prepared food for a program event, or attended a parent education meeting (p. 94).

One of the primary objectives of Head Start is to "strengthen families as the primary nurturers of their children" (Zill et al., 2003, p. 5). Results of FACES interviews conducted in 1997 and 1998 indicate that 94% of parents or primary caregivers in the study cited Head Start as "an important source of support in rearing their children" (p. 94). Parent reports also reflected a significant increase in the number of intellectually and socially stimulating weekly and monthly activities parents participated in with their children (p. 103). More than two-thirds of the parents reported reading to their children 3-5 times a week or more (p. iv), and parental spanking declined from fall to spring (p. 94). Many parents had increased their sense of "control over their lives" at the end of a program year compared with the beginning of the year (pp. 93-94). The authors note that the FACES interview can identify changes in household or family characteristics that may "assist in understanding factors among this population that might correlate with child development outcomes," but it is not meant to assess Head Start's impact on families (p. 48).

Bryant, Peisner-Feinberg, and Miller-Johnson (2000) examined the relationships among family factors, parental involvement in their children's learning activities within and outside of Head Start, and important school readiness related outcomes (e.g., literacy, social skills). The authors found that mothers' involvement in Head Start was linked not only to children's vocabulary development but also to higher ratings of children's social skills by teachers (Bryant, Peisner-Feinberg, & Miller-Johnson, 2000). It is not possible given the data presented to determine a causal relationship between maternal willingness to be involved in the program and children's social competence. It may be that parents of Head Start children who lack social skills are reluctant to come into the presence of the educational staff either because they

From its inception nearly 40 years ago, Project Head Start has had a major commitment to community action and the involvement of parents in all aspects of the program.

are embarrassed or because they feel inadequate as parents. Further, the results of the interview data also indicated that the higher the mother's level of education, the greater the extent of parental involvement in the Head Start program. This finding raises concern about how best to reach those parents who are most vulnerable and difficult to reach—the parents in the group who are likely to be less educated.

Research has also explored the barriers to the partnership between families and early childhood programs, a relationship to which Head Start has long been committed. Dreibe and Cochran (1996) explored which parents did not participate in the parent involvement opportunities provided by Head Start, and what might limit their participation. The subjects of the study ($N = 29$) were in their first year with one of three Head Start programs in upstate New York. They were interviewed twice, six months apart. Program staff members kept records of the participants' Head Start involvement activities during the study.

Driebe and Cochran (1996) note that previous research has suggested that lack of time, lack of transportation, feelings of being overburdened by poverty conditions, "an attitude of indifference, chemical dependency, and cultural traditions discouraging women from being assertive and participating in groups all could constitute barriers to parent involvement" (p. 5). Their results showed partial agreement with the findings of earlier studies. The study identified three main barriers to participation:

- High numbers of hours of employment and the subsequent increased financial resources seem to compete with parent involvement. Not surprisingly, the more hours a respondent was employed, the fewer volunteer hours she or he invested (p. 11).

- Change in household composition (e.g., additional child, marriage) may reduce the number of hours a parent has available to participate in Head Start activities. Parents whose families experienced no change in household composition were more than twice as likely to participate in Head Start activities than those who experienced changes (p. 13).

- Evening parent meetings were unappealing to many participants. The survey results show that 77% of the respondents who had attended parent meetings had no opinion or negative opinions of them. "Judging from these statements, a number of the Head Start parents interviewed found the parent meetings boring, unorganized, and confusing" (p. 14).

Reflecting on their findings, Driebe and Cochran (1996) note that many contemporary Head Start families do not fit a traditional model upon which parent involvement activities are based. They often work during the evenings, have more than one job, and have heavy family responsibilities. The authors recommend making the definition of parent involvement more flexible in terms of schedule and type of activity, and making evening meetings more interesting and useful to busy parents (pp. 19-21).

Connecting with Parents

Lamb-Parker and colleagues also focused on possible barriers to parental involvement in the Head Start program. They interviewed 68 mothers using a "Barriers to Parent Involvement" survey instrument. According to the authors, the results point to the need for Head Start programs to "modify some of their traditional activities, such as volunteering in the classroom, to accommodate the mothers with time constraints due to new and greater employment-related responsibilities" (Lamb-Parker, Piotrkowski, Baker, Kessler-Sklar, Clark, & Peay, 2001, p. 46).

In a study of 134 fathers and father figures of children in urban Head Start programs, Fagan (1999) found that characteristics of the child (e.g., gender), the father, the family, and the Head Start program all predicted paternal involvement in Head Start. For example, they noted that fathers were more involved in the Head Start program with sons than daughters, particularly if the program provided activities specifically directed at male volunteer involvement (e.g., cookouts, games). The fathers' levels of education were not related to involvement, but teachers' ratings of child behavior indicated that fathers of children with greater difficulties tended to be less involved. The direction of effects of this latter finding cannot be determined from the data available; however, it is reasonable to assume that providing the kinds of "extracurricular" activities (e.g., field trips, picnics) in which fathers might accept specific responsibilities might help to increase paternal involvement in their children's Head Start experience.

Concern about the evaporation of the gains children made during their Head Start experience once they reach formal schooling led to the development of 31 national Head Start-public school transition pilot projects across the country. The purpose of the transition projects was to carry forward from the preschool period into the school (up to the third grade) four major family-centered services: (1) developmentally appropriate education, (2) health provision, (3) family development, and (4) parent involvement. Outcomes for the children were studied by comparing those in the transition programs with comparison groups of children (Mulholland, Heffernon, & Shaw, 1998). The results of the study indicated that the transition projects produced few cognitive, social, or emotional results for the transition children. No significant differences were found between the transition projects and the comparison families.

Seefeldt, Denton, Galper, and Younoszai (1999) studied 133 families in a transition demonstration Head Start program in the outskirts of Washington, DC, focusing on the relationship between participation in the transition project, parental education level, self-efficacy, and children's academic abilities. The study used Bandura's construct of *self-efficacy*, namely "people's beliefs about their capabilities to exercise control over events that affect their lives" (Bandura, 1989, p. 1175). It was found, as expected, that participation in the transition project and parental education level were related to parents' sense of self-efficacy, and their self-efficacy, in turn, was related to children's academic abilities. The authors theorize that believing in one's own ability to influence one's child's behavior and learning increases

Driebe and Cochran (1996) note that previous research has suggested that lack of time, lack of transportation, feelings of being overburdened by poverty conditions ... could constitute barriers to parent involvement.

the parent's active involvement, which in turn has positive effects on children's learning (Seefeldt, Denton, Galper, & Younoszai, 1999). Their findings imply that parent involvement may be of substantial value if it is directed to increasing parents' feelings of efficacy with respect to their children's behavior and learning.

Machida, Taylor, and Kim (2002) also studied Head Start parents' beliefs in their own efficacy and control over their children. They defined self-efficacy as a parent's belief that he or she possesses the required parenting skills to meet specific child-rearing challenges (e.g., calming a distressed child). In a sample of 306 mothers (51% Mexican American, 36% Anglo American) in California and Arizona, they examined various mediators of parents' sense of control and effectiveness with their children. Not surprisingly, parents in all ethnic groups felt less self-efficacious with children described as "difficult" than with children who were not described as difficult. Furthermore, in both the Anglo American and Mexican American samples, "the mother's confidence in her parenting competence mitigated the negative impact of the child's difficult temperament" (p. 180). They reported wide variation among low-income families, emphasizing that not all low-income families are alike, and that many do provide stimulating experiences for their children (a sign of self-efficacy).

Although Head Start practitioners may themselves be under pressure because of being "understaffed and underpaid," they might "with some well-thought-out additional support ... be able to promote both family well-being and child development" (Pizzo, 1998, p. 9).

Starkey and Klein (2000) conducted two studies in the San Francisco Bay area of the effects of helping parents to engage their Head Start children in informal mathematical tasks at home or in the preschool classes. They report that the parents were willing and able to support their children's mathematical development once they were provided with the training to do so. The parents participated in classes on Saturday mornings for 8 weeks, were given access to a library of materials to use with their children, and were given mathematics kits to take home. The children whose parents participated in the program developed more extensive mathematical knowledge than a comparison group of low-income children. However, the authors do not indicate the characteristics of those families who dropped out of the program.

Finally, Pizzo (1998) conducted an in-depth review of 39 longitudinal studies of Head Start children and their families, 17 of which included measures of parent-related outcomes. Analyses of the studies with the best research designs indicated that Head Start parents in these studies consistently showed improved abilities to promote their children's educational achievement. All told, these studies involved more than 2,500 families in different parts of the country, at different points in Head Start's history. Among the main findings were that parental ability to promote early learning improved, including literacy skills, and parents' participation in children's later schooling increased.

Pizzo (1998) points out that the personnel working in Head Start are likely to be called upon by highly stressed parents for help. She recommends that

Head Start policy address this issue on a program-wide basis; although Head Start practitioners may themselves be under pressure because of being "understaffed and underpaid," they might "with some well-thought-out additional support ... be able to promote both family well-being and child development" (p. 9).

Finally, Pizzo (1998) concludes that the follow-up studies corroborate a pattern of parental progress. "Where parental teaching styles and later participation in children's schooling was reported ... a pattern of parent progress around evaluation of their own children's competence appears (p. 37).

In sum, the studies on connecting with parents in Head Start programs point to several issues worthy of further examination. One issue concerns the potential value of making more flexible arrangements for parents to partici- pate in Head Start related activities. Another issue is how to increase the kinds of activities likely to be favorably viewed by fathers and father figures. A third issue concerns the potential benefits of focusing on parents' sense of efficacy and power in parental roles as a way of engendering the cycle of more effective parenting strategies. More effective parenting may lead to increased social and intellectual competence in children, which in turn may further strengthen the parents' confidence in their parenting skills. Questions also arise about how best to communicate with parents regarding their self- efficacy and their involvement activities. All of these possible shifts in Head Start practices are likely to require substantial strengthening of the qualifica- tions, competencies, and wages of Head Start staff.

Home Instruction Program for Preschool Youngsters (HIPPY)

Established in Israel in 1969, the Home Instruction Program for Preschool Youngsters (HIPPY) was originally developed to engage the mothers of disadvantaged preschoolers ages 3, 4, and 5 in literacy activities that take only 15-20 minutes a day. HIPPY is founded on the assumptions that all children can learn basic skills and that parents want the best for their chil- dren. Over a 2-year period, mothers are taught to use puzzles, books, songs, and other school readiness activities that can help children cope with the kindergarten experience successfully. Mothers receive biweekly home visits with a parent educator, who leaves new activity packets for parents to share with the child. On alternate weeks, mothers, children, the home visitors, and the program coordinator meet to discuss the week's activities and talk about other family life or parenting-related issues. The program was introduced in the United States in 1984. Currently, approximately 161 programs operate in 27 different states. The program typically runs for 30 weeks out of the year and may be woven in as a preschool component in Title I funded programs or with other programs such as Even Start.

Research on HIPPY in the United States has been somewhat more difficult than in countries such as Israel partly because of the variety of ways that the programs are funded. In Israel, the program is funded by the Ministry of Education (Lombard, 1994, p. 9), and the decisions about which families will

HIPPY is founded on the assumptions that all children can learn basic skills and that parents want the best for their children.

participate in the programs are more consistent than in the United States, where programs are funded by a variety of foundations, each with its own program eligibility guidelines (Baker & Piotrkowski, 1996, p. 5). In a longitudinal study, using a quasi-experimental design, Baker and Piotrkowski found some positive results, although they were not uniformly shown in the two different groups studied. Either in one or both study groups, children who participated in the HIPPY program were rated as more ready to learn, had higher ratings from teachers regarding their adaptation to the classroom, were less likely to be retained in kindergarten, scored higher on tests of reading and math, had more positive academic self-images, and adapted more easily to the classroom at the beginning of second grade (Baker & Piotrkowski, 1996, pp. 28-47). Another recent quasi-experimental study, completed with five different HIPPY programs in New Zealand, showed that the performance of children who participated in HIPPY was higher on 11 measures than a control group (Barhava-Monteith, Harre, & Field, 1999, p. 152).

Hawaii Healthy Start

Established in 1975, Hawaii Healthy Start is a statewide program that focuses on preventing child abuse and neglect by assuring that every family has a primary health care provider, information on child development, and access to community resources, including parenting classes. Funded through Hawaii's State Department of Health, the program operates from a community-based resource center. A key aspect of the approach is early identification (EID) of families that may benefit the most before they leave the hospital with their newborns. Because Hawaii's system of health care coverage assures nearly universal access to care (Duggan et al., 1999, p. 77), the EID of families may be more successful there than in other states.

Hawaii Healthy Start home visits are made by paraprofessionals and organized around improving knowledge about child development, parenting, parent-child interaction, and nurturing the parent. An emphasis is placed on the parent-home visitor relationship. Home visits begin on a weekly basis but are reduced in frequency as the child grows and family goals are met. Children can stay in the program until they are 5 years old.

An early pilot study of the program showed positive results, such as decreased levels of stress and no cases of child abuse in the 234 participating families compared with other home-visiting programs (Duggan et al., 1999, p. 69). Although the study lacked a control group and may have had a bias in the administration of its pre- and post-tests, the Hawaii legislature judged the outcome sufficiently positive to warrant a significant increase in funding for the program between 1989 and 1995 (p. 69).

In 1994, a collaborative effort among the Hawaii Medical Association, Johns Hopkins University, and the Hawaii Department of Health initiated a more rigorous assessment of the effects of the Healthy Start program at three

Hawaii Healthy Start is a statewide program that focuses on preventing child abuse and neglect by assuring that every family has a primary health care provider, information on child development, and access to community resources, including parenting classes.

Connecting with Parents

different sites. Results raised concerns regarding issues such as delays in meeting with parents, fewer than weekly home visits, and high attrition (51% by 12 months) when compared with other universal home-visiting programs (pp. 73-74). The assessment also found no difference in maternal life skills or access to community services when compared with a control group (pp. 79-80). However, Healthy Start mothers reported more positive parenting behavior and a greater use of nonviolent discipline at the end of one year (p. 80). The study also noted higher retention rates at one site where home visitors were matched more carefully to families with similar interests or backgrounds. In addition, when home visitors persistently encouraged families to participate despite obstacles or missed appointments, the family viewed the home visitor positively and the program had a higher retention rate, affirming the importance of the relationship between the family and the home visitor (Duggan et al., 1999, pp. 74-75).

Parents As Teachers (PAT)

First introduced in 1981, Parents As Teachers (PAT) engages parents of young children through home visiting and group meetings with other parents and program professionals over a 3-year period. Mothers may enter the program when they are pregnant or have infants or toddlers and continue for 3 years until their child reaches the age of 5 years. PAT has developed its own curriculum, including variations that are sensitive to Native American and African American families. PAT is considered a universal program, so that any parent of a young child may participate. The goals of PAT include increasing parents' capacity to parent effectively through parenting education, building a strong foundation for school readiness through early literacy activities, preventing child abuse, and building strong partnerships between parents and schools, and between parents and other social support networks. Currently, all 50 states have PAT programs, and the program has been adopted in many other countries.

A longitudinal, quasi-experimental study that included videotaping of home visits reported that parents indicated benefiting from information provided in the program, such as learning about new ways to provide stimulating environments for their young children and a better understanding of normal child development and their child's behaviors. Approximately half of the mothers participating in the study were Latina, half of whom were English speaking. In addition, half of the mothers were first-time parents and under 20 years old (Hebbeler & Gerlach-Downie, 2002, pp. 31-32). The study participants were involved in parent focus groups and home visits, some of which were videotaped. Home visitors were interviewed and participated in a focus group. Children were given developmental assessments at 12, 24, and 36 months. Translation into Spanish was available as needed.

An interesting finding was that differences were noted between the home visitor and the parents in how they viewed the home visit. Parents viewed the time that the home visitor spent with the child as an intervention for the child, while the home visitor viewed the interaction as "modeling for the parent" (p.

The goals of PAT include increasing parents' capacity to parent effectively through parenting education, building a strong foundation for school readiness through early literacy activities, preventing child abuse, and building strong partnerships between parents and schools, and between parents and other social support networks.

43). Although parents spoke highly of the home visitor and the relationship, many parents did not believe that program participation had affected their parenting to any large extent. Home visitors focused on increasing parents' self-esteem by emphasizing that parents were "the experts," often avoiding telling parents how to modify their behavior. This approach conflicted with parents' views of the home visitors as the experts who were expected to provide information about ways to be a better parent. Home visitors may have overcompensated in attempting to help parents feel good about their parenting by minimizing concerns about the child's development that arose from their observations of the child at home. Home visitors tended to reassure parents that the child would "catch-up," but after 36 months, a majority of children participating scored below average on a standardized measure of development (Hebbeler & Gerlach-Downie, 2002).

The study results also raised questions about the validity of the "theory of change" that is implicit in home-visiting programs such as PAT, suggesting that parents may require more explicit goals to understand how the program is expected to work. Home visitors may also be required to include additional resources or strategies to ensure a child's healthy development (Hebbeler & Gerlach-Downie, 2002, p. 49).

Even Start

The family literacy approach began in the late 1970s and early 1980s, and by the late 1980s, "intergenerational" or "two-generation" education programs were being funded by state governments, school districts, private foundations, corporations, and universities (St. Pierre et al., 1995, p. 38). The Even Start family literacy initiative began as a part of Title I of the Elementary and Secondary Education Act (ESEA) in school year 1989-90 (St. Pierre, Gamse, Alamprese, Rimdzius, & Tao, 1998). Even Start legislation has been amended several times; programs are now administered at the state level, although some funding comes from the federal government. Even Start's purpose is to "help break the cycle of poverty and illiteracy by improving the educational opportunities of the Nation's low-income families by integrating early childhood education, adult literacy or adult basic education, and parenting education into a unified family literacy program...." (St. Pierre, Gamse, Alamprese, Rimdzius, & Tao, 1998).

Even Start programs include three "core services": (1) readiness-focused early childhood education for children from birth to age 8; (2) adult education services to enhance parents' basic educational and literacy skills, including adult basic education, adult secondary education, English as a second language instruction, or GED preparation; and (3) parent education to facilitate positive parent-child relationships and enhance parents' understanding and support of children's growth and development (St. Pierre, Gamse, Alamprese, Rimdzius, & Tao, 1998). Even Start activities can vary considerably from one setting to another, because decisions about implementing each requirement are left up to individual projects. However, a key goal of the program is to help participants identify parenting goals, such as using less

Even Start's purpose is to "help break the cycle of poverty and illiteracy by improving the educational opportunities of the Nation's low-income families by integrating early childhood education, adult literacy or adult basic education, and parenting education into a unified family literacy program...."

punitive discipline strategies, or personal educational objectives, such as attending adult education or job training, while their child is in preschool or elementary school. Recent revisions to the law may result in some changes such as the use of instructional programs based on scientifically based reading research for children and adults, to the extent that research is available (Public Law 107-110, 2001, Sec. 1235.10).

Parent group discussions, home visits, "parent and child together" activities, and links to support services are among the services that local Even Start programs have employed. National evaluations of Even Start indicate modest success. According to St. Pierre et al. (1995), parents at a number of Even Start sites reported that the parenting education component of the program influenced their interactions with their children; they indicated "having more patience with their children, using less physical punishment, and learning how to play with them" (p. 53). Children in Even Start appear to "get a 'boost' in cognitive development" when compared with control groups (St. Pierre, Gamse, Alamprese, Rimdzius, & Tao, 1998, p. 25).

Among the Even Start performance indicators are recruitment (St. Pierre, Gamse, Alamprese, Rimdzius & Tao, 1998, p. 12), retention, and participation (attendance) (p. 15). Even Start programs are charged with serving "those most in need." Face-to-face recruitment of such families (including door-to-door home visits) has been identified as a highly successful approach (St. Pierre et al., 1995, p. 59). "Word of mouth" referrals from friends or family members and exposure to a school brochure are also seen as important recruitment strategies among Even Start programs (Jacobvitz, Crosby, Wooley, & Smith, 1997, p. 11).

Retention is identified as a problem for Even Start. According to national evaluations in 1994-95 and 1995-96, about 60% of participating families remained in Even Start for one year or less, while 40% stayed with the program for longer than one year (St. Pierre, Gamse, Alamprese, Rimdzius, & Tao, 1998, p. 16). Many of these families apparently leave because they have completed their program goals or have become ineligible (St. Pierre et al., 1995, p. 59). Locally, retention figures may appear quite different from national statistics; a report on the ASPIRE Even Start program indicated that 46 of the original 49 families carried over into the third year of the program (Jacobvitz, Crosby, Wooley, & Smith, 1997, p. 24). Data are not provided on parents who drop out of Even Start programs for reasons other than ineligibility or program completion.

Programs reported employing a variety of incentives to enhance attendance and retention: contracts to clarify parental roles; attendance policies; use of participants to recruit and retain other families; special home visits; and tangible rewards such as prizes or credits, serving food to participants, and family field trips to local points of interest (St. Pierre et al., 1995, pp. 61-62). Some of these strategies rely on effective communication with families; however, no studies appear to have addressed the key factors and processes of communication in recruitment or retention of Even Start families. This situation may change in accord with provisions of the newly revised ESEA, which states that the National Institute for Literacy shall carry out research into how family literacy services can best provide parents with the knowledge and skills the parents need to support their children's literacy development (Public Law 107-110, Sec. 1241).

Healthy Families America

Launched in 1992, Healthy Families America (HFA) has attempted to build on the positive concepts of Hawaii's Healthy Start program and is designed to help expectant and new parents provide a good start for their newborns. Initiated by the Prevent Child Abuse America organization, HFA is partially supported by the Ronald McDonald House charities and the Freddie Mac Foundation.

HFA builds on the knowledge and experiences gained from Hawaii's Healthy Start program. New parents voluntarily participate in a home-visiting program designed to help the parents learn more about their new baby's behavior and healthy growth and development. The program uses a tool that assesses the presence of family risk factors such as social isolation, substance abuse, and a family history of child abuse or neglect. Parents who are identified as being in greatest need of services receive intensive home visiting by trained professionals, where the goal of building trust and connections is given a high priority along with adherence to common goals as identified by the HFA program (Daro & Harding, 1999, p. 156).

HFA also encourages collaboration with other community resources, such as health care providers, cooperative extension, local school districts, and Head Start, so that parents and children are more likely to make smooth transitions into other educational or support resources within the community. The National Committee to Prevent Child Abuse, currently known as Prevent Child Abuse America (PCA America), has established a network of researchers to evaluate HFA pilot sites (Healthy Families America, 2003).

Funding for research on HFA has been provided by state agencies, departments of health and social services, and foundations (Daro & Harding, 1999, p. 158). Results from 17 different HFA evaluations, located across the country, reported modest positive outcomes such as decreased reports of child abuse and neglect, increased use of appropriate health and well-baby care, increased parent-child interaction, and greater knowledge of alternative types of discipline and understanding of children's development. This combination of positive outcomes appears to be linked to an increased capacity in the parents to make appropriate parenting-related decisions. Outcomes varied across the programs with respect to decreased use of public assistance, welfare, and social supports (pp. 170-171).

Anecdotal evidence suggests that the quality of the HFA staff and parents' "connection" to a given worker are related to program outcomes (Daro & Harding, 1999, p. 171). Attrition ranged between 5% and 30% (p. 171) but was lower for mothers who were initially assessed while still in the hospital and for African American and Hispanic participants (p. 172).

Healthy Families America encourages collaboration with other community resources, such as health care providers, cooperative extension, local school districts, and Head Start, so that parents and children are more likely to make smooth transitions into other educational or support resources within the community.

Early Head Start

The federally funded Early Head Start (EHS) program was launched in 1995 with the goal of providing the highest quality resources to low-income families with infants and toddlers, beginning during the mother's pregnancy. Similar to Head Start, the EHS program is based on nine principles (EHS, n.d.). These principles include promoting prevention of developmental problems at the earliest possible time, promoting strong relationships between the parent and others within the community, providing culturally sensitive materials, encouraging parental involvement in the early childhood program, and increasing intensity in delivery of services to children and their families. Through a commitment to providing a high-quality program that incorporates what is known about best practices, EHS seeks to facilitate a smoother transition for the child and parent into Head Start or other educational programs. EHS program services are typically delivered through a combination of regular home visits and weekly small group meetings with other parents and children as part of a center-based approach.

The number of EHS programs has grown rapidly since 1995, and early research on the home-visiting component shows varied but promising results. Jean Ispa and colleagues found in a correlational study that when initiating a new program, mothers were unclear about the purpose of EHS and, in some cases, thought that their involvement would assure their child's place in full-time day care. Miscommunication of this type suggests that taking more time to clarify EHS goals and requirements would improve outcomes (Ispa et al., 2000, p. 2).

Parents also tended to have a more positive view of home visitors with characteristics similar to the parents (such as both having two children or coming from the same neighborhood) than of home visitors who were dissimilar or who might not have children. Other favorable qualities in home visitors, according to parent ratings, included the home visitor developing a warm relationship with the child and using gentle suggestions as parenting advice rather than commands. However, although Ispa et al. (2002, p. 6) found that parent ratings of the home visits tended to be lower than the staff ratings, Lori Roggman and colleagues (2001) found in a more extensive quasi-experimental assessment of another EHS program that the 92 families involved in the program were positive about the quality of the home visit and the home visitor (Roggman, Boyce, Cook, & Jump, 2001, p. 68). They also noted the importance of persistence of the home visitor combined with the parents' commitment to stay involved as characteristics that encouraged more successful outcomes (pp. 66-67).

A recent quasi-experimental national study of 17 EHS programs across the country has continued to show modest positive results for increasing parents' ability to use supportive, less punitive parenting strategies to guide their children. The study also suggested that EHS parents were more likely to provide a stimulating home environment that increased cognitive development, language development, and literacy than parents in a control group

The EHS program is based on nine principles ... [which] include promoting prevention of developmental problems at the earliest possible time, promoting strong relationships between the parent and others within the community, providing culturally sensitive materials, encouraging parental involvement in the early childhood program, and increasing intensity in delivery of services to children and their families.

(Love et al., 2001, pp. 150-154, 164). A concern revealed in the research was that despite parents' gains in knowledge of healthy child development, there was no evidence that parents had changed their behavior with regard to safety in the home for their children under 2 years (p. 165). Results included modest but sustained gains in the children's cognitive development at 3 years old for children who participated in EHS compared with a control group. Other results included increased vocabulary, improved social-emotional development and less aggressive behavior, increased parent self-sufficiency as evidenced through job training or work, and increased father involvement (Love et al., 2002, pp. 3-5). Programs that fully implemented the elements of the EHS program guidelines showed better outcomes than programs that were unsuccessful implementing the key elements. For example, programs that incorporated home visiting with center-based activities and other community support services were more successful despite the fact that collaboration with other agencies might have been difficult in some communities (Love et al., 2002, p. 6; Buell, Hallam, & Beck, 2001, p. 12).

Certain subgroups, including those who were pregnant when they enrolled, those with first-born children, African American families, and those who had a moderate number of risk factors (3 out of 5), tended to show better outcomes than families who enrolled later, who were from other ethnic groups, or who had either fewer or greater risk factors (Love et al., 2001, p. 286; Love et al., 2002, pp. 7-9) Two subgroups that were particularly difficult to serve were teen parents and parents at risk for depression (Love et al., 2002, p. 9).

Conclusion

In sum, research on these widely applied approaches to connecting with parents to assist in the education of their young children has been reviewed. Although no formal experimental studies have been reported, the available research indicates that these approaches have yielded some benefits. The reports also raised several issues that bear further attention:

- The literature regarding the approaches discussed here frequently suggested a need for deeper understanding of the causes of recruitment difficulties and the high drop-out rate in programs serving vulnerable families.

- A need has also been noted for programs to modify their conceptions of "the involved parent" so as to take into account the life stresses of overburdened parents, particularly the working poor who may have inflexible or extremely variable work schedules, or who may hold more than one job. Of the approaches included here, the one that is most dependent upon sustained direct involvement of parents is the parent-cooperative preschool system (Coontz, in press). However, it is reasonable to assume that the extent, types, and intensity of parent participation required in parent-cooperative preschools is too demanding for most of the parents who are hard to reach and to serve.

- Concerns were also raised regarding how responsible staff might make parent meetings more interesting and thereby encourage greater participation in them.

- The literature reviewed here also points to a need for explicit planning to involve fathers in the programs more consistently.

- Among the issues raised in the discussion of these approaches is whether the potential benefits of any of the types of parent involvement described in these reports are related to the age of the target child.

- Another issue is the focus of the services offered to the parent. Several programs are built upon the principle of taking a comprehensive approach to addressing both the direct and indirect effects of parents' actions on a child's readiness for school. Greater awareness of children's health issues, improved parental literacy, enhanced parenting skills, and increased employability are often considered important to promoting parents' efficacy for helping children become more ready for school. On the other hand, some programs with a specific focus have also reported success in facilitating children's school readiness. Whether specific focus on children's academic mastery is more beneficial to children in the long term than is assistance with wider aspects of parenting and family life is not clear from the available data.

- Another issue concerns the characteristics and strategies of home visitors in some of the programs. The current data are mixed as to whether parents are likely to make greater gains in relationships with home visitors similar to themselves, who serve as sources of support, as opposed to visitors who offer expert advice on parenting and related problems. The available data are also mixed regarding the relationship between program effectiveness, the frequency and regularity of home visits, and the duration of the home-visiting intervention.

- Finally, a theme throughout much of the available research is the cyclic nature of parenting and parents' involvement with children's education. Parents who feel that they can and should be involved in their child's education are more likely to be open to opportunities to participate in their children's educational programs. The reverse cycle has also been observed. Parents who believe they are not especially capable of being involved in ways requested by the program are less likely to take advantage of resources and supports offered to them. How to break the negative cycle remains the challenge facing all of these kinds of programs serving young children and their families.

Communication and the Exchange of Information

4

Introduction

Communication and the exchange of information (and other resources) are key components of the relationships between parents of young children and the staff of programs that serve them. This chapter calls attention to some ideas and research in communication and information science that offer insights into what works, and what creates barriers, in parent-staff interactions. Topics to be addressed include staff-parent communication practices, the identification of information needs, information-seeking behavior, information use, access to information, and social network analysis.

Investigating Staff-Parent Communication Practices

Although communication between parents and the staff of programs that serve them has been the topic of many practitioner-oriented articles and books in the fields of education, early intervention, health care, adult education, mental health, and social services, it has been less frequently addressed in the research.

In a summary of three related studies that he conducted in the late 1970s using in-person structured interviews with 212 working-class and middle-class parents and 89 full-day caregivers, Douglas Powell reported that the highest frequency of parent-caregiver communication in early childhood programs took place during transition times. However, he found that almost one-third of the parents (for unspecified reasons) did not come into the center during those times (Powell, 1989, pp. 59-62).

Similarly, Endsley and Minish (1991) collected observational data on parent-staff interactions during morning and afternoon transitions in 16 licensed proprietary urban and rural child care programs serving approximately 1,032 children. According to the authors, approximately two-thirds of the parents

Douglas Powell reported that the highest frequency of parent-caregiver communication in early childhood programs took place during transition times. However, he found that almost one-third of the parents (for unspecified reasons) did not come into the center during those times.

that they observed talked with a staff member during a transition time (p. 125). Slightly more than half of the observed conversations (53%) featured some "substantive information" about the children, adults, or the home or family. The authors also noted that in 43% of the observed situations, no communication took place, not even a greeting. (It was not clear whether the same parents consistently were not greeted.) Together, the Powell and the Endsley and Minish studies suggest that a number of parents may miss important opportunities to communicate with staff about their children, either because they do not enter the child care center during transition times or because no one on staff acknowledges them.

Communication practices are treated as indicators of the quality of services provided to parents of young children in the professional literature and in research. The Early Childhood Environment Rating Scale (ECERS), frequently used to assess quality of early childhood programs, includes standards in eight areas related to parent-staff relationships (Harms, Clifford, & Cryer, 1998, p. 46). National Association for the Education of Young Children (NAEYC) accreditation materials for early childhood programs include a variety of recommendations for good practice in parent-program relationships. Among the conditions for accreditation is having communication practices that "[convey] trust and respect" (NAEYC, 1998, p. 212). The National Parent Teacher Association (NPTA) also considers "regular, two-way, and meaningful" communication between home and school to be its first standard for parent/family involvement programs (NPTA, 2000, p. 25).

Research on the relationship between communication and the quality of programs that serve families with young children is sparse but may be growing.

Research on the relationship between communication and the quality of programs that serve families with young children is sparse but may be growing. In one such study, Ghazvini and Readdick (1994) analyzed communication channels in 12 child care settings (four subsidized, four contracted subsidized, and four nonsubsidized programs in a southeastern city of moderate size). Forty-nine caregivers and 201 parents responded to questionnaires about their perceptions of parent-caregiver one-way, two-way, and three-way communication and the importance of each to "the good of the child." Among their findings, the authors reported that higher child care quality (determined using a version of the ECERS) was significantly positively correlated with higher levels of two-way communication (p. 216).

Owen, Ware, and Barfoot (2000) examined possible correlations between parent-caregiver "partnership behavior" and the quality of child care. The authors looked at how 53 mothers of 3-year-olds and their children's caregivers communicated about the children. Data were collected from parents and caregivers through questionnaires and interviews. Live and videotaped observations of mother-child and caregiver-child interactions were also conducted in a lab, in family homes, and during child care visits. Partnership behavior was analyzed through parallel assessments that focused on three factors: "sharing information," "seeking information," and "adult relations" or "adult support." The authors reported that frequent partnership behavior was linked to indicators of higher-quality caregiver-child interactions and to higher-quality mother-child interaction. Quality was assessed using parallel scales that included "respect for the child's autonomy" and "stimulation of cognitive development" (p. 421). Correlations were found between quality and the frequency of two-way communication between parents and program staff. The authors caution that their results "may reflect personal characteristics of the caregivers and parents that result in both higher-quality caregiving and a propensity to seek and share information about the child" (p. 425).

Effective ommunication from home to school and from school to home is key to good-quality parent involvement programs, according to Joyce Epstein, whose research agenda on parent involvement in K-12 programs is perhaps the most comprehensive in the field of education. Optimal home-school communication, in the Epstein model, is an ongoing process of connecting via notices, phone calls, conferences, memos, conversations, and other media (Epstein, 2001, pp. 436-437). The National PTA's standards for parent involvement programs (NPTA, 2000) are based on a model of parent-school-community involvement developed by Epstein. (For further discussion of Epstein's partnership model, see Connors & Epstein, 1995; Epstein, 2001.)

Studies of communication practices between parents and the programs that serve them seldom frame "communication" in terms of any explicitly described model, although several such models exist. "Communication" itself appears to be rarely defined; a common understanding is assumed. Literature in the communications field reveals that communication is in fact a complex human activity with a number of components. Most definitions of *communication* involve the *transmission* or *exchange* of information, support, ideas, attitudes, expectations, and feelings between people or groups. Models of communication tend to have several elements in common. The *sender* (or source) initiates a *message* and *encodes* it by means of a *symbol* system (e.g., words, gestures, drawings) in a particular *medium* (e.g., print, oral, video), then sends it via a particular *channel*. (Multiple media may be involved, and messages need not be verbal for communication to take place.) The *receiver* (sometimes "audience" or "destination") *decodes* the message in order to construct its meaning, with some consequence or *effect* (McQuail & Windahl, 1993, pp. 4-6, pp. 46-53, pp. 184-192). One or both parties gain more knowledge, are convinced to think or believe differently, or are persuaded to act in a certain way. On the other hand, a receiver might also misunderstand, misinterpret, reject, or ignore a message. The *relationships* between senders and receivers are influenced by their individual capacities and personalities, by their relative autonomy, and by what they believe and assume (correctly or not) about one another.

Each of the components of a model of communication represents a point at which a connection can go well, or not so well.

Investigating Information Needs

Information is one of the principal resources that parents and program staff are likely to exchange when they communicate. *Information* is data that

Communication involves the transmission or exchange of information, support, ideas, attitudes, expectations, and feelings between people or groups. Models of communication tend to have several elements in common. The sender (or source) initiates a message and encodes it by means of a symbol system (e.g., words, gestures, drawings) in a particular medium (e.g., print, oral, video), then sends it via a particular channel. The receiver (sometimes "audience" or "destination") decodes the message in order to construct its meaning, with some consequence or effect.

individuals or groups use to "make sense" of (that is, to interpret and act upon) their experiences. Brenda Dervin's *sense-making theory* asserts that no one can ever know all the available information that might be relevant to his or her actions; yet, people must take action despite gaps in what they know (Dervin, 1999, p. 733). Information is one of the resources most likely to be exchanged when parents and program staff communicate with each other. An *information need* consists of the knowledge (cognitive, affective, or both) that a person or group requires, or believes they require, in order to accomplish a task or to solve a problem (Savolainen, 1995). A number of studies have examined how particular groups identify and meet their information needs. A few of these have focused on parents.

Information is data that individuals or groups use to "make sense" of (that is, to interpret and act upon) their experiences.

An *information need* consists of the knowledge (cognitive, affective, or both) that a person or group requires, or believes they require, in order to accomplish a task or to solve a problem.

In a small study in the United Kingdom, Nicholas and Marden (1998) conducted group interviews with 18 parents and individual interviews with 35 other parents, each of whom was the primary caretaker of a child under the age of 5. They reported that the most prominent information need was child health information (91%), followed by information about child care (86%) and child development (80%). Information about child behavior was sought by 51% of the parents. The authors note that staff of organizations that served these particular parents "seemed to be aware of the information needs of the parents" although "they also saw needs where parents did not" (p. 41). (The study does not address the differences between parents' perceived needs and those the professionals perceived.)

Jacobson and Engelbrecht (2000), investigating parents' needs and preferences regarding parenting education, distributed surveys to parents in 27 licensed child care centers and preschools in 13 cities in a county in Texas with both urban and rural populations. According to the authors, their analysis showed that when asked to rate 15 parenting topics, 95% of the 740 respondents indicated "strong interest" or "most interest" in "building your child's self-esteem." Helping children do well in school was rated "strong" or of "most interest" by 94%, "helping children have good relationships" by 91%, and "effective discipline" by 90% (p. 141). Parents who had not attended college rated several topics higher than those who had attended college, including "helping children have good relationships"; "helping children do well in school"; "preparation for parenting"; and nutrition, health, and safety (p. 143). The authors suggest that their findings indicate that these topics are "more salient in the ecologies of the parents without college experience" (p. 144), and that including information and support related to those topics would be important for professionals working with such parents (p. 144).

In a qualitative study of information needs of homeless parents in six urban shelters, Hersberger (2001) found that these parents ($N = 28$) tended to rank information on parenting and other family well-being issues second only to their need for information to address their financial concerns (p. 15). About half of the respondents also reported needing information about various aspects of their children's education (e.g., enrollment, transfer of records, conflict with a child's teacher).

Investigating Information Seeking

Information seeking is a communicative activity through which individuals or groups try to "create a meaningful order of things" (Savolainen, 1995, p. 267). Information seeking is not isolated in time or space, but rather something that people do in the varied contexts of their daily lives. Information theory differentiates between job-related information seeking and "everyday-life information seeking (ELIS)" (Savolainen, 1995, p. 259). Job-related information seeking is part of one's occupational tasks. Everyday-life information-seeking practices, on the other hand, are related to important daily activities such as family life, health care, household care, or hobbies (p. 266).

Program staff members may seek a great deal of information from parents in the context of their jobs. When a child care program director asks parents to fill out family information forms, for example, or when a home visitor asks a mother how she disciplines her preschooler, those professionals are engaging in job-related information seeking. Very little research has been done on this kind of activity in settings involving families of young children. One study by Squires and colleagues has some relevance, given the practice in some programs of asking parents to complete developmental assessments of their children. In a longitudinal study of 96 parent-infant dyads, they found that both low-income and middle-income parents who completed developmental screening tools regarding their children had a high degree of agreement with professionally administered assessments (Squires, Potter, Bricker, & Lamorey, 1998). Reports of case studies by Lubeck and colleagues refer to the Head Start practice of asking for parent preferences regarding workshop and adult education topics (Lubeck & deVries, 2000; Lubeck, Jessup, deVries, & Post, 2001). No details are provided of how the centers acquired information about the parents' preferences.

Parents' searches for books about parenting, child development, and school readiness constitute examples of everyday-life information seeking. Several studies have focused on parents' information-seeking behaviors. McKenzie (2002), for example, reports on the accounts given by mothers of twins regarding their information-seeking efforts during pregnancy; she notes that many of their questions concerned fetal and maternal health (pp. 37, 40-41) and that their physicians were not necessarily their most helpful sources of knowledge. Several mothers reported that they needed to persevere in order to find the information they sought.

Morisset (1994) found that parents in two low-income populations reported similar "preferred and most trusted" sources of advice and support regarding children's development (p. 13). Eighty-three percent of 59 mothers from a rural Colorado family center and 95% (of 60) in a Chicago family center indicated turning most often to other parents, including their own, when seeking advice and support about child development, health, or behavior problems. Health care and social service professionals were the second most preferred and trusted sources of such information, followed by service providers at their respective family centers (Morisset, 1994, pp. 13-14, 32).

> *Information seeking* is a communicative activity through which individuals or groups try to "create a meaningful order of things." Information seeking is not isolated in time or space, but rather something that people do in the varied contexts of their daily lives.

The homeless families in Hersberger's study reported that they used family and friends as sources of information regarding some needs, such as dependable transportation or family relationships. For other information needs, they used official sources, such as housing authority staff for information about housing or social services staff for child care referrals and information about children's behavior (Hersberger, 2001).

Overall, information studies indicate that most people, no matter how well educated, tend to rely heavily on informal sources such as friends and relatives for their information. They use formal sources only "when all else has failed in coping with a situation or when outside factors force them to" (Dervin, 1983, p. 158, in a discussion of theory and research). However, research has also shown that people within any specific population can be purposeful, highly motivated information seekers and users when they feel a compelling need for information (p. 159). Beth Harry, for instance, is one of a number of parents who have become experts on their children's particular disabilities. She writes that after her daughter was diagnosed with cerebral palsy,

> I embarked on several months of intensive reading of the current theories and instructional approaches regarding disabilities in young children. I have no idea how much of what I read I absorbed, engrossed as I was in the day-to-day realities of caring for an infant with severe feeding difficulties. (Kalyanpur & Harry, 1999, p. 47)

Investigating Information Use

Information use involves making meaning of information in order to "reshape, redefine, or reclaim [one's] social reality" (Chatman, 1996, p. 195). The forces of power and authority in society strongly influence both those who make or provide information and those who use it, although the ultimate control over an individual's sense-making processes and what he or she does with information rest primarily within that individual (Dervin, 1999, p. 738).

The staff of programs that serve vulnerable families usually expect that parents will use the information they provide in ways that enhance children's well-being. Parents are likely to expect that information that they provide to staff members will be adopted and used for the benefit of the child or the family. There is no guarantee that they will do so, however. Because information is not "a piece of reality that is knowable in an unbiased way," different people will make divergent uses of it (Dervin, 1983, p. 158)—adopting it, reinventing it, or resisting and rejecting it.

Even though information use was not explicitly addressed in the studies reviewed for this book, several indirect references were found in this literature review. For example, parents reportedly accepted ideas for home literacy activities (Serpell, Baker, Sonnenschein, Gorham, & Hill, 1996) and for math-related activities provided by a Head Start program (Starkey & Klein, 2000), using them at home with their children. Evaluations of Even Start, Head Start, and similar programs suggest that participating parents

Information use **involves making meaning of information in order to "reshape, redefine, or reclaim [one's] social reality" (Chatman, 1996, p. 195).**

Because information is not "a piece of reality that is knowable in an unbiased way," different people will make divergent uses of it (Dervin, 1983, p. 158).

Connecting with Parents

tend to accept and use the information offered in GED and other adult education classes (St. Pierre et al., 2003; Ames & Ellsworth, 1997).

Some examples of resistance to or rejection of information were also found. People may reject information when it does not mesh with how they construct their identities or the larger contexts of their lives. Wagner and colleagues note that some African American and Hispanic parents voiced doubts about some of the parenting strategies recommended in a home-visiting program. The practices were not what they had experienced in their own upbringing, and they considered the strategies to be "for white people." The authors also found that among white working-class families,

> advice that was more adult directed, such as turn off the television; stop smoking; provide a diet high in milk, fruit, and vegetables; and pursue higher education were in opposition to some parents' lifestyles and the lifestyles of their friends and families. (Wagner, Spiker, Gerlach-Downie, & Hernandez, 2000, p. 40)

Some studies suggest that people who reject information may do so because they consider the information source unreliable. In a discussion of observations made during a qualitative study of programs for pregnant high school students, Pillow (2000) relates that some of the young women objected vocally to the curriculum units about abstinence and other forms of birth control, and to the way content was presented. One mother-to-be remarked to the researcher and some friends,

> What is that teacher talking about when she says just say "no" to sex? What if I don't wanna say no! But they'll never talk about that with us— they look down their noses at you, like you're bad. [What does] she know anyway.... (p. 205)

Issues of Access to Information

In order for information to be useful, people must be able to acquire it and comprehend it. Issues of *access to information* include physical access and intellectual access.

Physical Access

Distance and sensory or physical disabilities may impede access to information. Programmatic factors such as scheduling may also interfere with people's ability to connect with information sources.

Geographic Factors. Sparse population and difficult terrain can make it especially difficult for programs to connect with parents in some rural areas (e.g., Alaska, Appalachia) (Beeson & Strange, 2003). Distance between homes and program sites contributes to the challenges. In a report of their ethnographic study of Head Start/Public School Transition programs in six rural South Dakota towns, Allen and colleagues noted that, although some of the sites could be considered "the centers of their communities" and a focal

In order for information to be useful, people must be able to acquire it and comprehend it. Issues of *access to information* include physical access and intellectual access.

point of parental involvement, other schools were not. Parents tended not to see schools as a focal point when children had to be bused to school in a neighboring community, when families in the community were highly mobile, and when a number of parents were employed outside the community where the school was located (Allen, Thompson, & Drapeaux, 1996, p. 17). In another publication based on the same study, the authors also reported finding that home visitors (family service coordinators) were viewed as important links when children's programs were located in communities distant from their homes (Allen, Thompson, Hoadley, Engelking, & Drapeaux, 1997a).

Disability. The difficulties that people with disabilities face in gaining access to information have been framed as aspects of "social exclusion" (Gleeson, 1998, in a discussion of disability and technology in urban settings). Typical written materials are of little use to visually impaired parents, for example, and services or information offered in spaces without accommodations for wheelchairs or walkers may be inaccessible to some individuals with physical handicaps. Overall, information access for parents with such disabilities has not received attention in the research literature.

Hoffmeister (1985) notes, in a discussion and review of literature regarding families with deaf parents, that technological advances have improved communication between deaf and hearing people (pp. 125-126). On the other hand, as Gleeson (1998) points out, assistive technology cannot completely overcome exclusion from mainstream activities. Some parents with disabilities will still be interdependent with other (usually nondisabled) people who are responsive to their particular needs (pp. 88-89).

Programmatic Factors. As suggested by previously mentioned work by Powell (1989) and Endsley and Minish (1991), the structure of the day in an early childhood program may limit contact between parents and child care providers so that high priority is placed on the exchange of information during transition times (i.e., when children are dropped off and picked up). In cases when parents do not enter a facility during transitions, they and the caregivers may not have access to important information about children or the program.

Descriptions of some early childhood programs indicate that special provisions are sometimes made to ensure that parents have access to information that they need. "Parent centers" and "family resource centers" are areas set aside for parents to facilitate their access to information and other resources. Parent room activities in the Chicago Child-Parent Centers, for example, include parent reading groups and inservice training sessions for parents in "child development, financial management, cooking, and home economics" (Reynolds, 2000, p. 41). In case studies of four programs with parent centers, Johnson (1994) describes what is offered by one center:

> During parent meetings, representatives of community agencies provide information about social agency assistance with fuel, day care, Head Start, and housing. A large information bulletin board ... includes job listings,

courses, and a listing of addresses of community agencies.... Teachers working with parents in the center have created learning games to send home.... The parent center has also offered a computer course for the last three years. (pp. 5-6)

In interviews with parents who used the centers, Johnson (1994, pp. 38-41) found that some parents reported that the centers provided information and experiences that helped them better understand how to take a more active role in their children's education.

Intellectual Access to Information

Intellectual access to information is another concern in information studies; information seekers cannot use what they cannot understand. Access to information can be seriously compromised by differences in literacy levels among parents and program staff. Insight into the kinds of literacy-related challenges that parents and professionals may face during their interactions can be found in a report by Serpell and colleagues (1996) on the Cooperative Communication Project conducted in four pre-kindergarten and kindergarten classrooms in Baltimore. A preschool teacher involved in the study recounted being confronted by a mother who claimed that the teacher had called her a "bad" name. The principal and an assistant teacher helped sort out what had happened. At the beginning of the school year, the mother's babysitter had tried to pick up the child without a note from the mother. The teacher had refused to let the child go with the sitter, saying that the mother was "adamant" about not releasing the child without a note from her. The sitter was not familiar with the word "adamant" and told the mother that the teacher used "a cuss word" (Serpell, Baker, Sonnenschein, Gorham, & Hill, 1996, fig. 4, pp. 2-3). Such reports suggest that professionals need to be mindful of their spoken vocabulary, as well as what they write, when working with parents who may have lower levels of English literacy.

Research in medicine and in education confirms the conventional wisdom that when professionals use technical terms and jargon without sufficient explanation, parents may not understand key information about their children. In a longitudinal qualitative study of 36 low- to middle-income African American families of young special education students, parents told the researchers that professional jargon made it difficult to understand what was being said about their children (Allen, Harry, & McLaughlin, 1993). On the other hand, in a British study that used a semi-structured interview with 95 parents of children with acute viral illness, a majority reported that although they did not want jargon, they also did not want the doctors to omit technical information that would help them make sense of their children's condition (Kai, 1996). These findings suggest a need to give high priority to developing ways to help parents move from one level of understanding to another when complex situations call for complex explanations.

The reading level of written material can affect its usefulness to readers. Easy-to-read materials are readily understood by more people; more difficult

Information seekers cannot use what they cannot understand. Access to information can be seriously compromised by differences in literacy levels among parents and program staff.

materials may confuse some readers or be ignored. Yet studies suggest that print materials for parents of young children are often written at levels too difficult for a significant part of their intended audience. Analysis of 107 sets of child safety seat instructions (Wegner & Girasek, 2003) revealed that all the instructions were between 7th- and 12th-grade reading levels, which meant that parents with lower literacy skills were less likely to fully understand them. Similarly, in a readability evaluation of 33 pediatric patient education materials for parents, Klingbeil, Speece, and Schubiner (1995) found that most of the materials examined had readability levels of 9th grade or higher, making them potentially inaccessible to parents with lower literacy skills or to second-language English speakers.

Language differences may cut off parents from important information and prevent them from sharing their own knowledge with the professionals who are involved with the family. For example, researchers in two related British studies found that communication about asthma symptoms was challenging for doctors even when parents spoke English, because not all parents used the same terms to describe their children's breathing sounds. When parents and physicians communicated through translators, the situation became even more complicated because some of the languages used by parents apparently had no equivalent for the term "wheeze" (Cane & McKenzie, 2001; Cane, Ranganathan, & McKenzie, 2000).

In a 10-year ethnographic study of intercultural interactions in a Hispanic community in a small coastal town in California, Delgado-Gaitan (1996) recorded how Hispanic (primarily Mexican American) parents experienced frustration over school-to-home communications. As non-native speakers of English, they had difficulty understanding what teachers and school officials wanted of them. They responded to the problem by creating an organization to improve their access to information from schools.

Information Poverty

Information poverty may have an impact on connections between parents of young children and the staff of programs that serve them. The term "information poverty" refers to a cluster of important problems related to information access. "Information-poor" individuals experience a generalized relative lack of information that might help them solve their problems and attend to the tasks of life. All the physical and intellectual barriers listed above are major contributors to information poverty, and research also strongly suggests a link with socioeconomic poverty. People who live in poverty are less likely to have access to the Internet, for example, giving rise to the concept of a "digital divide" in which people who lack access to computer technology for economic reasons stay not only technologically illiterate but also out of touch with the perceived wealth of information on the Internet (for further discussion, see Lazarus & Mora, 2000). Although the "digital divide" describes a gulf between the "information poor" and "information rich," there is evidence of a continuum of information poverty rather than a clear dichotomy (Sligo &

Williams, 2001, p. 4), and Internet access is by no means the only issue involved in information poverty.

Some research indicates that low income also is not the only factor in information poverty. Elfreda Chatman's qualitative studies of information seeking and use within specific populations (e.g., elderly women) led her to several conclusions regarding information poverty. She noted that information poverty was often found among groups that perceived themselves to be in some way isolated from, and less powerful than, the mainstream population. Chatman refers to them as "outsiders." The condition of information poverty is partly but not completely associated with power asymmetry and social class. Individuals and groups may experience it when others *have and withhold privileged access* to information (Chatman, 1996, p. 197). On the other hand, information poverty is also associated with a tendency to mistrust "mainstream" information sources. People who are information poor also believe (sometimes correctly) that negative consequences will result from sharing information with others who may have some power over them. So they keep their information needs to themselves, acting in ways that are self-protective but that serve to isolate them even further from potentially useful resources (pp. 199-201).

For example, early childhood teachers in a small midwestern community reported that parents of a number of children in their programs were undocumented immigrants and were reluctant to seek services if doing so required that they share some family information with program staff (D. Rothenberg & L. G. Katz, 2002, personal communication). The families thus remained cut off from resources that could have been useful to them, and their teachers were left without family information that might have aided their work with the children.

On the other hand, Chatman (1996) noted that people who are information poor are highly receptive to information from trusted sources when they perceive it to be relevant to their needs. A small qualitative study of parents in New Zealand who were involved in a PAT-like program appears to support Chatman's assertion. Williams, Comrie, and Sligo (2001) found that although most of the 16 parents experienced some degree of social isolation, most (13) had responded in positive ways to the information and support provided by home visitors in the program (p. 427). This response was attributed to the trusting relationships that developed between each of the visitors and the parents whom she mentored. Data for the study were collected during observations of the home visits and in interviews with 16 first-time parents and 6 educators. A significant barrier to trust, according to the authors, was a tendency of the mothers (10 of the 16) to prefer "self-sufficiency" to asking for help (p. 426); one commented, "You're better off being by yourself" (p. 429). At the same time, some said that they felt "really lonely" (p. 428) or "so scared" (p. 429). Nine of the 16 reported anxieties related to parenting small children and seemed to be "highly motivated" seekers of information (p. 427).

"Information-poor" individuals experience a generalized relative lack of information that might help them solve their problems and attend to the tasks of life.... People who live in poverty are less likely to have access to the Internet, for example, giving rise to the concept of a "digital divide" in which people who lack access to computer technology for economic reasons stay not only technologically illiterate but also out of touch with the perceived wealth of information on the Internet.

Williams, Comrie, and Sligo (2001) found that the home educators frequently showed flexibility in their approaches. When a family dealt with hardships connected with basic human needs—a sick baby, power supply cut-off, or phone service cut-off—the educators often had to work "within the particular circumstance of that particular moment in time with that family" (p. 432). "Sometimes the ... curriculum just doesn't even come into it," one of the educators remarked. One of them regularly drove a client to a young mothers' group where the mother found the support and information she wanted (p. 429). Another seemed to make a point of including the mother's partner in home activities and provided referrals to community resources (p. 429). According to the authors, the educators tended to indicate that trust is the result of conscious efforts to build common ground and shared understanding with the parents, while taking care that the involvement in the program does not "become like a coffee morning" (p. 433).

The authors of the study suggest that some components of these ongoing face-to-face parent-educator relationships provided a form of social connectedness that, much of the time, allowed parents to trust, accept, and use the "expert's" knowledge and professional support to direct their own processes of change (p. 435).

Taken together, the work on information poverty suggests that its dimensions "may take different shapes depending on the community in which they appear" (Sligo & Williams, 2001, p. 1) and that it need not be a permanent condition.

Analyzing Social Networks: Characteristics of Social Networks

Researchers and theorists in several fields use analysis of social networks to explore in depth the structures and processes of human interactions. *Social networks* consist of the patterns of relationships among individuals, groups, or organizations that permit or inhibit the exchange of resources, such as goods, services, social support, influence, and information (Haythornthwaite, 1996, pp. 323-324, in a discussion of the theoretical grounding of social network analysis). Significant aspects of social networks include characteristics of the participants, participants' access to resources, who interacts directly with whom, and the routes and methods used for exchanging information. A person's position in a social network will affect the flow of resources to and from him or her. A variety of societal, intrapersonal, and interpersonal variables may affect that position.

Social networks may include informal connections such as friendships and family relationships. More formal connections, such as those with colleagues or with professionals who provide services, are also considered social networks. One example of a study analyzing the social networks of the parents of young children was conducted by MacPhee and colleagues (MacPhee, Fritz, & Miller-Heyl, 1993). The findings of their social network analysis revealed significant differences in how parents of 2- to 5-year-olds in three ethnic

---

Social networks **consist of the patterns of relationships among individuals, groups, or organizations that permit or inhibit the exchange of resources, such as goods, services, social support, influence, and information.**

communities perceived and used social support networks. Their results were based in part on parents' responses to a Social Network Questionnaire (p. 8). The authors reported that participants from the Ute Mountain Indian community ($n = 136$) described having close-knit social networks that "[appear] to be governed by frequent interchanges with an interconnected web of kin" (p. 17). Participants from a low-income Anglo sample ($n = 93$), on the other hand, reported receiving emotional support from more members of their networks than either the Hispanic or Ute parents, and they indicated that they were more likely to have network members who did not know each other (p. 26). Hispanic parents ($n = 188$) reported the largest networks and tended to rely on a relatively small number of members for advice or other needs. The authors conclude their study by commenting that their findings "further underscore the need to ... tailor support programs to the specific ecologies of human development" (p. 19).

Analyzing Social Networks: Resources That Programs Offer to Parents

Descriptive reports of the types of programs described in Chapter 3 indicate that a wide range of resources are offered to the parents who are involved with them. These programs, and many others, offer one or more of the following resources:

- Child health services, including well-child information

- Prenatal and maternal health services, including wellness information

- Mental health care for individuals or families

- Early intervention services for children who have special needs or are "at risk"

- Child care, including infant/toddler care or preschool

- Adult education, including GED preparation, ESL instruction, adult literacy, life skills, and job skill training

- Experience with program governance and decision making for children's education

- Parent/family support services, including
    - Information about child development, family life, and how children learn
    - Parent education or training, including the modeling of activities that promote children's knowledge and skills
    - Social and emotional support, which may include support groups for parents

- Referrals to other sources of help

Some resources may be provided in the family home by nurses, therapists, parent educators, or family service coordinators. Others are offered at a particular site. Parenting classes, adult education programming, and child care are generally site based.

Analyzing Social Networks:
Resources That Parents Provide to Programs

Parents also provide resources to the programs that serve their families. Common examples include the forms for child and family information that are among the official requests for resources that parents receive when they become involved in programs that serve their young children. Parents who agree to participate in programs that are meant to augment family resilience or children's school readiness may provide support for program goals by attending the classes and meetings offered by the program and by being present for home-visiting appointments. They may also become actively involved in a child's intervention as co-therapists or assistants (see, e.g., Greene, 1999). Some research suggests correlations between parents' personal involvement in elementary and secondary schools and children's academic achievement. The link is less well established between involvement in children's early childhood education programs and an increase in school readiness.

Parents of children in early childhood programs are expected (at the very least) to have their children ready for the program day and to adhere to the center's policies. In addition, they may be expected to dedicate time and energy to the program's activities in person. The following examples of parent involvement opportunities in the Chicago Child-Parent Centers are found in Reynolds (2000, p. 41):

- Volunteer in the classroom (read to small groups, assist with field trips, supervise play activities, play games with small groups)
- Participate in parent room activities (participate with parent reading groups; complete craft projects; attend inservices in child development, financial management, cooking, or home economics)
- Participate in school activities (attend meetings and programs, attend parent-teacher conferences, attend social events)

The literature indicates that parents involved in programs may also give their time and energy to the following activities:

- Serving on governing boards or other decision-making bodies (see, e.g., Ames & Ellsworth, 1997; Abrams & Gibbs, 2002)
- Advocacy in the wider community on behalf of the program (e.g., through fund-raising, public relations, or social action efforts) (see, e.g., Epstein, 2001, p. 470; Shirley, 2002)
- Acting as liaisons to their home communities (see, e.g., Delgado-Gaitan, 2001)
- Working toward changes in programs to benefit a child or children (see, e.g., Delgado-Gaitan, 2001; McClelland, 1996; Shirley, 2002).

Although program staff may not welcome having parents advocate changing the system (Bryk & Schneider, 2002), parents may consider such activity to be in their children's best interests (see, e.g., Soodak & Erwin, 2000;

Parents who agree to participate in programs that are meant to augment family resilience or children's school readiness may provide support for program goals by attending the classes and meetings that are part of the services offered and by being present for home-visiting appointments. They may also become actively involved in a child's intervention as co-therapists or assistants.

Delgado-Gaitan, 2001; Shirley, 2002), and it can ultimately have positive results for the program and the community it is supposed to serve.

In general, parents and program personnel best serve children's interests when they freely provide each other with information, identify problems and strengths within the family and the child, and decide how best to employ resources and support those strengths, with the goal of enhancing the child's growth and development. In any social network, however, an individual or group may function as a "gatekeeper" who controls others' access to information and other resources. For example, medical personnel are likely to have knowledge that has a profound effect on the lives of parents. A qualitative study involving interviews with 19 women who were pregnant with twins (McKenzie, 2002) reveals that the behavior of individuals in the "gatekeeper" position sometimes created barriers to information seeking. One woman reported on her alarm during a conversation with medical personnel who appeared reluctant to share test results with her:

> And they said, "Well, when we took your blood, um, the results were abnormal." Like, they're scaring [me]. I'm like, "What do you mean, abnormal?" … So she just kept stalling, so she says, "Well, we think there might be more than one baby." (p. 35)

In another study, parents of children with cleft lip or cleft palate ($N = 100$), responding to a questionnaire about how they were informed about their child's diagnosis, reported that they preferred physicians to quickly get to the point soon after the child's birth with urgently needed news about the child's condition (Strauss, Sharp, Lorch, & Kachalia, 1995). In the same study, 67% of parents reported that they wanted to be referred to parents in similar situations, although only 16% received such referrals when being informed of the child's diagnosis. One father referred to this lack of information as "a gigantic burr under my saddle!" Some of the physicians in the parents' social networks thus used their gatekeeping position to increase the scope of the parents' social network, adding individuals who were especially likely to offer the parents information and emotional support.

Although caregivers and teachers are often in the "gatekeeper" position, in early childhood settings, staff members rarely deliberately withhold important information from parents. On the other hand, experience indicates that, for example, a teacher or caregiver may hesitate to tell a parent about a child's troubling behavior if it seems likely that the parent might then punish the child harshly. Experience also suggests that parents have been known to express frustration over hearing from a caregiver or teacher only when a child has had a problem; they also want more access to information about what goes well for the child.

Information Dissemination

Information dissemination refers to the intentional spreading of information by individuals or groups. Programs that serve young children and their parents frequently disseminate information to local program participants (e.g.,

In general, parents and program personnel best serve children's interests when they freely provide each other with information, identify problems and strengths within the family and the child, and decide how best to employ resources and support those strengths, with the goal of enhancing the child's growth and development.

when recruiting participants or distributing program-related materials to participating parents). Public "communication campaigns" may use larger-scale dissemination efforts (McQuail & Windahl, 1993, pp. 183-192, in a discussion of "planned communication"). The "I Am Your Child" campaign, for example, which began in 1997, included a television show for parents of young children that is said to have reached an audience of nearly 13 million (I Am Your Child Foundation, n.d.). The project currently maintains a Web site, which is one of a number of efforts to make content widely available to parents regarding the well-being and education of young children.

Results of a study in Turkey suggest that providing information via television can have positive direct effects on parenting attitudes and behaviors, and on children's school readiness (Baydar, Kagitcibasi, Kuntay, & Goksen, 2003). The information was provided via the television program *Benimle Oynar misin? [Will you play with me?]*, designed for children and parents to view together. The program aired 5 days a week for 13 weeks beginning in the fall of 2002. Families in the experimental group ($n = 139$) were asked to watch daily and were contacted afterward to reinforce the request. Families in the control group ($n = 127$) were asked to watch a different program at the same time and were followed up regularly to reinforce the request. The researchers found that children who watched the program more than 3 times per week (1) improved their own scores on measures of arithmetic readiness, spatial knowledge, and preliteracy skills, and (2) had higher scores than children who watched from 0-2 times per week. The scores of children who watched 1-2 times per week also improved significantly, although not as dramatically as those of the higher-frequency group. In addition, mothers who watched the television program with their children self-reported changes in their parenting behaviors, including (1) providing more cognitive stimulation to their children, (2) reducing use of harsh discipline, (3) reducing expectations that a child would fully and immediately comply with a parent's request, and (4) reducing suppression of children's self-expression. It should be noted that literacy among women in Turkey is lower than in the United States; in fact, the mothers who reported watching *Benimle Oynar misin?* most frequently had on average 5.7 years of education.

Other examples of efforts to reach large numbers of parents include the "shaken baby" campaigns conducted by child protection agencies via billboards and televised public service announcements.

The Public Broadcasting System, the federal government, as well as some cooperative extension services, public health agencies, and state boards of education also provide Web content for parents on a large scale via print and Internet sources. A few efforts are being made to study the use of the Internet as a means of supplying content, although parents have not been the specific target population. For example, a recent study by the Children's Partnership (Lazarus & Mora, 2000) focused on content needs and interests expressed by low-income and "underserved" Internet adults and children. They conducted a Web analysis of 20 community networks or "portals" (including library sites and commercial sites), group interviews with 56 adults and 51 children and youth (ages 10-22), more than 30 interviews with directors of community technology centers and community networks, and interviews with 60 additional experts.

Among their findings was the lack of Internet resources for adults with lower literacy skills. Of the 1,000 Web sites that they reviewed, they found only 10 that were appropriate for limited-literacy adults (Lazarus & Mora, 2000, p. 23); several easier-to-read sites were geared toward children. Only 20 of the Web sites that they reviewed had "content in languages other than English that provided practical information for a more productive life in the United States" (p. 23). They further noted that although Spanish-language information is becoming more widely available, much of it has been developed outside the United States, "limiting its usefulness in meeting the needs of the 33 million Hispanics in the United States today" (p. 23). The Illinois Early Learning (IEL) Project (http://illinoisearlylearning.org) is one of the few initiatives to intentionally focus on disseminating Web and print materials related to children's school readiness that meet the needs of parents who have low literacy skills or who speak languages other than English.

Effective dissemination is generally thought to depend on a variety of factors in addition to language and literacy, including how well defined the goals are; how appropriate the content, format, medium, and tone of the message are for its intended recipients; the timing of the messages; and the contexts in which the messages are received. (For more detailed discussion, see McQuail & Windahl, 1993, pp. 183-200.) It appears, however, that very little research is available to support or question the success of particular large-scale efforts to reach parents.

Conclusion

Communication is normal, desirable, and even indispensable among the individuals in the various settings in which children develop (e.g., family, child care, school), according to Bronfenbrenner's *bioecological paradigm* of human development (Bronfenbrenner, 1995, p. 620; Goodnow, 1995, pp. 279-282).

Communication is an intrinsic part of any relationship, including those between parents of young children and the staff of programs that serve them. The ideal is two-way open and frequent communication between parents and the people outside the family. This type of communication increases the likelihood that the exchange of information and other resources can be coordinated and provided in ways that have a direct or indirect positive impact on children's development.

Professionals who work with families are likely to be more effective when they are aware of how aspects of their own communication practices may affect parents' ability and willingness to engage with the program in the interests of their children.

Program staff will be in a better position to work with vulnerable children and families if they make a point of learning more about the information needs and the information-seeking and information-use activities common to the groups they want to serve. A deeper understanding of their role in the social networks consisting of themselves and the families they serve may facilitate better access to those families and more effective interactions with them.

Relationships between Parents and Programs

5

"Effective" Parent-Staff Relationships

Programs such as those discussed in Chapter 3 are considered "effective" when accountability measures indicate that they have directly or indirectly helped parents and children in areas related to school readiness. The dynamics are often treated as simple. The parents have encountered the programs, and some change has resulted: they have had their infants immunized, they have read to their toddlers at home, they have enrolled their preschoolers in Head Start, they have taken ESL or GED classes, they have joined a parent council. In any case, change has obviously occurred within individuals—the parents and the children who participated.

Yet it is unlikely that this change has happened in isolation. Research in communications and information science suggests that it is likely that the exchange of information, support, and other resources between the parent and individuals on the staff of the program has been a significant catalyst. In the social networks formed by their interactions, resources (information, support, referrals, etc.) have been exchanged that have probably enhanced parents' ability to help their children prepare for school.

This chapter begins with an exploration of variables, ranging from intrapersonal traits to within-program factors to issues of race and class, that seem to be linked to disconnections, misconnections, and good connections in the social networks of parent-program relationships. Two influential contemporary perspectives on effective program-parent relationships are also discussed. The chapter closes with a discussion of relational trust, which is seen as a key to positive relationships between parents of young children and the staff of programs that serve them.

Research in communications and information science suggests that it is likely that the exchange of information, support, and other resources between the parent and individuals on the staff of the program has been a significant catalyst [for change]. In the social networks formed by their interactions, resources (information, support, referrals, etc.) have been exchanged that have probably enhanced parents' ability to help their children prepare for school.

Variables That Influence Parent-Staff Connections

Our review of the literature suggests that demographic factors; characteristics of the community; family mobility; cultural factors; constructions of gender, sexuality, class, and race; parental disabilities; intrapersonal characteristics of individual parents and staff members; and program characteristics are among the variables that can influence interactions between parents and program staff.

Demographic Variables

Some studies have noted correlations between parent involvement in children's education and many of the demographic variables associated with family vulnerability: low income, low level of education, substance abuse, and single parenthood. Generally, vulnerable parents are portrayed as less likely to be involved extensively in their children's education than are parents who are not "vulnerable." Research by Hart and Risley (1995), for example, indicates that parents in very poor families engage in fewer basic preliteracy experiences (e.g., conversations) with their infants and young children than do parents in middle-income families.

On the other hand, some evidence suggests that parents with demographic characteristics associated with vulnerability can show high levels of commitment to programs intended to benefit their children. For example, mothers with one or more risk factors for mental health problems (e.g., depression, substance abuse, the experience of harsh or negative parenting as children) maintained active engagement in a parenting intervention program to the same extent as mothers without the mental health risk factors, according to a study by Baydar and colleagues. The study combined assessments from two quasi-experimental studies involving three groups of Head Start families ($N = 607$) in the Puget Sound area (Baydar, Reid, & Webster-Stratton, 2003).

Other qualitative studies also indicate that factors associated with vulnerability do not necessarily keep parents from actively participating in activities that benefit their children (see, for example, Lubeck & deVries, 2000; Ames & Ellsworth, 1997; Delgado-Gaitan, 1996, 2001).

Community Characteristics

Conditions within particular communities may create challenges to parents' full participation in programs that are meant to serve them. For instance, in a 3-year ethnography of an elementary school in California, Abrams and Gibbs (2002) found that the three parent decision-making groups at the school were divided along lines of race and socioeconomic class in their goals and attitudes about each other's contribution to the school. Although the problems had not resulted in open conflict, it was apparent from parents' comments that collaboration among the groups was virtually nonexistent.

Another example of the effects of community characteristics can be found in Skilton-Sylvester's work with ESL students who were part of the Cambodian refugee community in Philadelphia. In her case studies, she found hints that some irregular attendance may have reflected "possible ambivalence toward participation in educational programs" stemming from "the fact that so many of these women's relatives were killed [in Cambodia] because they were educated" (Skilton-Sylvester, 2002, p. 13). For some of the women, this concern was balanced by a belief that they could make better lives for their children if they learned English (p. 18).

The nature of the social networks in some communities might deter vulnerable families from interacting with the staff of programs that are meant to serve them. McClelland (1996) interviewed several parents in a small community whose children had problems in elementary school for a variety of reasons. Parents of a boy who was diagnosed with dyslexia in first grade related their struggle to have school officials acknowledge the diagnosis and use the teaching strategies recommended by a specialist. Their ongoing advocacy on behalf of their son was met with resistance and even resentment. The parents' relationship with the school principal eventually became "strained" despite the fact that they had known him for years and continued to see him in the community (p. 12). Other parents in that community recounted similar experiences. It seems likely that in such settings where lines between professional and personal lives are blurred, parents might hesitate to seek help for their family's problems for fear of similar social consequences.

Family Mobility

Statistics from the Government Accounting Office show a correlation between children's school performance and family mobility (Dolan & Haxby, 1995, p. 1). In particular, children's academic progress suffers when families move frequently, especially when children change schools in addition to changing their residence. Frequent moves also limit parents' ability to maintain ongoing relationships with teachers, caregivers, or health care providers.

Homeless families are likely to be among the most vulnerable and the hardest to serve. Newman (1999) points out factors related to homelessness that challenged parent-staff relationships for six families at a southern California homeless shelter. A majority of the 11 children in the case study experienced some difficulty in school: irregular enrollment and attendance, incomplete records, gaps in knowledge, or undiagnosed and unaddressed learning disabilities (pp. 176-177). According to Newman, the staff of one school made "heroic" efforts to work with two of the children but "simply did not have the resources to fully meet their educational needs" (p. 177). All six families had ongoing difficulties with child care, and the five families who did not have cars had significant transportation problems (p. 175). In such situations, parent-school connections, which might have helped the children, were made very difficult by the lack of child care and transportation.

Programs that serve migrant families with young children face similar obstacles. Lopez and colleagues conducted interviews and observations in

Statistics from the Government Accounting Office show a correlation between children's school performance and family mobility (Dolan & Haxby, 1995, p. 1). In particular, children's academic progress suffers when families move frequently, especially when children change schools in addition to changing their residence.

school districts in Texas and Illinois (Lopez, Scribner, & Mahitivanichcha, 2001) that had reported success in increasing parent involvement in migrant-impacted schools. A district administrator told the researchers,

> I went to visit [a family] the other day ... and they had candles inside the house.... They can't read a book or magazine or a newspaper, *porque no hay luz* [because there's no electricity]. Can you imagine going to the outhouse in the dark? So, that is why we ... [have to] know their whole life story, in order to serve them better. (p. 262)

The researchers described administrators and educators in these schools as "extremely committed" to meeting the migrant parents' needs and making "enormous effort" to do so. In many cases, these efforts stemmed from the professionals' firsthand knowledge of life in migrant families.

Military families are another highly mobile population, and the potential is great for programs that serve them to encounter difficulties in connecting with parents. Since passage of the Military Child Care Act of 1989, the U.S. Department of Defense (DOD) has made a concerted effort to improve education of military dependents, including care of young children. The U.S. military child care system serves more than 170,000 children worldwide, more than 50% of whom are age 3 or under (Lucas, 2001, p. 130). The National Association for the Education of Young Children has accredited 98% of military child development centers. On most military bases, parents who want child care for their young children have access to a free resource and referral service; referrals will be made to licensed nonmilitary providers when care is not available in a DOD facility (Campbell, Appelbaum, Martinson, & Martin, 2000). Programs are expected to be responsive to the extended work hours that military parents may encounter. They are also expected to provide parents with daily information about their children's experiences. The New Parent Support Program offers parent education classes, support groups, and crisis intervention services. Parents are included on program inspection teams and advisory councils (Lucas, 2001, p. 133). No research could be found regarding the practices or outcomes of the resources offered to parents by DOD early childhood programs.

Language and Literacy

Issues of language and literacy affect access to information, as discussed in the previous chapter. When differences in language and literacy level between parents and staff are not addressed adequately, the home-to-program connection can become strained. As one of the Hispanic parents in Delgado-Gaitan's study remarked, "We cannot argue with the schools because we have neither the means nor the language with which to do it" (Delgado-Gaitan, 1996, p. 4). The parents expressed awareness that school personnel had mistaken ideas about their willingness to communicate with the schools: "Teachers and principals ... say that our children aren't important to us because we don't attend meetings..." (p. 5).

Similarly, Hmong parents in a family literacy program, frustrated by difficulties communicating with their children's education program, wrote a letter in

Hmong to the principal, asking why the school did not give them information about their children in their own language so that they could participate more fully (Quintero, 1998, pp. 206-207).

Cultural Factors

As census figures reflect, the United States has a growing population with close ties to cultures other than what is considered "mainstream"—European American, English speaking, middle class. At the same time, in some fields such as early childhood education, the majority of professionals are white middle-class English speakers (Saluja, Early, & Clifford, 2002). Cultural variations in beliefs about child rearing, disabilities, health care, the parents' role in education, and how to deal with "help from outside" may become barriers to effective interaction when parents and program staff have different cultural backgrounds.

Cultural factors may also affect how parents' social networks are constructed and how they function, as indicated in work by MacPhee and colleagues (1993), who conclude their study by commenting that their findings "further underscore the need to ... tailor support programs to the specific ecologies of human development" (p. 19).

Possible barriers to providing culturally sensitive services to families have occasionally been examined in the research literature. For example, Lee and colleagues (2003) conducted a survey of early intervention (birth-3) professionals in a midwestern metropolitan area, representing agencies that served a total of 3,779 families. Of the 123 respondents, 91% were female. More than half of the 119 indicated that their own ethnicity was European American (60%); 20% African American, 11% Latino/Hispanic, and the remainder Latino, Asian American, Native American, or "other." These professionals frequently cited lack of agency support and lack of time as barriers to implementing culturally appropriate practices with the families they served. Obtaining information about specific cultures, for example, was seen as "time consuming" and had to be done outside of work hours. The authors note that lack of time and agency support may be interconnected, reflecting a misconception "that providing culturally appropriate services to families and their young children with special needs is an additional responsibility rather than an integral part of providing early intervention services" (Lee, Ostrosky, Bennett, & Fowler, 2003, p. 292).

Although matching programs to the ecology of a community is essential, at the same time, the mainstream "national culture" of the United States is a reality, and program staff may find themselves having to explain, interpret, or seek compliance with what the dominant culture expects. MELD (a national nonprofit family service organization based in Minneapolis) programs are among those that offer home-language materials explaining U.S. laws, customs, and mainstream expectations of child-parent relationships, as well as tips on how to navigate the school system.

An action research study by McInnis-Dittrich (1996) describes how staff members of a parenting education program adapted an established curriculum

Cultural variations in beliefs about child rearing, disabilities, health care, the parents' role in education, and how to deal with "help from outside" may become barriers to effective interaction when parents and program staff have different cultural backgrounds.

(Systematic Training for Effective Parenting) to the norms of an Appalachian community in order to accomplish the program's goals. Previously, parent educators had found that the program gained mixed acceptance in a community where typical parenting practices were considered abusive toward children by contemporary mainstream standards. Prior to the change, one parent who had been in the program for several weeks remarked, "This was good advice about talking to your kid, but we're mixed up as to when you're supposed to whip 'em!" (p. 416). The altered curriculum began with an emphasis on the parents' experiences with harsh parenting during their own childhoods, and gradually incorporated other aspects of the program after providing opportunities for them to consider the effects such treatment had on them and might have on their own children.

Communication between individuals of different cultures can be quite complex, as literature in the field of cross-cultural communication attests. This literature warrants a close look from any professional who works with parents of young children. For example, a growing body of research examines cross-cultural and intracultural variations in *communication patterns*. Differences have been noted in physical positioning, directness, topic raising, and the amount of talking that a person does (Tannen, 1994). Communication patterns may be influenced by such factors as orientation toward seeing oneself as independent of others or as interdependent with others (Morisaki & Gudykunst, 1994, in a meta-analytic review of literature on communication patterns in Japan and the United States) or by power asymmetries between groups (see also Shimanoff, 1994). (For discussions of the many variables involved in effective communication across cultures, see Gudykunst & Lee, 2002, or Ting-Toomey, 1994, 1999.)

Class and Classism

Socioeconomic inequities between parents and program staff are typical in programs that serve vulnerable families. The effects of social stratification on relationships between parents and program staff are not often addressed, or even acknowledged, in the research literature. To be sure, "low income" is often associated with low parental involvement in activities related to children's education, as well as with certain limits on information-seeking behavior and information access (see, e.g., Hart & Risley, 1995; Lazarus & Mora, 2000).

From low-income parents' point of view, it may be especially difficult to take part in parent involvement activities in their children's schools or out-of-home care situations, or to attend parenting classes, workshops, or meetings regularly (Yeung, Linver, & Brooks-Gunn, 2002; Chin & Newman, 2002). Irregular work hours, multiple jobs, inflexible leave policies, lack of child care or reliable transportation, and concerns about neighborhood safety are among the conditions that have been reported as complicating their participation in activities that could help them to enhance their children's readiness for school. Chin and Newman (2002) tracked 12 New York working poor families with children who were elementary age or younger and found that

Lott (2002) addresses prevalent negative beliefs about poverty and poor people that have been identified in research with adults and children, including the unwarranted assumption that poor people are likely to be less intelligent and inherently less capable of handling the tasks of life than higher-income people (p. 103).

Parents needed to handle homework, dinner, and bathing during the precious few hours they and their children had together before bedtime. Some households found ways to manage these burdens, but over the course of our fieldwork, it became more difficult for most of them, producing adaptations that cut into one bottom line—their workplace—or the other—children's school performance. (p. 20)

Socioeconomic class differences may also be associated with fundamental differences in what parents see as appropriate relationships with other adults who work with their children. For example, in a discussion of an ethnographic study that she conducted, Lareau (1996) cites working-class and poor parents who indicated during interviews that they sometimes complied with teacher requests that created some hardship out of fear that they would otherwise be reported to the child protection authorities for neglect. Middle-class parents in her study did not voice such concerns. Furthermore, although working-class and poor parents referred to "meeting with the school" even when they were meeting only with one person, middle-class parents tended to speak of their children's teachers by name and sometimes by first name (pp. 59-60).

Class issues may also complicate interactions between program staff and parents. Bernice Lott (2002), summarizing research into attitudes about poverty as expressed in social policy and research, calls upon professionals who work with families to interrogate their own "cognitive and behavioral distancing from the poor" (p. 100), which she argues is likely to negatively affect their ability to connect with families living in poverty. She addresses prevalent negative beliefs about poverty and poor people that have been identified in research with adults and children, including the unwarranted assumption that poor people are likely to be less intelligent and inherently less capable of handling the tasks of life than higher-income people (p. 103). She also argues against paternalism toward poor families, noting that parents who are poor may not want or need all the programs that might provide help.

Race

Researchers and policy makers have long treated racial categories ("White," "Black," "African American," "Asian American") as potentially, and potently, meaningful. Attitudes and beliefs about "racial" differences are often tightly interwoven with constructs of "class," "culture," and other social divisions. Cultural attributes such as language, religion, and traditions may also become identified with race.

A growing number of studies examine the meaning of race at a personal level. Sleeter (1993), commenting on research that involved a 2-year intervention with 26 K-12 public school teachers, noted that although several teachers professed to be "color blind" to their students' race, the same teachers exhibited stereotypical beliefs about the children's racial groups.

Lisa Delpit (1995) reported an excerpt from an interview with an African American woman who had trained to be a teacher but left the profession:

[My cooperating teacher] thought all black children were poor, but the kids in that school weren't poor. She kept talking about how we couldn't expect too much from them because they were poor. She even thought I was poor. She kept asking me questions like, "Is your father unemployed a lot?" (p. 107)

Susan Matoba Adler interviewed Asian American women from 12 families to learn their perceptions of how their "racial identity" developed; her findings suggest some ways in which ideas about race may influence parent-school interactions. For example, a Korean American woman indicated that her father's extremely negative views of non-Asians had influenced the behavior of others in the family (Adler, 2001, p. 276).

Adler (2001) notes the lack of a strong pan-ethnic "Asian" identity among participants in her study; they tended to identify more strongly with their ethnic or national backgrounds (e.g., as "Hmong" or "Korean American") (pp. 280-282, 287). Similarly, individuals from Native American groups in the United States are likely to identify first as members of their own tribe or nation (e.g., Klamath, Muscogee/Creek, Miami) and then as "American Indian" or "Native American."

Critical race theory (CRT) is emerging as a framework for scholars and educators to assess and discuss the impact of constructions of race on practice and research in a variety of disciplines, including law, disability studies (see, e.g., Asch, 2000), and educational policy and practice (see, e.g., Ladson-Billings & Tate, 1995). CRT has become a component of coursework in some professional preparation programs as well.

> **For the purposes of our discussion, suffice it to say that what participants believe race is, and what they believe racial differences mean, are likely to affect relationships between parents and staff members, especially when they have different racial backgrounds.**

For the purposes of our discussion, suffice it to say that what participants believe race is, and what they believe racial differences mean, are likely to affect relationships between parents and staff members, especially when they have different racial backgrounds.

Disabilities and "Ableism"

According to survey research by Bhagwanji and colleagues (1997), 85% of 269 Head Start disabilities services coordinators (DSCs) who responded indicated that their programs served children whose parents had disabilities. Of the programs serving parents with disabilities, 23% reported that working relationships were difficult with parents with emotional disabilities; 13% stated that working with parents with cognitive disabilities was difficult. Eleven percent had difficulty working with parents with sensory (hearing or vision) impairments, and 8% had difficulty working with parents with physical disabilities (Bhagwanji, Thomas, Bennett, Stillwell, & Allison, 1997, p. 13). Their report does not supply examples of the difficulties encountered; further qualitative studies could shed light on what such difficulties might be and how staff members meet the challenges. The authors also note that most of the respondents reported that their Head Start programs had no written policies regarding interaction with parents who have disabilities (Bhagwanji, Thomas, Bennett, Stillwell, & Allison, 1997). Given the interdisciplinary dearth of research on working with parents with disabilities, future investigations focusing on program policies and on current "best practices" regarding parents who have disabilities could contribute much to helping programs connect with parents.

Research by Ray and colleagues (1994) highlights some issues that might arise, for example, in working with parents who have cognitive disabilities. They conducted site visits to each of eight programs that provided parenting training and direct assistance to parents with cognitive disabilities (Ray, Rubenstein, & Russo, 1994). They also made home visits to 25 of the 86 families enrolled in the programs and reviewed services rendered to 41 of the families. Despite the parents' high level of need for help with household and parenting tasks, parents dropped out of the programs at a rate of about 40% per year on average (p. 734). According to the researchers, interviews with parents and staff members indicated that many of the parents at high risk of dropping out were "accustomed to ... making their own decisions" and felt "uncomfortable with having another adult frequently in their household, encouraging them to change accustomed habits and preferences" (p. 734).

In their discussion, the authors recommend creation of standardized risk- and progress-assessment protocols, which would incorporate parent involvement expectations, to assist professionals who work with parents who have cognitive disabilities. Such protocols would help staff members navigate between the need to assure that children's needs are being met, while at the same time respecting and fostering the right and the responsibility of the parents to make adequate decisions about their children (pp. 740-741).

Professionals, and the rest of the able-bodied public, commonly have concerns about the child-rearing abilities of parents with disabilities. Like classism and racism, bias regarding disability can make it difficult for parents and staff to work together effectively. Scholars as well as parents with disabilities point to tendencies of able-bodied staff members to behave paternalistically and to presume that any disabled person is not competent to be a parent. (For further discussion, see a review of the literature on parental disabilities by Kelley, Sikka, & Venkatesan, 1997.) Although federal and state laws may mandate that programs serving parents with disabilities provide the resources that they need to help them carry out their parenting roles (Kelley, Sikka, & Venkatesan, 1997), very little research has focused on parenting with disabilities, much less on the relationships between such parents and the programs that serve their young children. Discussion of effective strategies for staff working with parents who have disabilities has in general been confined to the professional literature (see, e.g, Strong, 1999). Adrienne Asch (2000), a scholar and disabilities activist who is blind, comments, "My own courses on motherhood ... include discussions of women with disabilities as mothers—something I have seen in none of the large numbers of recent books on the experiences of motherhood," including those that present the experiences of other "marginalized" populations.

Gender

Differences in what is expected of mothers and fathers can influence parent-program relationships. Historically, mothers have tended to have more contact than fathers with the staff of programs that serve them and their

Professionals, and the rest of the able-bodied public, commonly have concerns about the child-rearing abilities of parents with disabilities. Like classism and racism, bias regarding disabilities can make it difficult for parents and staff to work together effectively.

children. Most studies of "parent" involvement in fact use a sample consisting entirely of mothers. In the past decade, scholars and professionals have paid increasing attention to the roles of fathers and other males in children's lives, including their education. (For a comprehensive look at contemporary perspectives on fathers and fatherhood from a variety of disciplines, see Tamis-LeMonda & Cabrera, 2002.)

Fagan (1999) found that father and father-figure involvement in Head Start improved when the program made an effort to include activities that appealed to the men. Noting that men might "find excuses" for not volunteering in their children's programs, Fagan asserts that, "Men may say 'no' two or three times" to an invitation for involvement, but are likely to say "yes" the fourth time (p. 19). Specific programmatic support (such as providing guidance about how to become involved) was seen as a key to increasing the men's involvement in Head Start. (For further details of the Fagan study, see Chapter 3.)

A study by McBride and colleagues (2001) indicates that attitudes of female staff toward father/male involvement in early childhood classrooms may be mixed, and that some female staff may be resistant to having men involved in classrooms. As part of a larger study, the authors implemented an intervention in which female preschool staff ($n = 12$) had structured opportunities to express and critique their own attitudes about father/male involvement. Their findings indicated that overall father/male involvement in their children's classrooms was greater at the treatment site than at the control program following the intervention (McBride, Rane, & Bae, 2001). The authors report, however, that one teaching team out of three at the intervention site showed more commitment to involving men than did the other two teams. The latter, in contrast to their responses on a scale of attitudes toward father involvement, appeared to implement father/male involvement strategies in a very limited way and gave the impression of being resistant during consultations with members of the research team (pp. 90-91). The authors are not specific about what gave the impression of resistance, but their experience calls attention to the need for more research on relationships between fathers or father figures and the female staff of the programs that serve their young children.

Issues of Sexuality

Research and experience suggest that pregnant and parenting adolescents and gay/lesbian parents have found that responses of some program staff to their sexuality can increase difficulties in parent-staff relationships. Some evidence suggests that pregnant and parenting adolescents frequently believe that many teachers and administrators—particularly males—are openly uncomfortable about their pregnancies and about the presence of pregnant girls in the school (Pillow, 2000). Pregnant adolescents in Pillow's study repeatedly said they wanted to learn what other students were learning but reported many experiences when their wishes were put aside by school officials (p. 205).

Most studies of "parent" involvement in fact use a sample consisting entirely of mothers. In the past decade, scholars and professionals have paid increasing attention to the roles of fathers and other males in children's lives, including their education.

Casper and Schultz (1999) conducted interviews with 17 lesbian or gay parents of children ages 3-7, and with 20 staff members from their children's elementary schools, preschools, and child care centers. Results indicate that school staff revealed a continuum of attitudes about homosexuality and gay/lesbian parents, ranging from rejection of homosexual families as "disruptive to American life" to pride about the diversity of families in the child care center (Casper & Schultz, 1999, p. 140).

Bernstein (2000), in a narrative about her work with gay and lesbian couples in family therapy, notes that for a straight professional, "one's intellectual formulations are ahead of one's visceral responses to [sexual identity] issues" (p. 443), and that the professional can benefit from "an attitude inventory," including such questions as "What are the family therapist's 'family values' and how inclusive are they of gay, lesbian, bisexual, and transgender people and their families?" (p. 446).

The Seattle Gay and Lesbian Task Force used positive-focus interviews (rather than problem-focus interviews) with 33 gay/lesbian parents and 11 child care providers (Dispenza, 1999) with the goal of hearing what participants believed worked well in their relationships with their children's early childhood programs. Respondents repeatedly indicated that they felt most comfortable with child care settings in which staff members were willing to learn about the particular needs of families headed by gay/lesbian parents (p. 15). For example, one father related that his (adopted) son's center "called us just before the mother's day celebration and asked us how we would like to approach the issue. We told them to have our son simply write, 'To someone special'" (p. 15).

Variables within Programs

Characteristics of programs, official and unofficial, can influence relationships between staff and parents. The degree to which program schedules mesh with those of the parents can be a key to how much contact, and what kind, parents and staff are likely to have with each other. Opportunities to exchange information may be limited, for example, as suggested by findings in child care settings that show that parents and caregivers exchanged significant amounts of information during their few minutes of contact when children were being dropped off and picked up from child care (Powell, 1989; Endsley & Minish, 1991). Efforts of program staff to accommodate parents' needs may fail without input from all parents. Skilton-Sylvester (2002) comments that a Philadelphia community center offered ESL classes in the evening, so adults who worked could attend, "based on the assumption that work would happen during the day." This scheduling became a barrier for one of the women in her study who worked in a restaurant, because classes met during the "dinner rush" (p. 20).

Home visiting is seen as an optimal venue for parenting education and support in programs as varied as Head Start, HIPPY, and Hawaii's Healthy Start. However, an analysis of six home-visiting program evaluations indicates that, although evaluations often report success for home visiting, the

Characteristics of programs, official and unofficial, can influence relationships between staff and parents. The degree to which program schedules mesh with those of the parents can be a key to how much contact, and what kind, parents and staff are likely to have with each other. Opportunities to exchange information may be limited, for example, as suggested by findings in child care settings that show that parents and caregivers exchanged significant amounts of information during their few minutes of contact when children were being dropped off and picked up from child care.

programs vary so widely in purpose, services offered, and number of contact hours that it is difficult to generalize about the effects of home visits on parent or child outcomes (Gomby, Culross, & Behrman, 1999).

The longitudinal qualitative study of a home-visiting program by Hebbeler and Gerlach-Downey (2002) determined that the program was not as effective as expected because of a disconnection between the program's view of the home visitors' role and the practitioners' perspective. Although the purpose of the program was to provide school-readiness-related activities, the home visitors tended instead to see their primary role as one of social support. Consequently, they did not do as much teaching or modeling of desired behaviors as was officially prescribed (p. 42).

Attitudes of program staff may vary widely even when certain actions or policies are mandated. Soodak and Erwin (2000) investigated parents' reports of their experiences with being involved in the education of their children with severe disabilities. They conducted semi-structured interviews with 10 parents, all of whom lived in urban or suburban New York or New Jersey communities and had a child under 8 years old in an inclusive setting. Four were in pre-kindergarten settings. These parents reported that school personnel had a wide range of official responses to their efforts to participate in decision making for their children. Some experienced "open communication" involving transactions that were reciprocal, ongoing, uncensored, and informal (e.g., extending beyond the regular school day) (p. 34). They reported feeling "gratified" when school staff invited them to "tell us how" to work with their children (p. 35). Others experienced "restricted communication"—limitations on when and with whom they could speak. For instance, meeting times about a child were sometimes set despite a parent's schedule conflict (p. 34).

In a report on case studies of two Michigan Head Start programs, Lubeck and deVries (2000) noted that the atmosphere of the programs differed considerably with regard to fundamental ideas about parent-staff relationships. At a program serving mostly white families in a rural community, discourse analysis indicated that the administrators saw the program as "family-like," with the director as a "mom" figure and parents as relatively passive recipients of the help offered (Lubeck & deVries, 2000, pp. 644-645). Discourse analysis at an urban site with an African American population, however, suggested that administrators there emphasized the parents' agency, urging them toward further active involvement in a manner reminiscent of preaching; in fact, they referred to their program as being like a church (p. 649).

Although it is unwise to generalize from a pair of case studies, such comparisons can shed light on trends in the field and underscore the importance of contextual variables in understanding parent-staff relationships. These studies suggest that, even when certain types of involvement are mandated by law, as is the case with Head Start and inclusive programs serving children who have disabilities, local practices may create barriers to parent-staff communication in ways that are not aligned with the intent of the policies. Taken together, findings from these studies suggest that the goals of a program may or may not be well served by local policies or interpretations of policies.

Parents' Individual Experiences and Traits

The impact of any of the variables previously mentioned on parent-program relationships is likely to be interwoven with the effects of individual differences among the people involved. This review of the research indicates that parents involved in any program may have different and shifting forms and degrees of investment in participating. Research and theory suggest a variety of intrapersonal influences on their choices. Given the often-mentioned challenge of recruiting and retaining parents in programs, surprisingly little research has been done regarding parents' stated reasons for participating or not participating. Parents of toddlers from 11 licensed Chicago child care centers who enrolled in a 12-session mental health promotion/prevention intervention reported a variety of reasons for participating. Those who stated that they enrolled because they "wanted to share experiences with other parents" and to learn to discipline their children more effectively were found to be most likely to stay with the program for its duration. Parents who identified other motivations were more likely to drop out (Gross, Julion, & Fogg, 2001).

Dolan and Haxby (1995) noted that "time commitments and other responsibilities" and "personal problems" were the most frequently cited reasons given by parents who dropped out of a mental health intervention after attending one or more sessions (p. 14). Of the eligible parents that they contacted who chose not to take part in the program at all, on the other hand, more than one-fourth gave as their primary reason their belief that the program would not "make a difference" (p. 13). (The number of nonparticipant and dropout parents who were contacted for this study is not made clear in the report, and no data are given regarding race or ethnicity.)

The findings from these two studies underscore the obvious: that it is difficult for a program to serve parents who do not perceive that participating will be useful to them; these parents are clearly among the "hard-to-serve" parents. Furthermore, parents who believe that the program will be useful still may be unable to sustain their commitment because of external factors in their lives.

In their model of parent involvement in children's education, Hoover-Dempsey and Sandler (1995) emphasize the interconnection of three intrapersonal variables: (1) the parents' personal construction of the parental role that includes participating in the child's education (p. 313), (2) a positive sense of personal efficacy for being useful to the child's education (pp. 313-314), and (3) awareness of occasions or requests for involvement from the child or the school (p. 310). According to this model, parents then choose ways to be involved that suit their skills and knowledge, the demands on their time and energy, and specific requests from the program or their children.

It is difficult for a program to serve parents who do not perceive that participating will be useful to them; these parents are clearly among the "hard-to-serve" parents. Furthermore, parents who believe that the program will be useful still may be unable to sustain their commitment because of external factors in their lives.

Two studies involving parents of children with special needs provide examples of how these intrapersonal factors might work. Allen and colleagues (1993) followed 31 African American families (33 children) who were involved with early childhood special education programs. In their 3-year qualitative study using interviews, informal conversations, and observations, they found that the parents initially tried to be actively involved. However, parents reported difficulty with the special education jargon and found that over time, the structure of decision-making meetings severely limited their input and ability to ask substantive questions. The researchers were also told by parents and program staff that memos about important meetings were sometimes not sent in time for parents to fit the meetings into their work schedules (Allen, Harry, & McLaughlin, 1993). In terms of the Hoover-Dempsey and Sandler model, these parents seemed at first to see involvement in education as part of their role as parents, but they experienced a reduced sense of self-efficacy as a result of their encounters with professional jargon. In addition, the lack of meaningful roles for them in Individualized Education Program (IEP) meetings created a sense that they were not invited into the process.

Soodak and Erwin (2000), on the other hand, found that 8 of the 10 parents who they interviewed recounted taking strong action on behalf of their children, including filing a lawsuit or moving to a different area in order to secure the education that they wanted for their children. One might speculate that these parents maintained a sense of self-efficacy that enabled their continued active participation and advocacy for their children. These findings suggest that individual differences among parents or populations may influence whether and how they respond to challenges in their relationships with programs that serve their children.

Skilton-Sylvester (2002) asserts the importance of seeing participation not in terms of individual motivations to become involved, or limitations to involvement, but as part of the interaction between several factors: (1) how parents define themselves, (2) the social contexts of their lives, (3) "which identities are acknowledged and recruited" by the program, and (4) what they see as the potential return on their investment from becoming (and staying) involved (p. 10).

Individual Differences among Staff Members

Staff members' communication styles can affect how a parent responds to the individual, the program, and the resources offered. Some communication tasks that staff members are likely to encounter may require special skills. For example, Henry and Purcell (2000) point out that although confrontation is a difficult skill to learn and is likely to increase anxiety in parents and staff alike, it is sometimes necessary, as in situations when abuse may be occurring (p. 280).

Another situation that calls for strong communication skills is the sharing of "bad news" about a child. In a previously mentioned study by Strauss and colleagues (1995), parents who had been informed that their infants had cleft lip or cleft palate reported on their level of satisfaction with how they had been informed about the child's condition. High satisfaction was associated with physicians who projected confidence, let the parents talk, made an effort to make the parents feel better, gave enough information about the child's condition, and allowed the parents to show feelings (Strauss et al., 1995). These qualities of interaction appear to have made a long-lasting impression on parents, given that some were reporting on events that had occurred several years prior to the study.

Quine and Rutter (1994) had similar findings in a study of mothers' satisfaction ($N = 166$) with how physicians informed mothers of their children's severe learning disabilities. Results of multiple regression analysis suggest several components of parent satisfaction with how the physician handled the encounter. High satisfaction was related to (1) being told immediately about problems, even when professionals were unsure of details; (2) hearing the diagnosis from someone with a sympathetic approach who "was a good communicator" (p. 1282); and (3) subsequent access to information about the child's condition that was easy to remember and understand, and not highly technical (p. 1282).

Individual staff members' approaches to program policies may also influence parent participation. For example, Pillow (2000) describes significant differences in classroom atmosphere among programs serving pregnant high school students. In classrooms in which teachers departed from the curriculum guide somewhat by introducing topics—gender roles, sex, birth control—through such strategies as playing games, listening to popular music, or watching videos (p. 211), the resulting discussions often went beyond what was observed in classrooms in which teachers adhered to the curriculum guide. The young women appeared to be comfortable sharing "frank and explicit ideas on sex, sexuality, labor, and childbirth" (p. 211), which the teacher would confirm or correct. The teacher commented to the author that she believed, "The girls know what they need to know about, and this way gives the girls important information ... in a way they can hear it" (p. 212). According to the author, teachers who used a more informal approach in the classroom continued to monitor the young women's diets and home situations and to express clear goals for the students (p. 212).

Two Approaches to Parent-Program Relationships

Two contemporary perspectives on parent-program relationships shape much of the discourse related to working with families toward the goal of school readiness. Both the *partnership construct* and the *family centeredness* concept seem to have arisen from concern for creating parent-staff relationships that reflect confidence in parents as agents of change and growth in their own lives and those of their children. These perspectives differ in origin and in emphasis, but they have in common an emphasis on parents' responsibilities for determining the family life course and a belief in their right to do so.

Both the *partnership construct* and the *family centeredness* concept seem to have arisen from concern for creating parent-staff relationships that reflect confidence in parents as agents of change and growth in their own lives and those of their children. These perspectives differ in origin and in emphasis, but they have in common an emphasis on parents' responsibilities for determining the family life course and a belief in their right to do so.

The Parent-Professional Partnership

The concept of "partnership" between parents and program staff can be found in the literature of early childhood special education, early intervention, early childhood education, and elementary/secondary education. One particularly comprehensive model can be found in Epstein's work regarding family-school-community partnerships in K-12 education (Connors & Epstein, 1995; Epstein, 2001). (For other examples, see Davies, 1996; Easen, Kendall, & Shaw, 1992; Owen, Ware, & Barfoot, 2000; Swap, 1993; National Education Goals Panel, n.d.)

The concept of "partnership" represents an ideal or model for parent-professional relationships, based on the assumptions that parents and programs can gather and pool their strengths and resources to make decisions and take action toward the shared goal of creating optimal situations for children. The rise of partnership as an ideal signals a shift away from the historically dominant view of parents as passive learners who must depend on "expert" resources in order to accomplish their child-rearing tasks. (See Powell & Diamond, 1996, for a detailed descriptive and explanatory summary of this history.) The concept of partnership implies relationships among equals, with mutually agreed upon explicit goals, clearly negotiated roles, and decision-making authority equitably distributed among participants.

Some issues regarding partnership have been identified by researchers and practitioners. Perhaps the most obvious is that partnership is often only loosely defined, varying from author to author, program to program, and even among participants in a single program. An individual teacher's view of "partnership," for example, may entail a professional-client type relationship in which parents "[supplement] the classroom experience by preparing the child for school, reinforcing the curriculum, and showing support (often symbolic) by attending school events" (Lareau, 2000, p. 35), rather than by taking part in governance and policy setting.

Programs using a partnership model may assume that a parent's goals for the family or the child are aligned with the program goals. In fact, what parents want may be at odds with what staff members want. Some parents involved in "partnerships" have had to pursue or threaten due process, take part in mediation, relocate their families, or find schools on their own that were willing to accept their children in order to have their disabled children in inclusive early childhood settings (Soodak & Erwin, 2000, p. 34).

Some critics of the partnership model question whether relationships between parents and the professionals who work with their children can in fact be egalitarian enough to be called partnerships. Parents often perceive that program personnel have considerable power over a family's life, while they have little influence over a program or its staff. They may have this perception even when relationships are not meant to be coercive in the way that they are between, for instance, a child protection agency and a parent

Some critics of the partnership model question whether relationships between parents and the professionals who work with their children can in fact be egalitarian enough to be called partnerships.

accused of child abuse or neglect. Several qualitative studies have suggested that parents may hesitate to express opinions or ideas because of concerns about displeasing their children's teachers or school administrators. Graue, Kroeger, and Prager (2001), for example, suggest that new elementary school parents learned how to be "a Solomon parent" through discourse with administrators, teachers, and other parents. Among the most important information was how to avoid the "nasty image" of the pushy parent (p. 488), which might result in negative repercussions for their children and themselves. Lareau (1996) and Soodak and Erwin (2000) report similar concerns from parents in their studies.

A related criticism is that "partnership" tends to be defined by the more powerful parties in parent-program interactions. For example, although parent participation in decision making, framed as "empowerment," was an integral goal of the original Head Start, some observers have noted an official shift over the years away from parental advocacy and decision making in individual Head Start centers and across the Head Start system. Greenberg (1998), in a discussion of parent involvement in Head Start, asserts that rather than assuring that parents are "partners at the core," many programs instead teach parents (e.g., how to follow medical advice, how to help children learn at home), brief parents (e.g., tell parents what the program's philosophy and curriculum are), and permit parents to be involved peripherally (p. 50). (For more detailed discussions, see Kuntz, 1998, and Greenberg, 1998.)

The Family-Centeredness Continuum

Assumptions about family strengths and ability to make decisions strongly influence an organization's policies governing interaction, as well as how the parents and professionals interact within a program's social network. Drawing upon their research in early intervention, human services, and their "help-giving practices," Dunst and colleagues suggest analyzing assumptions and expectations about parents and professionals in programs that serve families (Dunst, 2002) on a continuum from *professionally centered* to *family-centered* (Dunst, Boyd, Trivette, & Hamby, 2002).

Professionally centered (sometimes called *medical help-giving* or *expert-based*) models emphasize family deficiencies and needs. Parental viewpoints and opinions carry little weight in the design of curriculum, interventions, or activities for the children or the family. Parents and other family members are expected to be passive participants in any intervention or activity in which the professional experts believe their help is needed. Contemporary research in medical settings suggests that the emphasis there is changing to become less professionally centered, as articles have begun to address such topics as "role negotiation" (see, for example, Callery & Smith, 1991) between medical staff and parents, as well as parents' perspectives on desirable characteristics of parent-pediatrician interactions (see, for example, Quine & Rutter, 1994, or Strauss et al., 1995).

At the other end of the continuum are *family-centered* programs. A family-centered approach (equivalent to *compensatory* or *empowerment* approach)

Assumptions about family strengths and ability to make decisions strongly influence an organization's policies governing interaction, as well as how the parents and professionals interact within a program's social network.

emphasizes the family members' ability to make decisions that benefit their families and to use available resources for their own benefit, when they are adequately informed and have access to other appropriate resources. The professionals act as agents of the family in identifying and facilitating access to key information, support, and other resources. The family's own expectations and resources are seen as guiding these processes (Dunst et al., 2002, p. 223).

Family centeredness is by no means universal either in help-giving practice or in early childhood programs. In a survey of 280 early childhood teachers (kindergarten, child care, and Head Start) in a large midwestern city, for example, Burton (1992) found significant differences among public school early childhood teachers and child care or Head Start teachers regarding attitudes associated with family centeredness. Head Start and child care teachers reported more positive beliefs about family strengths than did public school teachers. They also reported feeling more competent about interacting with families (pp. 54-55).

> **Parents have a deep personal investment in the well-being of their children and families. Given the many potential differences between program staff and the parents they serve, achieving trust is an important but potentially challenging part of parent-program relationships.**

This review of the literature also found debate, or at least tension, around the implementation of "family-centered" practice. Questions have arisen over whether family-centered practice is possible in inherently coercive relationships such as exist between child protection workers and parents who have abused their children (Henry & Purcell, 2000). As with the partnership model, there is debate over whether staff actually understand what information parents have and what they may need in order to participate fully in family-centered problem solving (Greene, 1999). A full cross-disciplinary discussion of family-centered practice is outside the scope of this review, but for readers interested in other perspectives, the following articles may be useful:

- Dunst's (2002) review and synthesis of qualitative and quantitative research evidence on family-centeredness, as well as the literature review of Dunst, Boyd, Trivette, and Hamby (2002, pp. 221-222).

- A report of a study by Romer and Umbreit (1998) and Winton's (1998) response in the same journal issue.

- A discussion in a special issue of *Topics in Early Childhood Special Education,* featuring Baird and Peterson (1997) and a response by Mahoney and Wheeden (1997).

Relational Trust

In this review of the literature on parent-program relationships, one concept stands out for its potential to bridge gaps in our understanding of effective parent-program relationships. *Trust* is mentioned many times as a key to effective interaction between parents and program personnel (see, e.g., Henry & Purcell, 2000; Meier, 2002; Bryk & Schneider, 2002; Bernstein, 2000). Parents have a deep personal investment in the well-being of their children and families. Given the many potential differences between program staff and the parents they serve, achieving trust is an important but potentially challenging part of parent-program relationships.

The construct of *relational trust* provides the framework for case study analyses of social networks in three elementary Chicago public schools (Bryk & Schneider, 2002). The authors note in a discussion of their findings that the day-to-day social exchanges between people in schools "fuse into distinct social patterns that generate (or fail to generate) organization-wide resources" (p. 122). "Discernment of the intentions of others" (p. 21)—that is, the interpretation one person makes of another's behavior—is basic to daily interactions, particularly among those who are involved with one another for some common purpose, such as "advancing the best interests of the children" (p. 16). Relational trust enables people to work cooperatively and is seen as a key factor in the ability of people to change their perspectives and behaviors and to influence organizational change.

In an overview of their theory, Bryk and Schneider (2002) identify four key "discernments" that form the foundation of relational trust: *social respect, personal regard, perceived competence of the participants,* and *perception of basic integrity. Social respect* is shown through interactions "marked by a genuine sense of listening to what each person has to say and in some fashion, taking this into account in subsequent actions or conversations" (p. 126). When social and political inequities are evident, social respect is especially important. One example can be found in the Ray et al. report on programs serving parents with mental retardation. In two of the programs, administrators asked volunteers or paid aides to leave when it became apparent that they did not "interact well" with persons with mental retardation or did not accept their rights as parents (Ray, Rubenstein, & Russo, 1994, p. 733).

Personal regard involves behaving in ways that reduce another person's feelings of dependency and vulnerability. In any situation involving parents and other adults interacting in the interest of children, any of the adults may be dependent on the others for information, support, and other resources. Bryk and Schneider (2002) note that anything one participant may do to offset another's feelings of dependency and vulnerability will affect the level of trust (p. 25). For instance, one mother told Soodak and Erwin (2000) that she avoided being in her child's classroom because "if I rock the boat with this teacher, I would have made it worse for my son" (p. 38). The teacher's behavior toward the mother obviously had not alleviated her sense of vulnerability. Personal regard is in part the result of a sense that participants truly care about one another; a key practice associated with personal regard is participants' perceived willingness "to extend themselves beyond what is formally required by, say, a job definition or a union contract" (p. 126).

Perceived competence of other participants is another criterion of trust. Parents want to believe that teachers and other professionals involved with them are capable of helping achieve the desired outcome (pp. 23-24) (e.g., a child's readiness for school). Likewise, staff members want to know whether the parents can be counted on to work with them (pp. 24-25). Perceptions of parental competence are at the core of family-centered programming as described by Dunst and colleagues (Dunst, 2002; Dunst, Boyd, Trivette, &

Bryk and Schneider (2002) identify four key "discernments" that form the foundation of relational trust: social respect, personal regard, perceived competence of the participants, and perception of basic integrity.

Hamby, 2002). Bryk and Schneider (2002) note that some parents may find it difficult to discern professional competence if their personal experience has not provided them with strong models (p. 24).

The *perception of the basic integrity* of others involved in the interactions is another key criterion of relational trust (Bryk & Schneider, 2002, p. 127). In any relationship, and especially in parent-professional relationships, participants need to see each other as reliable, as "keeping their word" (p. 25-26) or "meaning what they say." Perceptions of integrity may not be stable. Official policy changes, for instance, may influence parents' perceptions of a program's integrity. Ames and Ellsworth (1997) provide examples in a report of a case study that they conducted in a Head Start program. They document parental concerns over and negative responses to changes in the emphasis on parent decision making, including growing distrust of the administrators and policy makers.

Trust is also a major concern in parent-program relationships outside of schools. In a discussion of the difficulty of taking a family-centered approach and building rapport with families who have abused or may abuse their children, Henry and Purcell (2000) explore integrity-related issues. Although they propose that a family-centered approach is desirable, they assert the need to be straightforward with the families about the coercive aspects of the professional's official role. Although the professional may support the family's staying together, he or she must make clear the need for the family to do what is required by the state (p. 279).

Recent research, especially qualitative studies, suggest a generalized mistrust of "experts" on the part of the poor and marginalized members of society, who tend to be the most vulnerable and the most difficult to serve, but also among the population as a whole. It seems likely that if parents do not trust a professional who tells them what to do or how to change, they are less likely to accept that person's suggestions or directions for parenting or for involvement in their children's education.

Forging relational trust can be challenging, in spite of the common goal of furthering children's best interests. When the differences between parents and staff—the varied values, attitudes, and beliefs that they bring to their interactions—become barriers to effective communication, important resources such as information and support may not be exchanged optimally, if at all.

Emerging Issues in Connecting with Parents about School Readiness

6

Introduction

Several significant issues have emerged during our survey of the theoretical, descriptive, and empirical literature on connecting with parents of young children. The issues tend to be difficult to isolate and are interconnected across different fields (early childhood education, early intervention, information science, health care, etc.). In this chapter, we highlight four frequently addressed issues and some of their finer details, using literature discussed in previous chapters as well as supporting literature not previously mentioned. These issues are (1) the content of parent-program communication; (2) recruitment, retention, and commitment in programs serving families with young children; (3) the nature and nurturing of program-parent relationships; and (4) the potential of comprehensive, integrated programs to connect with parents. These are by no means the only issues that might be identified in our literature review.

Issue #1: The Content of Parent-Program Communication

We identified four key questions related to the content of information that parents and program staff may need from and attempt to provide for each other:

- What information do program personnel want to offer parents?
- What information do parents say they need?
- What information do program personnel need from parents?
- What information do parents want program personnel to have?

These questions are addressed both directly and indirectly in the literature that we reviewed on parent-program connections.

In this chapter, we highlight four frequently addressed issues and some of their finer details, using literature discussed in previous chapters as well as supporting literature not previously mentioned. These issues are (1) the content of parent-program communication; (2) recruitment, retention, and commitment in programs serving families with young children; (3) the nature and nurturing of program-parent relationships; and (4) the potential of comprehensive, integrated programs to connect with parents.

75

What Information Do Program Personnel Want to Offer Parents?

Some general agreement among professionals can be seen within the literature relative to what is considered important for parents to know in the joint effort to foster school readiness. Among the frequently noted types of content are

- basic prenatal or child health information, provided in such programs as Hawaii Healthy Start, Healthy Start America, Early Head Start, and programs for pregnant adolescents;
- information about a child's specific medical condition or need that may affect his or her development, provided by health care practitioners or intervention specialists;
- child development information, which is provided in Early Head Start and MELD for Young Moms (Treichel, 1995), PAT, and the National Black Child Development Institute's (NBCDI's) Parent Empowerment Project (PEP);
- information to enhance family or parent-child relationships (including how to understand and respond to children's needs, alternatives to corporal punishment, and awareness of parental responsibility toward a child), provided in such programs as Early Head Start, MELD for Young Moms (Treichel, 1995), Webster-Stratton's (2000) Incredible Years programming, and the Chicago Child-Parent Centers (Reynolds, 2000), and NBCDI's PEP;
- adult education content such as GED classes or ESL instruction, offered in such programs as AVANCE, Even Start, and the Chicago Child-Parent Centers;
- information about at-home learning activities for children, offered by such programs as PAT, HIPPY, Head Start, and NBCDI's PEP;
- information about the curriculum and services that specific programs provide for young children, offered by Head Start, parent cooperatives, and early childhood programs affiliated with Even Start;
- information about supporting children's classroom experiences through active involvement, provided in Head Start, parent cooperatives, Chicago Child-Parent Centers, and early childhood programs affiliated with Even Start;
- information about services in the community, offered by such programs as the Chicago Child-Parent Centers, Head Start, and NBCDI's PEP.

What Information Do Parents Say They Need?

Many programs position parents as learners in need of information from experts. Program staff may make many assumptions about what parents need to know, but very few studies have focused on the information needs that parents experience in the years before their children begin school.

Women who were pregnant with twins (McKenzie, 2002) and pregnant drug-addicted women (Dervin, Harpring, & Foreman-Wernet, 1999) expressed strong interest in maternal and infant health information specific to their own

Many programs position parents as learners in need of information from experts. Program staff may make many assumptions about what parents need to know, but very few studies have focused on the information needs that parents experience in the years before their children begin school.

situations. Parents who were being informed for the first time of their child's diagnosis of cleft lip or cleft palate reported that they wanted opportunities to discuss possible related problems with the physician and to be given referrals to other parents whose children had the same conditions. British parents of young children ranked child health information very high among their information needs (Nicholas & Marden, 1998).

Parents of infants and toddlers in two communities (one urban, one rural) placed questions about children's normal development very high among their concerns; however, parents from the rural community expressed significantly more concerns about health and physical development than did the urban parents (98% vs. 85%) (Morisset, 1994, pp. 28, 34-35). The author did not investigate reasons for this difference. All these findings suggest that desire for specific content may vary between communities of parents even when some factors (e.g., socioeconomic level) are similar.

For homeless parents, basic survival-related information may take priority over other knowledge, but these parents do want to know where their children might attend school and other information about education programs (Hersberger, 2001; Newman, 1999).

Surveys and interviews of parents and guardians in medical and education settings indicate that parents want to be informed regarding their children, especially when there are problems, in ways that they are able to understand. They want and need information that is free of jargon (Allen, Harry, & McLaughlin, 1993), but they prefer that it not be oversimplified (Kai, 1996). This finding suggests that opportunities exist for professionals to scaffold knowledge that will help parents better understand their children's situations.

Some research has shown that parents want information that will help them navigate the education system; this need is expressed most strongly among recent immigrants (see, e.g., Delgado-Gaitan, 2001) and parents whose children have special needs (see, e.g., Soodak & Erwin, 2000).

As with any other group of information seekers, parents are likely to feel the strongest interest in content that they believe will be useful to them—that is, information with the potential to "bridge a gap" that *they perceive* in their knowledge (Dervin, 1999).

What Information Do Program Personnel Need from Parents?

Little information is available regarding content that program personnel need or want from parents. Experience tells us that programs typically request specific family- and child-related information from parents (e.g., address, family composition, income level, parent's education level). The potential efficacy of parent-completed developmental questionnaires to assess children was supported in a study by Squires and colleagues (Squires, Potter, Bricker, & Lamorey, 1998).

As with any other group of information seekers, parents are likely to feel the strongest interest in content that they believe will be useful to them—that is, information with the potential to "bridge a gap" that *they perceive* in their knowledge (Dervin, 1999).

Lakey's (1997) narrative about a conflict in a parent-cooperative nursery school indicates that in such a setting, staff members actively solicit opinions and ideas from parents about the handling of curriculum matters. Dispenza's (1999) report on interviews conducted with gay and lesbian parents indicates that some caregivers and teachers ask parents how to adapt activities (such as making Mother's Day cards) so that gay/lesbian families will be fully included.

The practical and professional literatures of education and early intervention indicate that program personnel often want to know parents' expectations of their children and the program, and any plans they may have for participation in program activities, although no studies were found that dealt with the gathering of such information.

Although experience indicates that some programs actively solicit parental evaluations of services, that activity does not appear to have been a topic of research.

What Information Do Parents Want Program Personnel to Have?

Some reports of ethnographic studies in elementary schools indicate that educators and service providers may be unaware that they lack information about the communities in which they are located, particularly minority communities—information that would help them to work more effectively with parents to enable children to operate comfortably in both the mainstream culture and their own (see, e.g., Romero, in press; Delpit, 1995). Romero, for example, emphasizes the need for program personnel working with families from Pueblo communities to understand the "multicalendar lives" of the Pueblo families when scheduling program activities.

Susan Matoba Adler (2001) found in interviews with Asian American mothers that some of them wished that teachers would have more than superficial knowledge of the children's backgrounds. "I would like the teacher to do research and learn about the children's cultures," said one parent. "They should be sensitive and knowledgeable" (p. 282).

Evidence can be found in qualitative studies that language-minority parents want program personnel to understand that they are deeply concerned about and interested in their children's school experiences, despite the frequent misperception that such parents are uninvolved and uninterested (see, e.g., Quintero, 1998; Delgado-Gaitan, 1996, 2001). There is some indication that parents also want teachers and other staff to be aware that their work schedules and other responsibilities may impinge on their ability to be involved in expected ways (see, e.g., Allen, Thompson, Hoadley, Engelking, & Drapeaux, 1997b; Allen, Harry, & McLaughlin, 1993; Driebe & Cochran, 1996; Skilton-Sylvester, 2002).

Anecdotal evidence indicates that parents who have disabilities would like staff to be knowledgeable about what the parents' actual needs are regarding

Evidence can be found in qualitative studies that language-minority parents want program personnel to understand that they are deeply concerned about and interested in their children's school experiences, despite the frequent misperception that such parents are uninvolved and uninterested.

accommodation, including assistive technology, so that the parents can participate more effectively in activities that promote family resilience and children's school readiness. Parents with disabilities also want program personnel to know that they, as parents, are autonomous decision makers who are, with accommodations, capable of competent care taking (see, e.g., Reinelt & Fried, 1993).

Some studies include reports from parents of times when their information about their children and their families is sought and valued by program personnel (see, e.g., Soodak & Erwin, 2000). Despite the contemporary emphasis on empowerment and family-centeredness, however, several studies indicate that parents sometimes report that the child-related information that they offer may not be accepted or used. Examples can be found in reports of parents' efforts to communicate with personnel regarding their children with special needs (Soodak & Erwin, 2000; Allen, Harry, & McLaughlin, 1993) and in reports of parent experiences related to their children having trouble in school. A striking example of the latter can be found in McClelland's report of the difficulties one family faced in persuading school officials to accept the fact that their son was diagnosed with a learning disability (McClelland, 1996; also see Graue, Kroeger, & Prager, 2001; Lareau, 2000, p. 111).

Specific details about the content of communication between programs and parents are not usually offered in the research literature. An author is unlikely to show exactly what is included in a specific program's parent newsletter, in its handouts about home learning activities, or in parenting classes. Analysis of the content of actual conversations between staff members and parents is seldom provided (exceptions include Endsley & Minish, 1991; Owen, Ware, & Barfoot, 2000; Cane, Ranganathan, & McKenzie, 2000; Cane & McKenzie, 2001), although parent reports and staff reports of their interactions with one another can be found (see, e.g., Casper & Schultz, 1999; Ames & Ellsworth, 1997; Hebbeler & Gerlach-Downie, 2002; Strauss, Sharp, Lorch, & Kachalia, 1995; Quine & Rutter, 1994). Examples or models of communication practices are more often found in the practitioner-oriented literature, where they are likely to be in the form of suggested activities or hypothetical illustrations.

Issue #2: Recruitment, Retention, and Commitment in Programs

A number of studies suggest that even when parental stress is great and family resources are limited, parents still are likely to be interested in fostering their children's development and learning in whatever ways that they are able (see, e.g., Dauber & Epstein, 2001; Chin & Newman, 2002; Newman, 1999; Delgado-Gaitan, 1996). Parents of young children may use organizations or agencies as sources of information, services, or support for their child-rearing efforts—or they may not. In fact, a parent's willingness or ability to use what such programs offer may be a sign of their resilience.

The staff of these programs want to reach parents—in fact, often their mission is to provide resources for vulnerable families. The literature covered in our review indicates, however, that programs often report disappointing results of their efforts to recruit parents and to keep them engaged long enough for the program to be beneficial. Quite a bit has been said in the practical literature about techniques for gaining parent participation and support. Comparatively little appears in the research, however, regarding the variety of reasons that parents may not accept or use information or other resources even when regular attendance is not part of the program. The actual decisions that parents may make that result in some parents being "hard to serve" are often de-emphasized in research, however, and in professional discussions of how to foster relationships with them.

We have identified the following three key questions related to parents' participation in programs:

- What is known about how programs address challenges that arise in recruiting parents to take part in programs and activities intended to directly or indirectly benefit their children?
- What is known about how programs address challenges that arise in retaining parents in programs and activities intended to directly or indirectly benefit their children?
- What is known about how programs address challenges that have been identified in parental commitment to regularly attending programs intended to benefit their children?

Each of these questions is addressed below, accompanied by examples taken from the literature.

What Is Known about Challenges to Recruitment?

Recruitment, sometimes called outreach, entails persuading a parent to become involved by accepting a particular role (such as learner, observer, volunteer, "partner") for the direct or indirect benefit of the child's education and well-being. Home-visiting programs, as well as those that offer site-based resources, have reported challenges to recruitment. For example, Gomby and colleagues note in their meta-analysis of home-visiting program evaluations that data from Hawaii's Healthy Start and another visiting nurse program indicate that an estimated 10% to 25% of the parents who are invited to enroll do not choose to do so (Gomby, Culross, & Behrman, 1999, p. 16). (No information is provided regarding the characteristics of those who choose not to participate.)

The practical and professional literature addresses recruitment far more often than does the empirical work, offering suggestions based on practitioner experience and professional wisdom. Descriptive reports also provide sketchy summaries of recruitment activities. For example, the report of a Monongalia County (West Virginia) Even Start evaluation lists recruitment practices, including "door-to-door recruitment, awareness sessions, community information campaigns; and solicitation and referrals from Head Start and Title I teachers, classroom teachers, other service agencies, and clients in the program" (Meehan, Walsh, Swisher, Spring, & Lewis, 1999). Unfortunately, the authors do not indicate how many parents were recruited using these methods, and whether some methods were more successful than others.

Harachi, Catalano, and Hawkins (1997) documented recruiting efforts for a parent training program aimed at parents of late-elementary-age children from several ethnic populations in an urban area: African American, Latino, Native American, and Samoan. Three types of recruiting strategies were used: direct contact based on an existing relationship (e.g., a pastor's spouse contacted members of the congregation), direct contact with a person unknown to the recruiter (the so-called "cold call"), and indirect contact (e.g., brochures left at community social service agencies serving the target populations). Incentives to attend were offered: transportation, refreshments, and child care featuring structured activities. Bilingual individuals were recruited for the Hispanic and Samoan populations. Recruitment of Native parents was challenging, according to the authors, because their families were not geographically concentrated. The authors report that the most successful strategy in the Native community was hiring elders who were well known and respected in the Native community, who "made lengthy and repeated contacts to families to recruit them" (p. 31); advertising at pow-wows was also considered successful (p. 31).

In two pre-kindergarten and kindergarten classrooms in which parent partici-pation was low, Serpell and colleagues instituted an action research project with the teachers, designed to involve parents in literacy activities with their children. Planned interventions for the project included a home visit to each family, requests for items to be sent from home, and a week-long written or audiotaped "diary" to be kept by parents of their child's everyday activities. The teachers involved reported increased parent involvement in their children's literacy activities, and one teacher stated, "I'm seeing parents I've never seen before" (Serpell, Baker, Sonnenschein, Gorham, & Hill, 1996, p. 36). Another teacher commented that casual discussions with parents at arrival and departure had been at least as meaningful as the planned monthly meetings (p. 29).

What Is Known about Challenges to Retention?

Attrition appears to be a problem for many, if not all, programs that attempt to provide resources through activities that involve regular attendance. Researchers and programs find it difficult to follow parents who leave programs in order to hear the reasons that they give for no longer being involved with the programs. Results of studies that have been able to do so suggest that some parents stay with a program because their goals for participation are well matched to the program's goals—an especially impor-tant factor when the program is intended to bring about some change in parental behavior, because parents are likely to resist efforts to change if they see no reason to do so. Similarly, some parents who drop out do so because their reasons for participating in the first place do not mesh with what the program offers. Finally, some parents who leave do so because work and family schedules make it too difficult to keep the program among their commitments (Harachi, Catalano, & Hawkins, 1997; Chin & Newman, 2002; Dreibe & Cochran, 1996) or because the risks of continued involvement (e.g., leaving a teenage child at home alone, returning home under unsafe conditions) outweigh the perceived benefits.

The National Black Child Development Institute's Parent Empowerment Project uses a variety of strategies to hold parents' interest in their programs: "audio and visual aids, games, numerous interactive and participatory activities, and formal and informal presentations by professionals and role models from within the parents' own communities" (Moore & Barbarin, 2003). (No empirical data were provided supporting the use of these strategies over others, however.)

Harachi and colleagues speculate that one factor in retention for the parent training project that they studied may have been that workshops for Hispanic and Samoan parents were offered in their home languages (Harachi, Catalano, & Hawkins, 1997, pp. 29-30). They also note that workshop leaders (who had been recruited from the target communities) were "encouraged to adapt the curriculum ... or include other material as they felt would be appropriate" for their workshops (p. 31). The result was that most workshop leaders added sessions, and a majority (59%) added other topics, including definitions of child abuse (considered especially important to recent immigrants) and discussions on handling incidents of discrimination.

What Is Known about Challenges to Parents' Regular Attendance?

Commitment involves having parents participate in a program from start to finish so that they can gain the full perceived benefits of a program. Staff of programs for families considered vulnerable often report that few parents attend all the sessions or remain with a program for the duration.

Harachi and colleagues, for example, reported that approximately 54.5% of the 455 parents recruited for a series of parent workshops attended at least one-half of the sessions, while 14% attended all sessions (Harachi, Catalano, & Hawkins, 1997, p. 34). The various target populations differed in attendance, according to the authors. Of the African American parents, for example, 63.5% attended half or more of the sessions, while 42.2% of the Native American parents did so (p. 34). Workshop presenters at many sites in that study made phone calls to remind parents of upcoming sessions, and parents often reported that work schedule changes affected whether they could attend (p. 34). The study does not compare recruitment, retention, or commitment statistics with other programs.

The Third Annual National Even Start Evaluation includes mention of incentives used to maintain attendance: "parent's night out, family nights, holiday parties, picnics, and field trips" (St. Pierre et al., 2003, p. 85). Other such activities included a pizza party as a reward for 100% attendance at parent

Commitment involves having parents participate in a program from start to finish so that they can gain the full perceived benefits of a program. Staff of programs for families considered vulnerable often report that few parents attend all the sessions or remain with a program for the duration.

conferences and "attendance coupons" that could be used at local stores (p. 85). The Even Start evaluation also mentions that programs scheduled their early childhood classes to correspond with the times of adult education classes. One Even Start project required parents who were not employed to attend classes four days a week, while allowing those with jobs to attend two days a week. In addition, some projects provided transportation for parents and children, and some provided meals for parents and children (p. 85). The relative success of these strategies is not assessed in the evaluation.

Issue #3: The Nature and Nurturing of Program-Parent Relationships

Program personnel often feel frustrated when it is difficult to make or maintain optimum contact with those parents who are likely to be in greatest need of information, support, and other resources. In many settings, professionals' understanding of vulnerable and hard-to-serve parents remains inadequate, and working with them remains a challenge. Our review of the literature revealed a variety of analytical tools that might be applied to interactions between parents and program staff. In particular, an analysis of *relational trust* (Bryk & Schneider, 2002) in parent-program relationships might provide insights into "what works" when connections are successful and what has not worked at those times when parents remain hard to serve.

Trust is considered fundamental to parent-professional relationships in many settings. Although elementary schools, medical settings, preschool programs, and mental health services differ in significant ways, it is reasonable to assume that the components of trust between parents and program staff (teachers, doctors, counselors, etc.) remain similar across settings. Without trust, parents are unlikely to be forthcoming about their own concerns and needs, and they are unlikely to do what program staff members believe is important for them to do.

This discussion of issues in parent-program relationships is constructed around the four components of relational trust articulated by Bryk and Schneider (2002):

- social respect
- personal regard
- perceived competence
- perceived integrity

For each of these components of relational trust, we pose questions that a program might use for self-analysis if it is facing difficulty in connecting with parents. The questions are accompanied by relevant examples of research and theory from different fields.

Social Respect

Social respect involves viewing others as being one's "social equals"—as having equal worth. Many parties play important and interdependent roles in

Trust is considered fundamental to parent-professional relationships in many settings. Although elementary schools, medical settings, preschool programs, and mental health services differ in significant ways, it is reasonable to assume that the components of trust between parents and program staff (teachers, doctors, counselors, etc.) remain similar across settings. Without trust, parents are unlikely to be forthcoming about their own concerns and needs, and they are unlikely to do what program staff members believe is important for them to do.

the education of a child, and each party needs to feel that others value his or her contribution. It is reasonable to assume that, given a choice, parents will not commit many of their resources to a situation in which they do not feel sufficiently valued or respected. If for some reason they still must participate, they may exercise their autonomy by not fully cooperating with what program personnel want of them and by disregarding the staff as sources of useful information and guidance.

The very acts of identifying some families as "vulnerable" and of offering resources to them, however, suggests some inequalities at least with regard to knowledge of child development, child rearing, and education. Parents in vulnerable families may indeed be less knowledgeable, perhaps even less competent, than typical parents. In that case, they may be able to benefit from what "experts" and professionals offer them. Nonetheless, parents are autonomous decision makers, just as program staff are, and their influence on the child is powerful, perhaps even more powerful than any contribution made by teachers or other adults who may seek to help. In that sense, even the parents whose competence and efficacy are in doubt are very much on a par with the program staff members who would like to facilitate change in families.

Has an Effort Been Made to Offer Resources That These Particular Parents Feel They Need?

Parents are likely to feel a lack of respect by a "one-size-fits-all" approach to delivering information and other resources. For example, some of the pregnant high school students in Pillow's report expressed resentment of the set curriculum that they felt did not fit their view of themselves (Pillow, 2000, pp. 204-205). Some reports have indicated that parents from minority communities sometimes feel that materials for mainstream audiences are not especially meaningful to them. For example, some African American and Latino parents in a PAT evaluation commented that certain parenting techniques (e.g., "time-out") were "probably something those white folks use" (Wagner, Spiker, Gerlach-Downie, & Hernandez, 2000, pp. 39-40). In contrast, the National Black Child Development Institute has designed materials especially for African American parents, affirming the value of their experiences.

Understanding the social networks and information-seeking trends in the community served by a program would aid in deciding how to approach parents. Many parents of young children are likely to seek information about child health and development and parenting from trusted informal sources rather than from "expert" sources such as books or credentialed professionals (Morisset, 1994; Marden & Nicholas, 1997; Nicholas & Marden, 1998; Jacobson & Engelbrecht, 2000). If program staff can gain a sense of who or what the trusted sources are within a community, providing information and services to parents through those sources might prove more effective than a more direct, professional-centered approach.

When personnel directly involve parents in decision making about what resources are to be available, parents' satisfaction is likely to increase. For

Parents are autonomous decision makers, just as program staff are, and their influence on the child is powerful, perhaps even more powerful than any contribution made by teachers or other adults who may seek to help.

example, Lubeck and colleagues reported that one Head Start center offered workshops requested by parents on such topics as auto mechanics but also provided "employability grants" to help individuals acquire or finish training that they needed to get jobs (Lubeck, Jessup, deVries, & Post, 2001, p. 514). The center responded to the parental goal of improving family life through better employment by providing the programming that parents requested, an indication that parents' choices were valued.

Do Parents from Backgrounds Different from Those of the Staff Feel That Staff Members Treat Them with Social Respect?

Professionally developed guidelines for positive working relationships with diverse families can be found in position statements of organizations such as the American Psychological Association (2003) and the National Association for the Education of Young Children (NAEYC, 1995). Kalyanpur and Harry (1999, pp. 118-119) propose that program staff take a "posture" of *cultural reciprocity,* and they recommend a four-step process:

- Identify for oneself the assumptions—about child rearing, health care, disability, age, gender, education, etc.—that are embedded in the professional interpretation of a child's or family's situation, and in recommendations for service or action.
- Find out to what extent the parents share these assumptions; and if they do not, how their perspective differs from the professional view.
- Attempt to fully understand and respectfully acknowledge parents' beliefs about the situation, while providing a complete explanation to the parent about the professional interpretation.
- Work out a solution to the problem that is acceptable to the professional and the parent, taking into account both the family's cultural constructs and the parents' need to know how to operate within the laws and customs of the United States.

Following such recommendations for professional practice with diverse families does not, of course, guarantee that parents will always feel that the staff members are treating them with respect. On the other hand, working with the parents to generate a clear understanding of culture-based differences is likely to improve communication and to show that staff members at least do not treat the differences as unimportant.

Personal Regard

According to Bryk and Schneider (2002, p. 25), personal regard involves acting in ways that reduce another's feelings of dependence and vulnerability. Personal regard is particularly important in parent-staff relationships because asymmetries of knowledge, influence, and autonomy are likely to exist when parents of vulnerable families interact with professionals. Personal regard is shown when staff members and parents not only listen to one another but also go out of their way to provide for one another's needs and wants. A mother whose child has special needs told Soodak and Erwin

> If program staff can gain a sense of who or what the trusted sources are within a community, providing information and services to parents through those sources might prove more effective than a more direct, professional-centered approach.

(2000) how much she appreciated a teacher's spending extra time to understand what her child was saying: "And she'll sit there for five minutes and be late for a meeting until she can figure out what my child wants, and then answer her" (p. 37).

Do Parents Feel More Comfortable and Less Vulnerable when Staff Members Interact with Them in Particular Ways?

Program descriptions of Even Start, for example, indicate that if early childhood programs are available at the same time that adult education is offered, parents know that they have a safe learning environment for their children while they are in classes or workshops. Some descriptions indicate that when travel distance and neighborhood safety are problems for parents, some programs have offered transportation (St. Pierre et al., 2003, p. 84). Such strategies are intended to reduce parent discomfort and show awareness of their needs.

Parents are likely to feel especially vulnerable when learning that their child has a problem of some kind. Research suggests that they are likely to respond positively when they receive both information and interpersonal sensitivity from the informing staff members, and when they are given opportunities to talk and to ask questions (see, e.g., Quine & Rutter, 1994; Strauss, Sharp, Lorch, & Kachalia, 1995; Worchel, Prevatt, Miner, Allen, Wagner, & Nation, 1995). Research also suggests that for many such parents referral to other parents whose children have similar problems is an important factor in their level of comfort with being given "bad news" (Strauss, Sharp, Lorch, & Kachalia, 1995).

Some parents who are extremely vulnerable present challenges to the caring stance of program staff. Women who are pregnant and addicted to drugs, for example, may expect disapproval and rejection and have great difficulty finding helpful interpersonal connections. According to Dervin and colleagues, the pregnant addicted women in their study gave many cues that they needed (but did not receive) "communication which encourages, inspires, and reassures; exchanges with the potential to contradict the isolation, self-doubt, and hopelessness which they themselves characterized as the contextual background behind their struggles" (Dervin, Harpring, & Foreman-Wernet, 1999). In their interpretation of their findings, the authors recommended that health care providers and others who work with pregnant drug-addicted women strive to act as listeners, as "helpers and confidantes," in order to reduce the women's fear and help them to pursue the course of action that is most likely to ensure the birth of a healthy infant.

There is growing awareness of the need for information that is accessible to parents with lower literacy skills (see, e.g., Wegner & Girasek, 2003; Klingbeil, Speece, & Schubiner, 1995). The need also grows for information on child development, parenting, health care, and mental health in languages other than English. Some programs, such as AVANCE, offer information and services (e.g., literacy classes) in both English and Spanish; MELD provides

Parents are likely to feel especially vulnerable when learning that their child has a problem of some kind. Research suggests that they are likely to respond positively when they receive both information and interpersonal sensitivity from the informing staff members, and when they are given opportunities to talk and to ask questions.

parent education materials in English, Spanish, and Hmong. When programs ignore or fail to accommodate the need that parents have for information and services that they can understand, parents may feel discounted. Creating high-readability materials and providing translation and interpreting services require extra time and money but also increase the likelihood that parents will be able to understand what is said and written and to collaborate more effectively with program staff. Making this extra effort also signals that parents who need those services are valued members of the community and of the program (see, e.g., Delgado-Gaitan, 1996, 2001; Quintero, 1998).

Under What Circumstances and Conditions Do Parents and Staff Have Access to Each Other?

Programs may be structured in such a way that contact between parents and staff is limited or so that they have a variety of opportunities for interaction. For example, Allen and colleagues reported that home visits from family service coordinators enhanced the sense of connection between rural families and their children's early childhood centers and schools. The coordinators' roles sometimes included explaining information that had come from the school; at other times, a coordinator might listen to a parent's concern about an issue and then suggest contacting the teacher or the school administration (Allen, Thompson, & Drapeaux, 1996). On the other hand, in some home-visiting programs, visits have a very specific focus. They may be relatively infrequent and may even be set up to decrease in frequency as the parent progresses (Gomby, Culross, & Behrman, 1999); visits may also be irregular. This kind of scheduling raises questions about how strong a sense of personal regard is being conveyed—and how useful such connections ultimately are for vulnerable parents.

Studies of parent-caregiver interactions in child care centers (Powell, 1989, Endsley & Minish, 1991) and parent-teacher interactions in pre-kindergarten programs (Serpell, Baker, Sonnenschein, Gorham, & Hill, 1996) suggest that caregivers and parents may exchange quite a bit of information informally when children are dropped off and picked up. But parents and staff may benefit from more frequent or sustained access to each other. Those parents who for whatever reason do not come into the center at those two key times may be missing some significant opportunities for talking about their children.

Lightfoot (1978) notes that education programs traditionally "organize public, ritualistic occasions that do not allow for real contact, negotiation, or criticism between parents and teachers" (pp. 27-28). She advocates instead "opportunities for ... meaningful, substantive discussion" in light of the fact that parents and teachers must continually negotiate areas of overlapping responsibility and "fuzzy boundaries" where distrust may grow (p. 26). Some evidence suggests that good-quality early childhood programs make a variety of efforts to communicate with families, and make such efforts frequently (Ghazvini & Readdick, 1994). Epstein (2001) advocates establishing clear two-way channels between home and school, with opportunities for discussions that include parents, staff, and sometimes children. She also suggests the frequent use of newsletters, notices, and memos, with "clear information" provided on policies and program changes (p. 411).

Perceived Competence

It is reasonable to assume that actual competence of parents and program staff is essential to providing resources that help foster children's school readiness, but no matter what the realities are concerning staff competence, it is the parents' perceptions of staff capabilities that matter in the formation of relational trust. It is easier to trust others if one believes that they are competent to carry out their roles than if one has real doubts about their competence. It helps when parents and staff members alike know that they can count on one another to "do their jobs" and when each participant knows that the others acknowledge his or her competence.

Do Staff Members Emphasize Parents' Competence to Make Decisions and to Carry Them Out?

Controversy continues over the roles that parents ought to have in making decisions that affect their children's development and early learning. The "expert" holds professionally accepted or established knowledge of child development, family life, literacy, and other domains that could be useful to parents in vulnerable families. Teachers, parent educators, home visitors, interventionists, and other staff members also have some control over the parents' access to information, support, adult education, and other resources, and perhaps even over what happens when the parent decides whether or how to use those resources. On the other hand, the parent's knowledge of his or her child and family is practical, "everyday" knowledge (Kalyanpur & Harry, 1999, p. 62), which may have a great deal to offer professionals interested in the benefit of the child. Staff members are likely to have as limited a picture of home activities as the parent has of the child's activities at preschool. Difference in perspective is not to be mistaken for lack of knowledge or competence. Parents are (appropriately) not objective and perhaps not even realistic about their own children, whereas the professional strives for a kind of optimal emotional distancing and rationality regarding a child (Katz, 1995, p. 165).

Although experts certainly have resources to offer, overemphasis on "parents as learners" neglects parents' role as decision makers. By definition, the more family centered a program is, the greater is the confidence at the official level in parents' abilities to make positive changes in family life (Trivette, Dunst, & Hamby, 1996; Dunst, Boyd, Trivette, & Hamby, 2002; Romer & Umbreit, 1998). It is clear that, no matter what the philosophies of the programs in which they participate, parents make the following decisions:

- What "school readiness" means for their children (Graue, 1993, pp. 82-88, 122-131)
- How they will support a child's development and education (Grolnick & Slowiaczek, 1994; Hoover-Dempsey & Sandler, 1995)

- What information and other resources they will seek (Marden & Nicholas, 1997; Nicholas & Marden, 1998; Morisset, 1994; Dervin, Harpring, & Foreman-Wernet, 1999)
- What information and other resources they will make available to program staff
- Their preferred means of communicating with program staff
- What use they will make of the resources offered (Pillow, 2000; Dervin, Harpring, & Foreman-Wernet, 1999; McInnis-Dittrich, 1996)
- Whether they will become involved in a child's intervention, child care, or education program, and in what ways (Hoover-Dempsey & Sandler, 1995; Grolnick & Slowiaczek, 1994)
- What to do when their goals for their child or family differ from those of the program (Soodak & Erwin, 2000; Ray, Rubenstein, & Russo, 1994; Ames & Ellsworth, 1997)
- What to do when dissatisfied with their relationships with program staff (Quintero, 1998; Delgado-Gaitan, 1996, 2001; Bryk & Schneider, 2002; Ames & Ellsworth, 1997)

Do Program Personnel Communicate Reasonable Expectations of Parents' Competence?

Parents who have experienced success with programs such as Head Start have reported being strongly influenced by staff members' assumption that they are competent to do what their families need. For example, a Head Start parent who later became a staff member told Ames and Ellsworth (1997), "[The director] said, 'Lila, you need to get your high school diploma.' So I did.... And I like to see parents when they would come to us [and say], 'I'd like to get my high school diploma.' 'Well, gal, I know how you can do that'" (p. 76).

Although most parents are active and capable decision makers, many may need more information than they have in order to make choices that serve the best interest of their children and families. When parents lack confidence in their ability to do things that help their children prepare for school, two questions arise: Are they really unable to understand or to make use of the resources provided here, or can they do so with some guidance? What, if any, guidance will be beneficial? Greene (1999), writing from her experience as the parent of a child with special needs, asserts that family-centered service providers can better assist parents like her by guiding parents toward a full understanding of their roles and options as collaborators in early intervention (p. 150).

Program staff must be sensitive to their own use of specialized vocabulary when providing such information or discussing a child's needs. Use of jargon can make it difficult for parents to understand what is being said (Lashley, Talley, Lands, & Keyserlingk, 2000; Allen, Harry, & McLaughlin, 1993; Kalyanpur & Harry, 1999; Lareau, 2000). On the other hand, parents do not want important information to be left out, especially when a child has a problem or condition that will require extra attention (Kalyanpur & Harry, 1999; Kai, 1996).

Parents who have experienced success with programs such as Head Start have reported being strongly influenced by staff members' assumption that they are competent to do what their families need.

Beth Harry, a special education researcher, provides the example of her own first encounter with "the language of special education in the United States" after her child was born with a disability. The phrase "multiply-handicapped" in written material confused her because she was accustomed to thinking of "multiply" as a verb—"to multiply" two amounts together (Kalyanpur & Harry, 1999, pp. 47-48)—rather than as an adjective meaning "in many ways." She thus found the material challenging, although she had more education than many other parents facing such a situation.

When a professional and a parent spend time talking with and listening to each other, they may be able to arrive at a common vocabulary that lets them exchange information effectively, as suggested by a medical study in which physicians, interpreters, and parents whose first language was not English sought ways to describe children's asthma symptoms (Cane, Ranganathan, & McKenzie, 2000; Cane & McKenzie, 2001). (For an extended discussion of professional expertise and language in parent-staff relationships in special education settings, see Kalyanpur & Harry, 1999, pp. 47-74.)

Do Parents Believe the Staff Members Are Competent at What They Do?

If parents do not perceive staff as competent to provide resources useful to them and their children, the program will lack the credibility to persuade parents to participate or to maintain their involvement. An extreme example can be found in Pillow's (2000) account of her research with pregnant high school students. One student, who seemed to feel that a particular teacher was unaware of the reality of their lives, openly dismissed the teacher's ability to inform them about abstinence and birth control options—"Whatta she know?" In other programs, a less forthright parent who believed that a staff member did not know enough to do his or her job might simply leave the relationship, and the program, without explanation.

Some studies indicate that being perceived as a competent communicator is important. Quine and Rutter (1994), investigating doctor-to-parent communication, found that parents' satisfaction with the way that physicians informed them about a child's disability was related to several factors, including "being a good rather than a poor communicator" (p. 1275). Competence in communicating across cultures is particularly important in contemporary society. A parent's or professional's failure to recognize and account for cultural differences in verbal and nonverbal communication styles can lead to misperceptions about one another's politeness or sincerity, and perhaps even to conflict (for further discussion, see Ting-Toomey, 1999).

Perceived Integrity

Belief in others' integrity involves the perception of consistency between a person's words and a person's actions.

Do Parents Feel That Staff Members "Say What They Mean and Mean What They Say?" Are Staff Members Seen as "Genuine" Rather Than "Phony?"

The work of Ames and Ellsworth (1997) illustrates the effect on parents of inconsistency between policies and the behavior of administrators. During a 3-year qualitative study in northern New York state, they witnessed a shift on the part of administrators in three Head Start centers away from having parents in meaningful roles of governance and decision making for their children's programs. The authors reported that parental trust was damaged as administrative decisions increasingly conflicted with—and usually superceded—the authority of the Policy Councils (the primary source of parental power in local Head Start programs) (p. 4). Some parents responded with defiance—continuing to object when administration terminated the contract of an employee on leave without Parent Council approval, for example (p. 175)—and others with discouragement. The authors quote one especially involved parent as saying, "I know I told you [earlier] that Head Start gave me self-esteem.... It's so different now. They *try* to make me feel stupid" (Ames & Ellsworth, 1997, p. 189).

Bryk and Schneider (2002) assert that asymmetries of autonomy and authority must be understood (especially by those with more power) and handled straightforwardly and tactfully in order to preserve trust (pp. 26-28). Program staff may be unaware of some aspects of power asymmetries between themselves and parents; and even if they are aware of their "legal and social prerogatives ... to confront parents when they are concerned about children's welfare" (Lareau, 1996, p. 61), they may not understand that parents might view these inequities as coercive. One parent interviewed by Lareau (1996), for instance, indicated that she sometimes did what the school had requested despite the hardship it created in her schedule, because she believed she might otherwise be reported to the state for neglect. Lareau observed that although middle-class parents did not voice such concerns in their interviews with her, several working-class parents did so. She attributes the difference in part to working-class parents' awareness that their typical methods of disciplining children differ from what is considered acceptable by school officials, who are likely to be middle class. In the working-class homes that Lareau observed, physical punishment was the norm, while punishment was more likely to be verbal in middle-class homes. "Parents are generally not at risk for being turned in to child protective services on the basis of a verbal comment," she notes, whereas "beating a child with a belt does place a parent at risk for consideration" by child protection agencies (p. 62).

Similarly, professionals other than teachers who work with families of young children may have control over some information and services that a family receives. These professionals are likely to be mandated reporters of suspected child abuse and neglect. In a discussion of the challenges of doing family-centered work with families in which abuse or neglect are suspected or occurring, Henry and Purcell (2000) stressed the need for staff to be honest about their own prerogatives when working with such parents.

Bryk and Schneider (2002) assert that asymmetries of autonomy and authority must be understood (especially by those with more power) and handled straightforwardly and tactfully in order to preserve trust (pp. 26-28).

Perhaps relationships with parents in other settings benefit when staff members are forthright about their role as mandated reporters of child abuse and neglect—without giving the impression that they are predisposed to suspect that parents are abusive.

Do Staff Members Believe That These Particular Parents Are Likely to "Say What They Mean and Mean What They Say?"

Studies in several settings have illustrated that cultural differences in communication style can result in the impression that someone is hypocritical or dishonest. For example, in some cultures, norms of politeness and respect dictate that one must not openly disagree with an elder or a teacher. Service providers may be surprised when a parent who appeared to agree to a request does not actually comply. Greater cultural awareness may help teachers or other personnel understand what such parents really mean.

Chatman's (1996) studies of information poverty indicate that people withhold information from others when self-disclosure increases their sense of vulnerability to an intolerable level. This behavior may be especially true for parents who will be in trouble with the law if the authorities learn certain things about them. Thus, parents who are undocumented immigrants (D. Rothenberg & L. G. Katz, personal communication, 2003; Chin & Newman, 2002) and drug-addicted pregnant women (Dervin, Harpring, & Foreman-Wernet, 1999) are among the groups likely to maintain a certain level of secrecy in their relationships with program personnel, for obvious reasons.

More subtle power asymmetries may also create barriers, especially in schools and early childhood programs. Some gay and lesbian parents hesitate to give details of their family life to their children's teachers (Casper & Schultz, 1999; Dispenza, 1999). In several studies involving children's education programs, Soodak & Erwin (2000), Graue (1993), Lareau (2000), and others have noted that parents sometimes refrain from discussing concerns with a teacher because they fear repercussions for the child. One example comes from Lareau's ethnographic study of two schools, in which a working-class mother told Lareau her reason for not complaining about a teacher's behavior: "I am sure if I went up to her and said something about her yelling, it would just make her madder and that might put more pressure on [my daughter]" (Lareau, 2000, p. 111).

Some Reflections on Power Asymmetry and Trust

Some of the approaches to parent-program relationships in the literature reviewed for this project were clearly oriented toward enhancing parental autonomy and democratic processes. Other approaches appeared to support more autocratic types of interaction, with professionals or program staff having greater degrees of authority to tell parents what to do and how to proceed. Often, it was clear that parents and program staff members desired equitable relationships. On the other hand, it was also clear that professionals and policy makers expected or wished to have parents change or to behave

Studies in several settings have illustrated that cultural differences in communication style can result in the impression that someone is hypocritical or dishonest.

in certain ways that many perceive as enhancing the family situation or directly promoting a child's school readiness. The line between care and coercion is sometimes blurred, especially in situations when a child's health and safety may be in jeopardy.

As Bryk and Schneider (2002) suggest, administrators, educators, social workers, and home visitors are likely to have a greater degree of influence and connection to the power structure than parents. They are thus in the position to take the lead in working toward more symmetrical relationships with parents than may currently exist in their settings. They can do so by showing social respect and personal regard, by emphasizing parental competence and efficacy, by exhibiting the competence to fulfill their own obligations, and by "saying what they mean, and meaning what they say." Although maintaining these components of relational trust can be difficult, their positive effects can be powerful. In the context of these kinds of trusting relationships, parents may come to view program staff as among their preferred sources of information and support, and they may begin to make optimal use of the resources that they offer.

Issue #4: The Need for Comprehensive Programming

Early intervention services, child care and preschool programs, parenting education and adult education programming, child protection and welfare agencies, dental care, medical care, and mental health services—each can play a role in family resilience and in fostering children's readiness to begin school. But there is some indication that the current systems for providing information, services, and other resources to families do not serve the needs of vulnerable families—or of communities—as well as they could.

Our review of the literature found several calls for "coordinated," "comprehensive," or "integrated" programming for families of young children, especially those considered vulnerable (see, for example, Melaville, Blank, & Asayesh, 1993; Dryfoos & McGuire, 2002; Schorr, 1997; Zuckerman & Parker, 1995; Raver, 2002). Such approaches to connecting with parents, especially vulnerable parents, are increasingly seen as essential to supporting family resilience. In fact, in a "review of reviews" ($N = 35$) of program evaluations, Nation and colleagues found that "comprehensiveness" was the most frequently mentioned of eight commonly cited characteristics of effective programming (Nation et al., 2003, p. 452). Four questions arose as we examined the literature about comprehensive programming to serve vulnerable families with young children:

- What is the nature of comprehensive, integrated programming?
- On what basis is such programming believed to be particularly important for vulnerable families?
- What are some challenges encountered when attempting to provide comprehensive, integrated programming?
- What are some current efforts to provide comprehensive, integrated programming for vulnerable families?

The line between care and coercion is sometimes blurred, especially in situations when a child's health and safety may be in jeopardy.

What Is the Nature of Comprehensive, Integrated Programming?

Providing comprehensive resources entails making resources available that address the widest possible range of family issues and problems. When such services are integrated, they are connected by a common vision and by careful planning and coordination on the part of the administrators and program staff. Integrated and comprehensive services are part of a holistic approach to working with families, drawing from the principle of the interconnected contexts in which children grow and develop: family, community, and education settings (e.g., early childhood programs and schools) (such as expressed by Bronfenbrenner, 1995, 1998). Such services involve intentional interface and coordination among professionals who deal with families of young children. These programs bring together specialists from a variety of fields, including early intervention, medicine and public health, social work, mental health, information/library science, early childhood education, and child care. Each professional's knowledge of a family can be integrated with the others' perspectives into a more complete picture of that family's strengths and needs. Such services may be provided in a common location—perhaps a school building—or at least with some form of common administration.

Full-service community schools, for example (Dryfoos & Maguire, 2002), house a number of community services within a public school building that is ideally "open to students, families, and the community before, during, and after school, seven days a week, all year long" (p. 4). Resources offered (in addition to the regular school program) may include:

- primary health clinics;
- before- and after-school learning components;
- youth development programs (including substance abuse counseling, sports and recreation, and community service learning);
- early childhood programs;
- a family resource center to help parents address literacy, child rearing, employment, housing, immigration, and other issues (including programs for teen parents);
- support from college faculty and students, business people, youth workers, neighbors, and family members (pp. 4, 20).

Other models of comprehensive or integrated programming may include some or all of these components, as well as ESL classes, GED preparation, and household management workshops.

On What Basis Is Such Programming Believed to be Particularly Important for Vulnerable Families?

In their call for integrated or comprehensive service provision for families, Melaville and colleagues note that there has been little research on such systems and little evidence to support claims that they improve academic achievement or child well-being. They assert, however, that the flaws apparent in the current practical strategies are good reason to try integrated

> Providing comprehensive resources entails making resources available that address the widest possible range of family issues and problems. When such services are integrated, they are connected by a common vision and by careful planning and coordination on the part of the administrators and program staff.

approaches to providing services related to families. First, current methods tend to be crisis oriented, rather than prevention focused. Second, the authors note that although children and families are likely to need a mix of resources, current systems are designed to address "discrete problems, commonly referred to as categorical problems," and programs tend to provide services within, not across, categories (Melaville, Blank, & Asayesh, 1993, p. 9). Third, communication about children and families rarely, if ever, takes place among the public and private agencies that provide resources, severely limiting opportunities to work in ways that complement one another, often because of statutory limitations on sharing information. Finally, highly specialized agencies have difficulty collaborating with one another to plan, finance, and implement creative, comprehensive solutions to complex problems that many families and communities face (p. 9).

An example of the lack of interagency connection is provided by Ray, Rubenstein, and Russo (1994) in their report of a study of programs serving parents with mental retardation—a population with especially high needs. The authors found that staff of the programs reported that relationships with local child protection/prevention services were often "strained and precarious." According to the authors, "Effective coordination and communication with the caseworkers of these service agencies, including regular progress reports and consistent reporting of the problems encountered, were not a part of the standard protocol of any of the programs" that were meant to help the parents (p. 739).

Lack of coordination between services to a child with special needs causes severe family stress and alienates parents from those who are providing services, according to Marci Greene, author and mother of a child with special needs. In her case, the burden of many meetings and multiple home assignments resulted in serious time pressure, emotional stress for all family members, and even marital strife. As a result, there were times when she said, "I didn't want to keep the appointments to discuss our daughter's progress" (Greene, 1999, p. 150).

On the other hand, coordinated services work well when they focus on a particular goal. Head Start, Even Start, and AVANCE represent efforts to offer multiple services to families, including early childhood programming, parenting education, and adult education. However, these services usually do not include comprehensive medical, dental, or mental health services, or school-age child care.

Vulnerable families may experience multiple needs for service and, at the same time, disconnection from potential resources. In particular, parents who are by definition "hard to serve" do not have access to, or do not avail themselves of, information and services that professionals feel would be useful to them. The comprehensive service program can be seen as a social network that potentially facilitates parents' access to early childhood programs, parenting information and parent support groups, adult education, mental health providers, and a wide range of other resources, interrupting their isolation and (possibly) substantially enhancing their resilience.

"Entry points" for services are an important consideration in service provision for vulnerable families. Cybele Raver and Jane Knitzer (2002), in a review of research on children's mental health, comment that center-based child care and Head Start programs are often entry points for families with children who have mental health issues (p. 15). Similarly, in comprehensive, integrated programs, the different components can easily provide entry points for one another. With coordinated services, a parent concerned about her child's behavior might be referred to a family counselor who keeps office hours in the same facility as the child's Head Start classroom.

Ideally, parents are invited or expected to provide some resources themselves, perhaps as home educators for their children, as volunteers in a preschool classroom, as members of a parent support group, as community advocates, or as participants on a parent council.

What Are Some Challenges Encountered when Attempting to Provide Comprehensive, Integrated Programming?

A number of challenges to integrated, comprehensive programming are discussed in the literature. Three issues arose that are directly related to connecting with parents: (1) creating a climate of relational trust, (2) meeting the challenges posed by the difficulty of collaborating to coordinate services to families, and (3) defining appropriate roles of parents.

It seems reasonable to assume that the more family centered the comprehensive programming is, and the greater the level of relational trust, the more likely parents are to be engaged in a program and make use of what is offered. With the potential to have many professionals familiar with a single family, however, it may be imperative to avoid giving the impression of "ganging up on" the parent. It may become especially important for all program staff to be clear with parents about their own roles and to be straightforward about responsibilities. For example, policies regarding confidentiality (e.g., when a pregnant high school student does not want her parents to know she is seeking services) must be made clear and so must the organization's relationship to Immigration and Naturalization Services. Parents should also know staff members' roles as mandated reporters of child abuse and neglect. At the same time, program staff may find that parents remain distant unless the staff members make it clear that "We are not the truant officer. We are not the counselor. We are not the principal" (Smrekar, 1996).

Raver and Knitzer (2002) note that research seems to indicate that the effectiveness of flexible mental health strategies (e.g., having on-site mental health consultants in early childhood programs) may depend on "complex factors such as the fit of the consultant's approach with the philosophy of the center" (p. 17). This finding supports the common wisdom that the more people are involved, the greater the need for clarity among them about their roles and for fundamental agreement about the goals and methods of the program. For example, McDowell (1999) recommends that marital and family therapists who would like to be consultants with Head Start programs ask such questions as, "What is your mission statement?" "What are important ways I can support the way you work?" and "What are common mistakes that employees make who do not fit in?" (p. 1). Frequent and open communication among staff members, including negotiation of roles and "turf," is likely to be a key to achieving and maintaining a good fit, and must be built into the schedule of integrated programs. (For further discussion of the challenges of collaborating to provide coordinated services, see a report on a set of case studies of five programs by Crowson & Boyd, 1996.)

According to family therapist and author William Doherty (2000), parents are often cast as consumers of professional services, rather than as "producers of support, growth, and learning for themselves and their communities" (p. 322). The limitations of this role can hamper a program's effectiveness. Integrated programs for children with special needs, for example, may be stronger from the parents' point of view if they feature parent/professional education (Greene, 1999, p. 150), in which program staff members learn about a particular child from his or her parents. Parents have inside knowledge of the child's needs and behavior, and they may be self-educated experts about the particular disability (p. 150). The same may be true of parents from diverse cultures, who can provide program staff with important information about their communities.

Three issues arose that are directly related to connecting with parents: (1) creating a climate of relational trust, (2) meeting the challenges posed by the difficulty of collaborating to coordinate services to families, and (3) defining appropriate roles of parents.

It seems clear that providing integrated, comprehensive services to parents of young children entails many challenges. Its effectiveness within and across communities has yet to be fully evaluated, and those evaluations may themselves be complex and challenging (Knapp, 1995). Still, a number of programs can serve as exemplars, suggesting that we are on the way to learning whether providing comprehensive integrated resources to parents is worth the time, cost, and effort required.

What Are Some Current Efforts to Provide Comprehensive, Integrated Programming for Vulnerable Families?

Many programs focused on young children offer at least two forms of connection with parents. For instance, parents involved in Early Head Start, PAT, and HIPPY receive home visits with an instructive focus, and parents attend group meetings that involve support, parent education, and connection to other community resources. The Chicago Child-Parent Centers also offer multiple services: early childhood programming through the early elementary school years; a parent resource center staffed with a teacher; parenting classes; parent involvement opportunities; home visits; health screenings for preschoolers; access to speech therapists, school psychologists, and social workers; and referrals to appropriate medical care (Reynolds, 2000).

Several full-service community schools (Dryfoos & Maguire, 2002) are operating around the country, including schools in Bennington, Vermont; Buffalo,

New York; and Chicago. Dryfoos and Maguire's description indicates that many of these programs begin with a K-12 school, sometimes with an early childhood component, gradually adding community services over time.

Head Start programs in some communities have been the targets of pilot efforts to add other services. For example, McDowell (1999) states that some success has been attributed to a university-Head Start collaboration in which marital and family therapy (MFT) interns serve as consultants to Head Start centers, facilitating discussion groups and workshops based on parent interests, consulting with staff and families, and providing brief therapeutic interventions and referrals when families identify a need for therapy. In similar university-Head Start collaborations, MFT interns provide in-home family and marital therapy (Thomas, McCollum, & Snyder, 1999), center-based play therapy, and filial therapy (Johnson, Bruhn, Winek, Krepps, & Wiley, 1999).

Another potential component of comprehensive programming can be seen in a report of a case study of a dual-focus "digital divide" pilot project in Connecticut (Salovey, Moward, Pizarro, Edlund, & Moret, 2002). The investigators provided a six-hour computer training course to parents (young mothers, fathers, and grandparents), and they then gave them refurbished Internet-ready computers. Head Start staff members were trained as "technology coaches." This quasi-experimental study involved the use of cancer-relevant information embedded in the training materials (e.g., a word-processing exercise that involved copying a paragraph about sunscreen use). (Findings were not yet available on the effectiveness of the embedded information in raising parents' cancer prevention awareness or on the usefulness of the training to parents.)

A recent national initiative—Starting Early Starting Smart (SESS)—which targets mental health of children and families, integrates behavioral health services, child care, Head Start, and primary health settings. Through its 12 demonstration sites, the project is designed to see whether such comprehensive and integrated services increase families' access to and use of services for parenting, mental health, and substance abuse prevention (Casey Family Programs & U.S. Department of Health and Human Services, 2001). According to the summary of preliminary findings, SESS seems to increase participating families' access to resources and to strengthen parents' use of positive guidance and support of their children.

The four topics addressed in this chapter do not constitute an exhaustive list of issues that have emerged in the research and the theoretical literature regarding parent-program connections. They do, however, represent areas of complex decision making that many programs face in their efforts to provide resources for vulnerable families with young children.

Connecting the Threads

7

Introduction

This chapter suggests some future directions in research and practice related to connecting with parents in the early years. These recommendations are based in part on the literature that we have reviewed in Chapters 2 through 6. They are also built upon the recommendations and visions for the future shared at the symposium of specialists that met in March 2003 at the University of Illinois's Conference Center at Allerton Park, Illinois. These specialists focused on improving connections between parents of young children and the program staff who work with them.

Recommendations Related to Research

Recommendation #1: Develop Coherent, Comprehensive, Interdisciplinary Research Agendas for the Study of Connections between Parents and Programs That Serve Young Children

Our survey of the literature in several fields has confirmed the impression of Douglas Powell, the first symposium presenter, that scholarship has been theory-heavy in this area. Other scholars have also noted a dearth of comprehensive research *agendas* regarding connections between parents and programs that serve young children. In the area of school-family relationships alone, for example, Ryan and Adams (1995, p. 5) note:

> Research in the field is still largely unintegrated and underutilized. The large variety of constructs that have been investigated, let alone the even more various strategies that researchers have used to measure these constructs, leaves the would-be reviewer of literature gasping.

Even when relationships between parents and professionals are studied, the findings are rarely shared across disciplines or fields. As a result, the research

Even when relationships between parents and professionals are studied, the findings are rarely shared across disciplines or fields.

is fragmented and lacks the power that it might have if a series of carefully planned, interrelated, interdisciplinary studies contributed to our understanding of the parent-program connection across the fields of early childhood education, early intervention, health sciences, social services, adult education, information science, and communication science. Investigators from all fields who share interest in parent-program relationships during early childhood could participate in concerted interdisciplinary research efforts that creatively incorporate qualitative, quantitative, and meta-analytical methods.

Recommendation #2: Promote Interdisciplinary Understanding of Parent-Program Relationships, Using Mixed Research Methods to Approach Complex Questions and Situations

The use of mixed methods allows simultaneous focus on both broad and specific aspects of connection between programs and parents in the years before school.

Qualitative studies permit (even demand) attention to the central role of *context* in program-parent interaction. Budget, type of governance, and the nature of parents' and staff members' existing social networks are among the contextual factors that can influence parent-staff relationships. Qualitative research also allows critical examination of what may be unexamined or even unrecognized in quantitative studies—for instance, the differences in information needs and information-seeking behaviors among parents in different communities, or the presence of unofficial lines of communication that affect parents' responses to a program.

Policy makers and practitioners want to know "what works" in parent-program relationships, so the prospect of finding cause-effect relationships between practices and positive outcomes for parents and children has strong appeal. Experimental studies, large and small, are the potential sources of evidence of cause and effect. They can provide evidence about which strategies and techniques actually facilitate parents' skills or promote their engagement with programs meant to promote family resilience.

Critical reviews have indicated, however, that true experimental designs are rarely found in the literature on parent-program relationships. Reviewers have also found that correlations are sometimes mistaken for causal connections. Correlations are themselves useful, but they do not provide the clear evidence of "what works" that is often sought.

Keeping in mind that rigor is possible and desirable in any research methodology, investigators who plan an integrated, interdisciplinary research agenda might consider incorporating the following research methods:

- *Social network analysis* contributes to an understanding of how information and other resources flow among parents and staff through official and unofficial channels. It sheds light on information access, information

Critical reviews have indicated that true experimental designs are rarely found in the literature on parent-program relationships. Reviewers have also found that correlations are sometimes mistaken for causal connections. Correlations are themselves useful, but they do not provide the clear evidence of "what works" that is often sought.

Connecting with Parents

poverty, and asymmetries of power and knowledge in parent-program relationships and can prove essential to discerning why some efforts to connect with parents work better than others.

- *Discourse analysis* is "the study of actually occurring language in specific communicative contexts" (Schwandt, 2001, p. 57). It can provide insight into verbal aspects of parent-program connections through its attention to such aspects of discourse as turn taking, vocabulary, "overlaps" (interruptions), and conversational gaps (Solomon, 1997, in a discussion of a framework for analyzing information-seeking conversations, pp. 222-226). Similarly, textual analysis of written communications between programs and parents can pinpoint such problems as a reading level that does not match parents' skill levels and materials that are culturally inappropriate. Discourse analysis might also help clarify how parent-staff conversation may differ in family-centered versus professionally centered practice.

- *Behavioral observation* of the interactions of parents, staff members, and children addresses "the classic fieldwork question, 'What's going on here?'" (Schwandt, 2001, p. 179). Behavioral observation and analysis can augment or conflict with the self-reports that are often a part of both qualitative and quantitative studies. Use of audio and video technologies to record observations can facilitate quantitative and qualitative coding and analysis of the actions in naturalistic, experimental, and quasi-experimental settings.

- *Ethnographic studies* provide thorough descriptions of programs, families, and communities, and the interactions that characterize them. Ethnographies are well suited to uncovering what occurs in terms of power inequities; cooperation and conflicts between parents and staff; and the ways that beliefs and attitudes about culture, race, ability, class, and gender play out in parent-staff relationships. Ethnographic studies can also lay the groundwork for later studies targeting specific situations at a site.

- *Case studies*, like ethnographies, are suited to revealing context and multiple layers of interaction in particular places. They are well suited to evaluation and cross-case analysis of practices and outcomes.

- *Action research* allows participants (such as parents and staff members) to study their own activities, with the goal of improving practice. Although practitioners often informally assess what happens when they try a new approach to a task, action research permits more formal, reflective study of problems, plans, and actions.

- *Experimental studies*. Experimental studies might be used to establish causal connections between particular aspects of program-parent interaction and particular results. The complex contextual, interpersonal, and intrapersonal factors within programs and families make it difficult, if not impossible, to isolate specific practices and control external influences. However, close examination of the results of qualitative studies may reveal research questions related to parent-staff relationships that can best be approached through experimental methods.

The complex contextual, interpersonal, and intrapersonal factors within programs and families make it difficult, if not impossible, to isolate specific practices and control external influences. However, close examination of the results of qualitative studies may reveal research questions related to parent-staff relationships that can best be approached through experimental methods.

Longitudinal studies using a variety of methods can play a valuable role in understanding parent-program relationships. Ongoing studies that are primarily quantitative (e.g., the Chicago Longitudinal Study) might benefit from adding a qualitative component to support and illustrate their statistics about program success with semi-structured interviews with parents and professionals, or social network analyses of the various sites. Ethnographies and case studies, conducted over a period of years, have the potential to build sufficient trust between researchers and participants to allow more candid responses to questions about the complexities of the relationships between parents and the staff of programs that operate in the community.

Recommendation #3: Construct Studies That "Ask the Right Questions" and Have the Potential to Evoke Still More Questions about Parent-Program Relationships

Symposium participants also voiced concerns about the importance of developing methods of study that "ask the right questions"; some wondered aloud whether the field of parenting has a solid enough knowledge base to know the "right questions."

Symposium discussions and the literature featured in this review identified the following topics for further study: (1) What exactly is "school readiness" and how is it accomplished? (2) What resources (information, support, etc.) are most likely to be useful for parents who would like to promote their children's readiness for school? (3) What exactly constitutes "effective parent-staff relationships" and how are they achieved, particularly with parents who are considered "hard to serve?" (4) Do parents, children, and communities reap benefits other than enhanced academic achievement when program staff and parents actively collaborate in children's early education? (5) How can we best represent for inservice and preservice practitioners what is known about working with families? (6) What role can mass distribution of readiness-related resources or targeted national campaigns play in public awareness and understanding of school readiness? These questions are explored in greater detail below.

What Exactly Is "School Readiness" and How Is It Accomplished?

The wide range of definitions of "readiness" is potentially confusing for parents of young children and for those who work with them. Several approaches to addressing the interconnected issues of what readiness is and how it might be achieved have been recommended, including the following suggestions:

- Ethnographic studies of school communities (parents, teachers, caregivers, and administrators) to uncover local conceptualizations of readiness and how they compare with state and national policies and with what research suggests.
- Long-range case studies, across cultural and socioeconomic groups, of "silent learning" (Romero, in press, p. 17) in the home, as a means by which young children learn problem-solving and life skills that they may

The wide range of definitions of "readiness" is potentially confusing for parents of young children and for those who work with them.

need in school. Following the Hart and Risley (1995) model, such studies would employ in-home behavior observation, as well as interviews and other methods.

- Longitudinal studies of groups of children who have participated in readiness-related programs to see if what constituted "readiness" when they entered kindergarten has translated into later academic success.

What Resources (Information, Support, etc.) Are Most Likely to be Useful for Parents Who Would Like to Promote Their Children's Readiness for School?

Many programs that work with parents of young children provide them with a great deal of information. Some offer social support (e.g., parent support groups), counseling, volunteer opportunities, and opportunities to take part in decision making that affects the program. It is possible that some resources are more valuable than others in helping parents promote school readiness. The following types of research provide information on the usefulness of resources for parents:

- Profiles of how individual parents or families participate in a program, including how they change (or do not change) their attitudes, beliefs, or actions, with particular attention to parents' perspectives.
- Action research on parenthood itself. University investigators might collaborate with parents and practitioners in the programs that serve young children to examine what parenting means to individuals and how individuals approach opportunities to change their parenting practices.
- Case studies (prominently featuring parents' perspectives) of how parents in vulnerable families go about marshalling resources for their interactions with early childhood programs, schools, and other programs that are designed to help them.
- Comparative case studies of programs that focus on parents' ability to work toward ensuring that the schools are "ready" for their children, to find out what tends to be most likely to help parents prepare for proactive relationships with schools.

What Exactly Constitutes "Effective Parent-Staff Relationships" and How Are They Achieved, Particularly with Parents Who Are Considered "Hard to Serve?"

The following approaches have been suggested to investigate this topic:

- Profiles of how individual program staff members interact with the parents who are involved in their programs.
- Surveys of parents regarding what they consider to be effective parent-staff relationships.
- Comparative case studies, using thorough descriptions, of how programs get resources to families, and what challenges they may face in doing so.

Many programs that work with parents of young children provide them with a great deal of information. Some offer social support (e.g., parent support groups), counseling, volunteer opportunities, and opportunities to take part in decision making that affects the program.

- Comparative, long-range case studies of the trajectories of families who participate in "family-centered programs" to determine how they are doing months and years after receiving resources from the programs.
- Case studies focusing on relational trust in a variety of settings: home-visiting programs such as PAT, HIPPY, and Early Head Start; Head Start programs; parent-cooperative nursery schools; preschools; child care centers; family literacy programs; parent education classes; parent support programs; full-service community schools.
- Comparative case studies of "typical practice" and "best practice" (per Knapp, 1995, p. 13) to learn how programs successfully engage fathers and father figures in programs concerned with children's learning and development.
- Case studies of "typical practice" and "best practice" regarding efforts to recruit and retain parents in the programs that are intended to promote family resilience and/or children's school readiness. These studies would include analyzing parents' self-reported reasons for not using what a given program offers.
- Experimental or quasi-experimental designs to examine whether some intensities of service are more likely than others to produce improvement in the targeted behaviors in specific interventions.
- Comparative case studies of sites that are part of national programs (e.g., Even Start, Early Head Start, Head Start) to identify trends in parent-program relationships across the varied but similar contexts. Understanding of relationships within individual sites may suggest how specific practices contribute to or detract from the overall effectiveness of the national programs.

Do Parents, Children, and Communities Reap Benefits Other Than Enhanced Academic Achievement when Program Staff and Parents Actively Collaborate in Children's Early Education?

Improved academic achievement is usually treated as the primary goal of parent-staff collaboration. However, in our literature review and in symposium discussions, the possibility was raised that families and communities may benefit in other ways as well. The following approaches may begin to address the issue of nonacademic benefits of parent-staff collaboration:

- Ethnographic studies of communities before, during, and after such collaborations.
- Action research at the community level with parents, practitioners, community members, and perhaps university affiliates involved together in identifying mutual concerns, planning how to address them, instituting an action plan, observing outcomes, reflecting together on their activities, and creating more critically informed plans.

How Can We Best Represent What Is Known about Working with Families for Preservice and Inservice Practitioners?

Effective preparation of practitioners to work with families is crucial, but little consistency has been found within disciplines regarding preservice and

Effective preparation of practitioners to work with families is crucial, but little consistency has been found within disciplines regarding preservice and inservice curricula and materials. Even within a field, such as early childhood education, great variation can be found among teacher training programs with regard to required coursework and practical experience.

inservice curricula and materials. Even within a field, such as early childhood education, great variation can be found among teacher training programs with regard to required coursework and practical experience. Several possible approaches to understanding current practices of professional preparation were suggested.

First, comparative analysis within a field can shed light on how different professional training programs approach the task of helping their students learn to connect effectively with parents of young children. Colleges of education might be compared with one another, schools of social work, or counseling certification programs. Points of comparison might include the following elements:

- coursework (available, required, and optional);
- the explicit or implicit empirical and theoretical base for recommended practice;
- the nature of preservice practical experience in working directly with families;
- novice professionals' perspectives on how well prepared they were for working with families, one year after they begin work in the field; and
- parent perspectives on novice professionals' communications with them.

Comparison of professional training across fields might also be informative, shedding light on possible gaps in how novice professionals are prepared to work with families. This comparison may be particularly important in fields such as early childhood education where professionals sometimes find themselves in conversations with parents that would normally be the domain of a social worker or psychotherapist. Points for evaluation would include the issues mentioned above: coursework, empirical and theoretical base for recommended practice, preservice practical experience in working directly with families, novice professionals' perspectives on their preservice preparation, and parent perspectives on how the novice professionals interact with them.

Some programs provide ongoing training for staff members regarding their interactions with parents. Comparative analysis of frequently used practitioner-oriented or inservice resources on parent-program connections within a field might include evaluation of the following:

- explicit or implicit theoretical orientations within the materials,
- research cited,
- recommended practices,
- approach to presenting the material (e.g., lecture, role-play),
- the degree of "fit" between recommended practices and what research shows,
- practitioner perspectives on their experiences in implementing recommended practices, and
- parents' perspectives on practitioners' interactions with them following the additional training.

Comparison of professional training across fields might also be informative, shedding light on possible gaps in how novice professionals are prepared to work with families.

What Role Can Mass Distribution of Readiness-Related Resources or Targeted National Campaigns Play in Public Awareness and Understanding of School Readiness?

Although a great deal of money and time is spent in mass campaigns or in large-scale efforts to reach specific groups with information about school readiness, little is known about the effects of such activities on public knowledge and parental behavior. Suggestions for ways to begin to study this issue include the following:

- Cumulative case study evaluations of targeted national campaigns such as Reach Out and Read (a program focused on helping pediatricians encourage at-home literacy activities).

- Pilot studies of the use of mass media campaigns to create a climate of awareness and concern about children's school readiness. For example, how effective are public service announcements, messages on billboards, or appearances by guest "experts" on popular television programs such as the *Oprah Winfrey Show* in raising awareness about school readiness? How effective are Internet-based materials such as those provided at the PBSparents Web site? What might be the effects of a television series aimed at parents and children such as Turkey's *Benimle Oynar misin* (Baydar, Kagitcibasi, Kuntay, & Goksen, 2003)?

Recommendation #4: Through Critical Literature Review, Including Meta-analysis, Increase Interdisciplinary Awareness of Common Challenges in Studies on Specific Aspects of Parent-Program Relationships

Some authors have argued that it may be "too early" for meta-analysis of studies of such topics as comprehensive integrated programming (Knapp, 1995, p. 14) or parent-school partnerships (Chavkin, 2001, p. 86), for example, because there is no widespread agreement about concepts, outcome measures, and independent variables. On the other hand, some symposium participants spoke of a need for critical literature reviews and meta-analyses to identify research trends and to shed light on problems within the literature with regard to research design and methods. Critical reviews of the literature on specific aspects of parent-staff interaction can uncover the extent to which "knowledge" in that area may be based on studies that suffer from design flaws, flawed methods, flawed reporting, ill-defined key concepts, or absence of crucial information about populations or interventions.

Among the critical reviews of research related to parent-staff relationships are Mattingly, Prislin, McKenzie, Rodriguez, and Kayzar (2002) on evaluations of parent involvement programs; Gomby, Culross, and Behrman (1999) on evaluations of home-visiting programs; White, Taylor, and Moss (1992) regarding research on parent involvement in early intervention; and Baker and Soden (1997) on parent involvement research. Some of these reviews may have their own flaws in conceptualization or definition of basic concepts.

Some symposium participants spoke of a need for critical literature reviews and meta-analyses to identify research trends and to shed light on problems within the literature with regard to research design and methods.

We found, for instance, that even among studies deemed higher quality by Mattingly et al., some lacked key information such as an adequate definition of the concept central to its premise or contextual details that might have had a bearing on the results.

Discussion at the symposium aligned with the work of some researchers in noting that critical reviews of the literature of parent-staff relationships should address the following questions:

- Have researchers clarified what they are studying? That is, what do they mean by "parent education" or "parent involvement?" How does a particular quantitative study isolate one variable from another within potentially complex interactions? Have they defined key terms?

- Do the authors adequately describe the situation being studied? That is, do they provide a clear picture of the context in which the study takes place, including mention of the policy environment, how resources are shared, etc.?

- Is the approach constructively skeptical about what is claimed by the program being studied or by the participants? That is, are the researchers trying to evaluate a program too early in its development? Do they privilege one source of information over others? Does the report make clear who has funded the study and the funders' position, if any, regarding what is being studied?

- How are variables related to human diversity handled in the study? In some studies, for example, effects of gender may be overlooked when "parents" are actually all "mothers." Similar problems may arise when social class is not considered as a potential source of difference in responses, or when ethnicities are racialized (as when "Hispanic" is treated as a racial category along with Caucasian/White or African/ African American/Black). Researchers should be accountable for the constructs of race, culture, class, ability, and gender that they use.

- What evidence of rigorous methods is apparent in a qualitative study? Do the researchers employ thick description, member checks, and triangulation?

Symposium discussions confirmed the impression created in the research, that relationships between parents of young children and the staff of programs that serve them are multilayered and involve complex questions regardless of the setting studied or the methods employed. It is crucial for researchers to focus on how parents and staff members navigate the ongoing tensions in their relationships—between suspicion and trust, domination and collaboration, professional-centeredness and family-centeredness—in order to support and learn from each other, in the interest of children.

Recommendations for Practice and Policy

Both practice and policy were directly and indirectly addressed in the research reviewed on program-parent relationships in the years before school, especially in the case studies, ethnographies, and descriptive studies that reported the experiences of parents and staff members. (Our review did not concentrate heavily on the large body of work for practitioners and policy makers that describes tips and strategies for creating and improving connections with parents.) The recommendations for future directions in practice and policy in this section of the chapter are based on points raised in the literature review and during in-depth discussions at the Kellogg symposium.

Recommendation #1: Programs Working with Parents of Young Children Should Put a High Priority on Creating a Culture of Mutual Trust

Although the importance of trust seems obvious, it is nevertheless difficult to achieve. No one offering a program for parents knowingly or deliberately plans to create distrust, and yet some factors clearly can and do undermine trust. These program qualities probably require ongoing attention and should not be taken for granted. It is important, then, that program personnel convey their trust in parents, and that they strive to create a climate in which parents can also trust the program and its staff. These goals are most likely to be achieved when staff members consider the needs and preferences of parents as well as those of the program, so that the program's policy environment and the actions of individual staff members foster an atmosphere of trust. Symposium participants suggest several strategies for administrators and other program policy makers, and for staff who work directly with families.

To increase the trust in a program setting, administrators and other program policy makers can consider the following suggestions:

- Clearly define the basic constructs that their programs use (e.g., "partnership," "family centeredness," "relational trust," "helping," "school readiness," "parent involvement").
- State these basic constructs in language that all parents and staff members can understand and be particularly clear about what is expected of parents and of staff members.
- Look critically at whether their policies and actual practices are conducive to relational trust. Do these policies and practices convey social respect and positive personal regard for parents, as well as staff competence and integrity? How are power asymmetries handled? Are policies and practices regarding relationships with parents congruent with the program's goals of supporting family resilience and enhancing school readiness? Are practices reasonably consistent among staff members?
- Set high standards for self-awareness, sensitivity, and personal growth in relation to their attitudes, beliefs, and behaviors regarding differences in race, class, culture, gender, ability, sexual orientation, language, and literacy.
- Hire personnel who share those standards of self-awareness and sensitivity.
- Actively but tactfully encourage and facilitate staff members' development of self-awareness and personal growth in these areas.
- Make concerted efforts to tailor the program to the local community's primary resource needs, perhaps using local channels of communication

Although the importance of trust seems obvious, it is nevertheless difficult to achieve. No one offering a program for parents knowingly or deliberately plans to create distrust, and yet some factors clearly can and do undermine trust.

and information exchange (e.g., church contacts, conversation at the hairdresser's or on the front step), to determine what parents would like to see offered.

- Critically examine the formal and informal channels through which resources (e.g., information, support) are exchanged between staff and parents at a site. Do resources flow smoothly and equitably among parents and staff members? If not, where are the problem areas? How might practice be improved with input from parents and staff?

- Avoid distrust, confusion, and conflict by establishing regular times and places for in-depth discussions between parents and staff in order to clarify responsibilities and roles, share information and other resources, and reach consensus about actions to take.

- Given the "time crunch" that many families and early childhood professionals experience, foster collaboration between program personnel and parents to create convenient opportunities for ongoing substantive interactions between parents and staff members.

Program staff members who provide direct services to parents and children are in key positions to foster strong positive relationships with parents. Symposium participants suggested that staff members who work directly with families can build optimal relationships with parents when they provide parents with information about their children's needs and activities that is accessible but does not oversimplify complex situations or concepts. The following suggestions are based on approaches that have been tried in a variety of contemporary settings:

- Invite some parents to collaborate with staff to create informative materials, including virtual library materials, for other parents with similar information needs. These materials would incorporate parent-friendly definitions of professional terms.

- Share videotapes with parents to demonstrate a child's daily activities in his or her early education setting. These could be sent home, or a place could be provided on-site for viewing. Parents' comments and questions can be solicited.

- Make available audiotapes of important meetings or conversations between a parent and a staff member (e.g., between a father and his child's teacher, or between a doctor and the mother of a pediatric patient). Parents can use the tapes to review what took place in a meeting, or share them with a spouse or partner who was not able to attend.

- Inform parents early and offer as much information as possible when a child has a disability or other such problem. Many parents also welcome referrals that let them connect with other parents who have had similar experiences, and program staff should make a point of being aware of and offering such resources.

- Adjust what is expected of parents in line with the understanding that they may not have adequate resources to be involved in their children's education in the ways that have been traditionally expected.

Symposium participants suggested that staff members who work directly with families can build optimal relationships with parents when they provide parents with information about their children's needs and activities that is accessible but does not oversimplify complex situations or concepts.

Recommendation #2: Acknowledge That Parents Share Responsibility for Defining School Readiness, and Support Parents' Efforts Relative to Their Children's Readiness to Begin School

Our review of the literature encountered a wide range of programs intended to support or enhance parents' ability to meet their responsibility to help their children become ready for school. The programs vary in scope, population served, expectations of parents, and the type of information and other resources available, but they share a commitment to providing resources that parents of young children may use to enhance their own resilience and to foster their children's school readiness.

In every case, programs can help parents best when they have channels in place for meaningful parental input. Often, parents report that they cannot get program personnel to listen to their perspectives, or that staff members let them talk but do not take what they have said into account. Conversely, staff members report that some parents reject information and resources that might help them or that parents do not seem to understand what their children need in order to be ready for school. Several suggestions were raised during the symposium for ways that programs might better support parents' efforts, based on research and experience.

Some symposium discussion focused on the importance of recognizing that many parents are unsure of how to define school readiness, and they may not know what makes a school "ready" for children. Staff members might try a variety of formal and informal collaborations with parents to define and address the goals of having "ready schools" as well as "ready children," including the following:

- alleviating some of the basic discomfort many parents feel in their relationships with schools;

- encouraging parents to be members of decision-making bodies in their children's early childhood programs, with attention to (1) the fact that some parents are likely to feel that they do not know enough about the programs or children's education, and (2) the possibility that policies or actions of administration may conflict with the goal of having parents in leadership roles;

- offering information about what schools will expect of children and ways parents might help children to be ready meet those expectations; and

- offering information to parents about how to approach school personnel when conflicts arise over a child's needs.

Research suggests that disseminating information via lectures, pamphlets, tip sheets, Web sites, and listserv services may not be effective with many vulnerable parents, especially those who are hardest to serve. Like anyone else, however, such parents seek and benefit from ideas and insights pertinent to their particular hopes for and struggles with their own families. They also tend to rely more upon trusted sources of information (friends, family members, or even television talk show hosts) than impersonal written information or seemingly anonymous reports of findings of scientific research. Symposium participants suggested that programs could reach more parents with information if they followed these strategies:

- Recognize that "hard-to-serve" parents probably gain little from superficial periodic meetings in which, for example, such basic elements as how to read to a young child are offered (although such offerings may do no harm).

- Have people on staff (e.g., family coordinators) who spend time with parents in a community to learn what they think their information needs are and how they are most likely to accept information.

- Make a point of hiring and training staff members from the communities being served, as MELD, AVANCE, HIPPY, Head Start, and some others have done. They are likely to know the community intimately and can serve as liaisons and offer insight into the kinds of resources and service delivery most likely to reach and be useful to the parents in the program.

Recommendation #3: Sustain the Capacity of Programs to Work with Parents Effectively by Allocating Adequate Resources

Funds and human capital are crucial to supporting effective work with families of young children, particularly vulnerable families that may lack resources that would enable them to increase the family's resilience and foster children's school readiness. Symposium participants made several recommendations regarding policies to enhance the functioning of vulnerable families. A need was expressed for government policies that reflect a strong sense of "what's good for children" in the "big picture" as well as for the short term, with the main goal of making it possible for parents to focus on and provide for their children's educational needs. Federal and state decision makers can have a positive impact if they consider the following suggestions:

- Continue or increase WIC, TANF, paid family leave, medical insurance for children, as well as subsidies for child care and early childhood programs. These are crucial to supplementing family resources and reducing parents' stress in difficult times.

- Provide or increase funds for neighborhood safety and for community-based programs that provide job skills training, mental health resources, and respite care for families with members who have special needs.

- Create a cadre of people who are trained to work effectively in poor communities.

- Support or establish comprehensive, integrated approaches to connecting with vulnerable families, fully acknowledging the challenges of funding and staffing such programs. Early childhood and elementary programs can serve as "hubs" of such programs.

Symposium participants suggested that, at the program level, decision makers also contribute to effective allocation of resources by (1) doing what is

Funds and human capital are crucial to supporting effective work with families of young children, particularly vulnerable families that may lack resources that would enable them to increase the family's resilience and foster children's school readiness.

necessary to recruit and retain well-qualified staff who are bilingual or multilingual and are fluent in the languages that families in the setting use and (2) advocating for adequate compensation for staff members and for program budgets that reflect the true costs of striving to work effectively with the parents being served.

Recommendation #4: Take Deliberate Steps to Strengthen the Capacity of Program Staff to Work Effectively with Parents

In the literature and in symposium discussions, three areas were often identified as essential to enhancing staff members' ability to work effectively with parents of young children: (1) preservice training and education, (2) professional development, and (3) the production of educational materials for both kinds of training.

Preservice Training and Education

Although we found no relevant comparative data, experience indicates that preservice training and education in fields such as mental health and social work appear to require more substantive preparation for interacting with parents than do early childhood and elementary education, or medical training. Experience also indicates that most preservice early education students, for example, are overwhelmed by the prospect of dealing with a class full of preschool children, so that classroom issues may take priority over gaining sensitivity to vulnerable or hard-to-serve parents.

On the other hand, our review of the literature included strong calls for teacher education programs that give attention to parent-staff relationships. From that perspective, teacher preparation curricula should include specific competencies for working with families, including knowledge of family systems theory, communication skills, and family-based curriculum development (Shores, 1998). It seems reasonable to assume that similar competencies ought to be addressed in training in health care, social services, school administration, or any other field that will involve program staff in substantial interactions with parents.

Other recommendations, based on points raised in the literature and at the symposium, include bringing preservice professionals into "communities of practice," which would involve the following:

- Assign preservice and novice practitioners to support staff who have ample direct experience of working with families, to help support their initial efforts in this area of professional responsibility.

- Provide introductory opportunities to collaborate with professionals from other fields who also work with families, with attention to differences and similarities in their concerns.

- Maintain channels for ongoing reciprocal communication among practitioners, preservice professionals, and university teaching staff regarding issues in program-family relationships.

In the literature and in symposium discussions, three areas were often identified as essential to enhancing staff members' ability to work effectively with parents of young children: (1) preservice training and education, (2) professional development, and (3) the production of educational materials for both kinds of training.

- Provide training and guidance for novice and veteran staff members in conducting action research into their own practices.

Such provisions are rarely available at present, in part because of cost and high attrition among the ranks of staff who work with young children and their families.

Professional Development

Symposium participants suggested that programs are likely to better serve more parents if they consider the following suggestions for inservice training:

- Expand inservice training to include mentoring of novice professionals by veteran staff members.

- Recruit mentors on a voluntary basis, or make mentoring relationships part of job descriptions so that prospective employees will be aware of the expectation that they will participate. Mentors should receive inservice training and professional support for their mentoring.

- Create opportunities for novices to meet as a group with a group of more experienced staff members (including paraprofessionals) to exchange insight, ideas, and strategies for meeting challenges.

- Offer conversational second-language instruction in languages other than English that are most common in the setting as inservice training, or use staff development funds to pay for individual staff members to learn the languages.

- Provide ongoing inservice workshops on communicating with parents, working with families in poverty, and understanding information needs.

Hope was expressed at the symposium that such provisions might help reduce high turnover among staff serving parents of young children.

Production of Educational Materials for Preservice and Inservice Training

Materials used in preservice and inservice training could be designed, or redesigned, to help preservice and novice practitioners to gain insight, sensitivity, and understanding of the complex issues involved in communicating with families. These materials should clearly illustrate more-effective versus less-effective practices. Producers of these materials might consider the following suggestions:

- Support all suggestions for practice with explicit theoretical and empirical grounding in human development, family systems, communication studies, and information studies.

- Include case books written at least in part by family members so that teachers and other professionals can gain parents' perspectives on the issues, joys, and challenges of parenting young children.

- Emphasize the experiences of vulnerable families and families from culturally, economically, and racially diverse backgrounds.

Materials used in preservice and inservice training could be designed, or redesigned, to help preservice and novice practitioners to gain insight, sensitivity, and understanding of the complex issues involved in communicating with families.

- Use "vignettes"—video clips or brief "case-study" type presentations in print—to illustrate particular aspects of interacting with parents. These vignettes should bring into sharp relief how things can go badly—in spite of good intentions—as well as illustrate how to increase the chances that they can go well. (See the Appendix for examples of potential vignettes and case study topics.)

- Use audio and video feedback sessions of role-plays of interactions with parents, through which staff can review and critique their own practices.

Recommendations for Charitable Organizations

Recommendation #1: Foundations Can Support the Development of Coherent, Comprehensive, Interdisciplinary Research Agendas for the Study of Connections between Parents and the Programs That Serve Young Children

A number of possible areas for research into program-parent relationships have been identified in this chapter. Representatives from foundations can collaborate with federal, state, and local agencies and with researchers from universities, research institutes, or professional organizations to identify (1) the most pressing questions for investigations and (2) the types of research that might be most fruitful in addressing those questions.

One potentially fruitful approach to funding studies of parent-program relationships would be to support pilot programs in a variety of sectors aimed at helping vulnerable parents promote their children's school readiness. In particular, funding might be geared toward learning more about aspects of programs not frequently addressed, such as the "nuts and bolts" of staff-parent communication—the methods used to provide information to parents, the formal opportunities for interaction, the literacy level of verbal communications, and so on. Support of rigorous practitioner research is especially recommended in order to ensure that the voices and firsthand experiences of parents, teachers, social workers, health care providers, and others can be fully integrated into the body of knowledge about effective and ineffective parent-program relationships.

Recommendation #2: Foundations Can Provide Substantial Support for the Development of Research-Driven Tools to Assist Parents with Helping Their Young Children Prepare to Begin School

Symposium participants pointed out the importance of creating a climate of awareness in the general public regarding children's school readiness. Foundations might fund pilot studies of efforts to reach the public with information about the roles that parents and other adults play in helping children prepare to begin school.

Support of rigorous practitioner research is especially recommended in order to ensure that the voices and firsthand experiences of parents, teachers, social workers, health care providers, and others can be fully integrated into the body of knowledge about effective and ineffective parent-program relationships.

Possible projects might include development and dissemination of short parent-oriented videos that emphasize the social aspects of school readiness. These videos might be especially useful if produced at a basic literacy level. They could be distributed for two venues: use by parent education programs or use by commercial and public television stations. (See the Appendix for a list of potential topics for such projects.) These episodes could be made more instructive by showing adult strategies that are most likely to be effective, compared with strategies that are less likely to work, using either actors or cartoon characters. The episodes could be brief enough to serve as Public Service Announcements for commercial and public television channels. Longer versions could serve as television programs. Audio clips might be used on radio programs. The video or audio segments could be augmented by brief printed "tip sheets" for parents and by information available on an accompanying Web site.

Foundations might collaborate with researchers and professional training programs to produce a set of video- or audio-teaching vignettes demonstrating common problems, typical practice, and best practice in working with parents, particularly those considered "hard to serve." The information in these vignettes would draw from both research and professional wisdom regarding parent-staff relationships. These vignettes could become part of university professional preparation curricula, or they could be used for staff development.

Conclusion

In closing, we note that many approaches to parent-program connections have been developed, tried, and implemented over extended periods of time. Head Start, the Chicago Child-Parent Centers, HIPPY—all have served families for more than a generation, while Healthy Start America, AVANCE, MELD, and others have done so for more than a decade. As far as we can tell, given the difficulties of conducting formal scientific studies of the long-term effectiveness of these and similar programs, they have been sufficiently successful with most of those to whom their services are directed to earn our support and to be continued. The challenge remains to find ways for these worthy programs, and others, to reach still more parents of young children who can benefit from the information and other resources offered, thereby increasing overall family resilience and improving school readiness on the part of young children in vulnerable families. It seems clear that much can be gained from increased understanding of the relationships between parents of young children and the staff members of the programs that serve them.

It is apparent that programs are most likely to help parents prepare their children to begin school when parent-staff interactions are characterized by mutual trust and by two-way and open communication, when the resources offered by the programs are accessible, and when parents perceive those resources as potentially useful. The questions of how best to achieve such interactions are many and varied. Researchers, professional organizations, governmental policy makers, foundations, program administrators, and

Foundations might collaborate with researchers and professional training programs to produce a set of video- or audio-teaching vignettes demonstrating common problems, typical practice, and best practice in working with parents, particularly those considered "hard to serve."

individual practitioners all have roles to play in addressing these questions and in promoting effective parent-program interactions. This document may be a step toward fuller realization of those roles.

References

8

Abrams, Laura S., & Gibbs, Jewelle Taylor. (2002). Disrupting the logic of home-school relations: Parent involvement strategies and practices of inclusion and exclusion. *Urban Education, 37*(3), 384-402. (ERIC Journal No. EJ660359)

Adler, Susan Matoba. (2001). Racial and ethnic identity formation of midwestern Asian-American children. *Contemporary Issues in Early Childhood, 2*(3), 265-294.

Allen, Norma N.; Harry, G. Elizabeth; & McLaughlin, Margaret J. (1993). *The parent professional partnership: African American parents' partici-pation in the special education process. Final report.* College Park: University of Maryland, Institute for the Study of Exceptional Children and Youth. (ERIC Document No. ED403726)

Allen, Sharon M.; Thompson, Ray; & Drapeaux, Jane. (1996, April). *Schools as the center of rural communities.* Paper presented at the national meeting of the American Educational Research Association, New York. (ERIC Document No. ED398040)

Allen, Sharon M.; Thompson, Ray H.; Hoadley, Michael; Engelking, Jeri; & Drapeaux, Jane. (1997a, March). *Improving school climate: Creating a circle of communication between educators and families.* Paper pre-sented at the annual meeting of the American Educational Research Associa-tion, Chicago. (ERIC Document No. ED408097)

Allen, Sharon M.; Thompson, Ray H.; Hoadley, Michael; Engelking, Jeri; & Drapeaux, Jane. (1997b, March). *What teachers want from parents and what parents want from teachers: Similarities and differences.* Paper presented at the annual meeting of the American Educational Research Association, Chicago. (ERIC Document No. 408097)

American Educational Research Association (AERA). (2003). *Resolution on the essential elements of scientifically-based research* [Online].

Available http://www.aera.net/meeting/councilresolution03.htm [2003, October 29].

American Psychological Association. (2003). Guidelines on multicultural education, training, research, practice, and organizational change for psychologists. *American Psychologist, 58*(5), 377-402.

Ames, Lynda J., & Ellsworth, Jeanne. (1997). *Women reformed, women empowered: Poor mothers and the endangered promise of Head Start.* Philadelphia, PA: Temple University Press. (ERIC Document No. ED404397)

Asch, Adrienne. (2000). Critical race theory, feminism, and disability: Reflections on social justice and personal identity. *Ohio State Law Journal* [Online], *62*(1). Available: http://moritzlaw.osu.edu/lawjournal/asch.htm [2003, October 1].

Baird, Samera, & Peterson, JoEllyn. (1997). Seeking a comfortable fit between family-centered philosophy and infant-parent interaction in early intervention: Time for a paradigm shift? *Topics in Early Childhood Special Education 17*(2), 139-164. (ERIC Journal No. EJ550596)

Baker, Amy J. L.; & Piotrkowski, Chaya S. (1996, August). *Parents and children through the school years: The effects of the Home Instruction Program for Preschool Youngsters. Final report.* New York: National Council of Jewish Women, Center for the Child. (ERIC Document No. ED402406)

Baker, Amy J. L., & Soden, Laura M. (1997, March). *Parent involvement in children's education: A critical assessment of the knowledge base.* Paper presented at the annual meeting of the American Educational Research Association, Chicago. (ERIC Document No. ED407127)

Bandura, Albert. (1989). Human agency in social cognitive theory. *American Psychologist, 44*(9), 1175-1184.

Barhava-Monteith, Galia; Harre, Niki; & Field, Jeff. (1999). A promising start: An evaluation of the HIPPY program in New Zealand. *Early Child Development and Care, 159,* 145-157. (ERIC Journal No. EJ602202)

Baydar, Nazli; Kagitcibasi, Cigdem; Kuntay, Aylin; & Goksen, Fatos. (2003). *Evaluation of an early childhood educational television program in Turkey.* Istanbul, Turkey: ACEV.

Baydar, Nazli; Reid, M. Jamila; & Webster-Stratton, Carolyn. (2003). The role of mental health factors and program engagement in the effectiveness of a preventive parenting program for Head Start mothers. *Child Development, 74*(5), 1433-1453.

Beeson, Elizabeth, & Strange, Marty. (2003, February). *Why rural matters 2003: The continuing need for every state to take action on rural education. A report of the Rural School and Community Trust Policy Program* [Online]. Available: http://www.ruraledu.org/streport/pdf/WRM_2003.pdf [2003, October 1].

Berger, Eugenia Hepworth. (2000). *Parents as partners in education.* Upper Saddle River, NJ: Prentice-Hall.

Bernstein, Anne C. (2000). Straight therapists working with lesbians and gays in family therapy. *Journal of Marital and Family Therapy, 26*(4), 443-454.

Bhagwanji, Yash; Thomas, Dawn; Bennett, Tess; Stillwell, Marge; & Allison, Anita. (1997). *Relationships with parents with disabilities: Perceptions and training needs of Head Start staff.* Champaign: University of Illinois at Urbana-Champaign. (ERIC Document No. ED433152)

Blair, Clancy. (2002). School readiness: Integrating cognition and emotion in a neurobiological conceptualization of children's functioning at school entry. *American Psychologist, 57*(2), 111-127. (ERIC Journal No. EJ646501)

Brody, Gene H.; Dorsey, Shannon; Forehand, Rex; & Armistead, Lisa. (2002). Unique and protective contributions of parenting and classroom processes to the adjustment of African American children living in single-parent families. *Child Development, 73*(1), 274-286. (ERIC Journal No. EJ649384)

Bronfenbrenner, Urie. (1995). Developmental ecology through space and time: A future perspective. In Phyllis Moen, Glen H. Elder, Jr., & Kurt Lüscher (Eds.), *Examining lives in context: Perspectives on the ecology of human development* (pp. 619-647). Washington, DC: American Psychological Association. (ERIC Document No. ED394667)

Bronfenbrenner, Urie. (1998). The ecology of developmental processes. In William Damon & Richard M. Lerner (Eds.), *Handbook of child psychology. Vol. I: Theoretical models of human development* (5th ed., pp. 993-1028). New York: Wiley.

Brooks-Gunn, Jeanne. (1995). Children in families in communities: Risk and intervention in the Bronfenbrenner tradition. In Phyllis Moen, Glen H. Elder, Jr., & Kurt Lüscher (Eds.), *Examining lives in context: Perspectives on the ecology of human development* (pp. 467-519). Washington, DC: American Psychological Association.

Bryant, Donna; Peisner-Feinberg, Ellen; & Miller-Johnson, Shari. (2000, April). *Head Start parents' roles in the educational lives of their children.* Paper presented at the annual conference of the American Educational Research Association, New Orleans, LA. (ERIC Document No. ED446835)

Bryk, Anthony S., & Schneider, Barbara. (2002). *Trust in schools: A core resource for improvement.* New York: Russell Sage Foundation. (ERIC Document No. ED469022)

Buell, Martha J.; Hallam, Rena A.; & Beck, Heidi L. (2001). Early Head Start and child care partnerships: Working together to serve infants, toddlers, and their families. *Young Children, 56*(3), 7-12. (ERIC Journal No. EJ635765)

Burton, Christine B. (1992). Defining family-centered early education: Beliefs of public school, child care, and Head Start teachers. *Early Education and Development, 3*(1), 45-59. (ERIC Journal No. EJ441921)

Callery, Peter, & Smith, Lorraine. (1991). A study of role negotiation between nurses and the parents of hospitalized children. *Journal of Advanced Nursing, 16*(7), 772-781.

Campbell, Nancy Duff; Appelbaum, Judith C.; Martinson, Karin; & Martin, Emily. (2000). *Be all that we can be: Lessons from the military for improving our nation's child care system* [Online]. Washington, DC: National Women's Law Center. Available: http://www.nwlc.org/pdf/military.pdf [2003, October 6].

Cane, R. S., & McKenzie, S. A. (2001). Parents' interpretations of children's respiratory symptoms on video. *Archives of Disease in Childhood, 84*(1), 31-34.

Cane, R. S., Ranganathan, S. C., & McKenzie, S. A. (2000). What do parents of wheezy children understand by "wheeze"? *Archives of Disease in Childhood, 82*(4), 327-332.

Casey Family Programs & U.S. Department of Health and Human Services. (2001). *Starting Early Starting Smart: Summary of early findings.* Washington, DC: Casey Family Programs and the U.S. Department of Health and Human Services, Substance Abuse and Mental Health Services Administration. (ERIC Document No. ED466899)

Casper, Virginia, & Schultz, Steven B. (1999). *Gay parents/straight schools: Building communication and trust.* New York: Teachers College Press. (ERIC Document No. ED435462)

Chatman, Elfreda A. (1996). The impoverished life-world of outsiders. *Journal of the American Society for Information Science, 47*(3), 193-206. (ERIC Journal No. EJ520208)

Chavkin, Nancy Feyl. (2001). Recommendations for research on the effectiveness of school, family, and community partnerships. In Sam Redding & Lori G. Thomas (Eds.), *The community of the school* (pp. 83-96). Lincoln, IL: Academic Development Institute. (ERIC Document No. ED452981)

Chin, Margaret M., & Newman, Katherine S. (2002). *High stakes: Time poverty, testing, and the children of the working poor* [Online]. Working Paper Series. New York: Foundation for Child Development. Available: http://www.ffcd.org/ourwork.htm [2003, October 1]. (ERIC Document No. ED466304)

Christenson, Sandra L., & Sheridan, Susan M. (2001). *Schools and families: Creating essential connections for learning.* New York: Guilford. (ERIC Document No. ED456941)

Clingempeel, W. Glenn, & Henggeler, Scott W. (2002). Randomized clinical trials, developmental theory, and antisocial youth. *Development and Psychopathology, 14*(4), 695-711.

Coe, Gwendolyn, & Shelby, Debra. (1998). Practitioner's perspective: Relative efficacy of parent and teacher involvement in a shared-reading intervention for preschool children from low-income backgrounds. *Early Childhood Research Quarterly, 13*(2), 293-294. (ERIC Journal No. EJ574141)

Connors, Lori J., & Epstein, Joyce L. (1995). Parent and school partnerships. In Marc H. Bornstein (Ed.), *Handbook of parenting: Vol. 4. Applied and practical parenting* (pp. 437-458). Mahwah, NJ: Erlbaum. (ERIC Document No. ED389419)

Coontz, E. Kim. (in press). *Bringing families together: A guide to parent cooperatives.* Davis, CA: Center for Cooperatives, University of California.

Crowson, Robert L., & Boyd, William Lowe. (1996). Structures and strategies: Toward an understanding of alternative models for coordinated children's services. In James G. Cibulka & William J. Kritek (Eds.), *Coordination among schools, families and communities: Prospects for educational reform* (pp. 137-169). Albany: State University of New York Press. (ERIC Document No. ED395718)

Curtis, W. John, & Cicchetti, Dante. (2003). Moving research on resilience into the 21st century: Theoretical and methodological considerations in examining the biological contributors to resilience. *Development and Psychopathology, 15*(3), 773-810.

Daro, Deborah A., & Harding, Kathryn A. (1999). Healthy Families America: Using research to enhance practice. *Future of Children, 9*(1), 152-176. (ERIC Journal No. EJ589000)

Dauber, Susan L., & Epstein, Joyce L. (2001). Parents' attitudes and practices of parent involvement in inner-city elementary and middle schools. In Joyce L. Epstein, *School, family, and community partnership: Preparing educators and improving schools* (pp. 205-220). Boulder, CO: Westview Press. (ERIC Document No. ED454322)

Davies, Don. (1996). *Partnerships for student success: What we have learned about policies to increase student achievement through school partnerships with families and communities.* Baltimore, MD: Center on Families, Communities, Schools, and Children's Learning, Johns Hopkins University. (ERIC Document No. ED399079)

Davies, Don. (1997). Crossing boundaries: How to create successful partnership with families and communities. *Early Childhood Education Journal, 25*(1), 73-77. (ERIC Journal No. EJ554394)

Delgado-Gaitan, Concha. (1996). *Protean literacy: Extending the discourse on empowerment*. Washington, DC: Falmer Press.

Delgado-Gaitan, Concha. (2001). *The power of community: Mobilizing for family and schooling*. Lanham, MD: Rowman & Littlefield. (ERIC Document No. ED464797)

Delpit, Lisa. (1995). *Other people's children: Cultural conflict in the classroom*. New York: New Press. (ERIC Document No. ED387274)

Dervin, Brenda. (1983). Information as a user construct: The relevance of perceived information needs to synthesis and interpretation. In Spencer A. Ward & Linda J. Reed (Eds.), *Knowledge structure and use: Implications for synthesis and interpretation* (pp. 154-183). Philadelphia, PA: Temple University Press.

Dervin, Brenda. (1999). On studying information seeking methodologically: The implications of connecting metatheory to method. *Information Processing and Management, 35*(6), 727-750.

Dervin, Brenda; Harpring, Jayme E.; & Foreman-Wernet, Lois. (1999). In moments of concern: A sense-making study of pregnant, drug-addicted women and their information needs. *Electronic Journal of Communication* [Online], *9*(2, 3, 4). Available: http://www.cios.org/getfile\Dervin2_V9N23499 [2003, October 1].

Dispenza, Mary. (1999). *Our families, our children: The Lesbian and Gay Child Care Task Force report on quality child care*. Seattle, WA: Lesbian and Gay Child Care Task Force. (ERIC Document No. ED437174)

Doherty, William J. (2000). Family science and family citizenship: Towards a model of community partnerships with families. *Family Relations, 49*(3), 319-325.

Dolan, Lawrence, & Haxby, Barbara. (1995). *Removing barriers to learning: Factors that affect participation and dropout in parent interventions*. Baltimore, MD: Center on Families, Communities, Schools, and Children's Learning, John Hopkins University. (ERIC Document No. ED380231)

Driebe, Nicole M., & Cochran, Moncrieff M. (1996, June). *Barriers to parent involvement in Head Start programs*. Paper presented at the Head Start National Research Conference, Washington, DC. (ERIC Document No. ED400108)

Dryfoos, Joy, & Maguire, Sue. (2002). *Inside full-service community schools*. Thousand Oaks, CA: Corwin Press. (ERIC Document No. ED466829)

Duggan, Anne K.; McFarlane, Elizabeth C.; Windham, Amy M.; Rohde, Charles A.; Salkever, David S.; Fuddy, Loretta; Rosenberg, Leon A.; Buchbinder, Sharon B.; & Sia, Calvin C. J. (1999). Evaluation of Hawaii's Healthy Start program. *Future of Children, 9*(1), 66-90. (ERIC Journal No. EJ588996)

Dunlap, Katherine M. (1997). Family empowerment: One outcome of cooperative preschool education. *Child Welfare, 76*(4), 501-518. (ERIC Journal No. EJ549477)

Dunst, Carl J. (2002). Family-centered practices: Birth through high school. *Journal of Special Education, 36*(3), 139-147. (ERIC Journal No. EJ655573)

Dunst, Carl J.; Boyd, Kimberly; Trivette, Carol M.; & Hamby, Deborah W. (2002). Family-oriented program models and professional helpgiving practices. *Family Relations, 51*(3), 221-229.

Early Head Start (EHS) National Resource Center Home Page. (n.d.). Available: http://www.ehsnrc.org/AboutUs/Index.htm [2003, October 1].

Easen, Patrick; Kendall, Pippa; & Shaw, Janet. (1992). Parents and educators: Dialogue and development through partnership. *Children and Society, 6*(4), 282-296. (ERIC Journal No. EJ492334)

Educate America Act of 1994, H.R. 1804, 103d Cong. [Online]. Available: http://www.ed.gov/legislation/GOALS2000/TheAct/index.html [2003, December 5].

Elementary and Secondary Education Act of 2001, Pub. L. 107-110, 115 Stat. 1425 [Online]. Available: http://www.ed.gov/policy/elsec/leg/esea02/107-110.pdf [2003, October 1].

Endsley, Richard C., & Minish, Patricia A. (1991). Parent-staff communication in day care centers during morning and afternoon transitions. *Early Childhood Research Quarterly, 6*(2), 119-135. (ERIC Journal No. EJ431695)

Epstein, Joyce L. (2001). *School, family, and community partnerships: Preparing educators and improving schools.* Boulder, CO: Westview Press. (ERIC Document No. ED454322)

Fagan, Jay. (1999). *Predictors of father and father figure involvement in pre-kindergarten Head Start.* Philadelphia, PA: National Center of Fathers and Families. (ERIC Document No. ED454982)

Gallagher, Peggy A.; Fialka, Janice; Rhodes, Cheryl; Arceneaux, Cindy. (2002). Working with families: Rethinking denial. *Young Exceptional Children, 5*(2), 11-17. (ERIC Journal No. EJ643013)

Galley, Michelle. (2003). Math and science get own research center. *Education Week, 23*(1), 34, 36.

Garbarino, James. (1992). *Children in danger: Coping with the consequences of community violence.* San Francisco: Jossey-Bass. (ERIC Document No. ED346217)

Ghazvini, Alisa S., & Readdick, Christine A. (1994). Parent-caregiver communication and quality care in diverse child care settings. *Early Childhood Research Quarterly, 9*(2), 207-222. (ERIC Journal No. EJ493682)

Gleeson, Brendan. (1998). A place on earth: Technology, space, and disability. *Journal of Urban Technology, 5*(1), 87-109.

Gomby, Deanna S.; Culross, Patti L.; & Behrman, Richard. (1999). Home visiting: Recent program evaluations—Analysis and recommendations. *Future of Children, 9*(1), 4-26. (ERIC Journal No. EJ588993)

Goodnow, Jacqueline. (1995). Differentiating among social contexts: By spatial features, forms of participation, and social contracts. In Phyllis Moen, Glen H. Elder, Jr., & Kurt Lüscher (Eds.), *Examining lives in context: Perspectives on the ecology of human development* (pp. 269-302). Washington, DC: American Psychological Association. (ERIC Document No. ED394667)

Graue, M. Elizabeth. (1993). *Ready for what? Constructing meanings of readiness for kindergarten.* Albany: State University of New York. (ERIC Document No. ED355012)

Graue, M. Elizabeth; Kroeger, Janice; & Prager, Dana. (2001). A Bakhtinian analysis of particular home-school relations. *American Educational Research Journal, 38*(3), 467-498.

Gredler, Gilbert R. (1992). *School readiness: Assessment and educational issues.* Brandon, VT: Clinical Psychology Publishing Company. (ERIC Document No. ED375979)

Greenberg, Polly. (1998). The origins of Head Start and the two versions of parent involvement: How much parent participation in early childhood programs and services for poor children? In Jeanne Ellsworth & Lynda J. Ames (Eds.), *Critical perspectives on Project Head Start: Revisioning the hope and challenge* (pp. 49-72). Albany: New York State University Press.

Greene, Marci. (1999). A parent's perspective. *Topics in Early Childhood Special Education, 19*(3), 149-151. (ERIC Journal No. EJ594947)

Grolnick, Wendy S., & Slowiaczek, Maria L. (1994). Parents' involvement in children's schooling: A multidimensional conceptualization and motivational model. *Child Development, 65*(1), 237-252. (ERIC Journal No. EJ478223)

Gross, Deborah; Julion, Wrenetha; & Fogg, Louis. (2001). What motivates participation and dropout among low-income urban families of color in a prevention intervention? *Family Relations, 50*(3), 246-254. (ERIC Journal No. EJ632177)

Grotberg, Edith H. (1997). *The International Resilience Project: Findings from the research and the effectiveness of interventions* [Online]. Available: http://resilnet.uiuc.edu/library/grotb97a.html [2003, March 11].

Guba, Egon G., & Lincoln, Yvonna S. (1989). *Fourth generation evaluation.* Newbury Park, CA: Sage.

Gudykunst, William B., & Lee, Carmen M. (2002). Cross-cultural communication theories. In William B. Gudykunst & Bella Mody (Eds.), *Handbook of international and intercultural communication* (2nd ed., pp. 25-50). Thousand Oaks, CA: Sage.

Harachi, Tracy; Catalano, Richard F.; & Hawkins, J. David. (1997). Effective recruitment for parenting programs within ethnic minority communities. *Child and Adolescent Social Work Journal, 14*(1), 23-39.

Harms, Thelma; Clifford, Richard M.; & Cryer, Debby. (1998). *Early Childhood Environment Rating Scale* (Rev. ed.). New York: Teachers College Press. (ERIC Document No. ED422128)

Harrist, Amanda W. (1992, April). *Parent-child synchrony and later competence with peers: Do interaction styles at home forecast success in kindergarten?* Paper presented at the meeting of the American Educational Research Association, San Francisco.

Hart, Betty, & Risley, Todd R. (1995). *Meaningful differences in the everyday experience of young American children.* Baltimore, MD: Paul H. Brookes. (ERIC Document No. ED387210)

Haythornthwaite, Caroline. (1996). Social network analysis: An approach and technique for the study of information exchange. *Library and Information Science Research, 18*(4), 323-342. (ERIC Journal No. EJ558525)

Head Start Bureau. (1996). *Communicating with parents. Training guides for the Head Start learning community.* Washington, DC: U.S. Department of Health and Human Services, Administration for Children, Youth, and Families. (ERIC Document No. ED407138)

Head Start Bureau. (1998). *Training guides for the Head Start learning community: Family partnerships: A continuous process* [Online]. Washington, DC: U.S. Department of Health and Human Services, Administration on Children, Youth, and Families. Available: http://www.headstartinfo.org/pdf/family_partnerships/family_partnerships_a_continuous_process.pdf [2003, October 6].

Healthy Families America. (2003). *Research findings* [Online]. Available: http://www.healthyfamiliesamerica.org/research/index.shtml [2003, October 1].

Hebbeler, Kathleen M., & Gerlach-Downie, Suzanne G. (2002). Inside the black box of home visiting: A qualitative analysis of why intended outcomes were not achieved. *Early Childhood Research Quarterly, 17*(1), 28-51. (ERIC Journal No. EJ651042)

Henderson, Anne T., & Mapp, Karen L. (2002). *A new wave of evidence: The impact of school, family, and community connections on student achievement.* Austin, TX: Southwest Educational Development Laboratory, National Center for Family and Community Connections with Schools.

Henry, Jim, & Purcell, Roberta. (2000). Exploring the tensions: Being family-centered with parents who abuse/neglect their children. *Infant-Toddler Intervention, 10*(4), 275-285. (ERIC Journal No. EJ626366)

Hersberger, Julie. (2001). Everyday information needs and information sources of homeless parents. *New Review of Information Behaviour Research, 2,* 119-134.

Hewes, Dorothy W. (1995, November-December). *The changing role of fathers in co-op nursery schools.* Paper presented at the annual conference and exhibition of the National Association for the Education of Young Children, Washington, DC. (ERIC Document No. ED399039)

Hoffmeister, Robert J. (1985). Families with deaf parents: A functional perspective. In S. Kenneth Thurman (Ed.), *Children of handicapped parents: Research and clinical perspectives* (pp. 111-130). Orlando, FL: Academic Press.

Hoover-Dempsey, Kathleen V., & Sandler, Howard M. (1995). Parental involvement in children's education: Why does it make a difference? *Teachers College Record, 97*(2), 310-331. (ERIC Journal No. EJ523879)

I Am Your Child Foundation. (n.d.). *Mission and goals* [Online]. Available: http://www.iamyourchild.org/aboutus.html [2003, October 1].

Ispa, Jean; Sharp, Elizabeth; Brookes, Sheila; Wolfenstein, Miriam; Thornburg, Kathy; Fine, Mark; & Lane, Valeri. (2000, June). *Mother and home visitor personality characteristics, the mother-home-visitor relationship, and home visit intensity.* Paper presented at the Head Start National Research Conference, Washington, DC. (ERIC Document No. ED443561)

Jacobson, Arminta Lee, & Engelbrecht, JoAnn. (2000). Parenting education needs and preferences of parents of young children. *Early Childhood Education Journal, 28*(2), 139-147. (ERIC Journal No. EJ618672)

Jacobvitz, Deborah; Crosby, Danielle; Wooley, John; & Smith, Ralph. (1997). *ASPIRE: An Even Start program of communities in schools. Final evaluation report, year 3, 1996-97.* Publication no. 96.20. Austin, TX: Austin Independent School District, Department of Accountability, Student Services, and Research. (ERIC Document No. ED419828)

Johnson, Laura; Bruhn, Rick; Winek, Jon; Krepps, Jeff; & Wiley, Kelly. (1999). The use of child-centered play therapy and filial therapy with Head Start families. *Journal of Marital and Family Therapy, 25*(2), 169-176. (ERIC Journal No. EJ600947)

Johnson, Vivian. (1994). *Parent centers in urban schools: Four case studies.* Baltimore, MD: Center on Families, Communities, Schools, and Children's Learning, Johns Hopkins University. (ERIC Document No. ED375197)

Juffer, Femmie; Hoksbergen, Rene A. C.; Riksen-Walraven, J. Marianne; & Kohnstamm, Geldolph A. (1997). Early intervention in adoptive families: Supporting maternal sensitive responsiveness, infant-mother attachment, and infant competence. *Journal of Child Psychology and Psychiatry, 38*(8), 1039-1050.

Kai, Joe. (1996). Parents' difficulties and information needs in coping with acute illness in preschool children: A qualitative study. *British Medical Journal, 313*(7063), 987-990.

Kalyanpur, Maya, & Harry, Beth. (1999). *Culture in special education: Building reciprocal family-professional relationships*. Baltimore, MD: Paul H. Brookes.

Katz, Lilian G. (1995). *Talks with teachers of young children: A collection*. Norwood, NJ: Ablex. (ERIC Document No. ED380232)

Kelley, Susan D. M.; Sikka, Anjoo; & Venkatesan, Sivaraman. (1997). A review of research on parental disability: Implications for research and counseling practice. *Rehabilitation Counseling Bulletin, 41*(2), 105-121. (ERIC Journal No. EJ560572)

Klingbeil, Carol; Speece, Mark W.; & Schubiner, Howard. (1995). Readability of pediatric patient education materials: Current perspectives on an old problem. *Clinical Pediatrics, 34*(2), 96-102.

Knapp, Michael S. (1995). How shall we study comprehensive, collaborative services for children and families? *Educational Researcher, 24*(4), 5-16.

Kochanska, Grazyna; Murray, Kathleen; & Coy, Katherine C. (1997). Inhibitory control as a contributor to conscience in childhood: From toddler to early school age. *Child Development, 68*(2), 263-277. (ERIC Journal No. EJ545077)

Kochanska, Grazyna; Murray, Kathleen T.; & Harlan, Elena T. (2000). Effortful control in early childhood: Continuity and change, antecedents, and implications for social development. *Developmental Psychology, 36*(2), 220-232. (ERIC Journal No. EJ605483)

Kuntz, Kathryn R. (1998). A lost legacy: Head Start's origins in community action. In Jeanne Ellsworth & Lynda J. Ames (Eds.), *Critical perspectives on Head Start: Revisioning the hope and challenge* (pp. 1-48). Albany: State University of New York Press. (ERIC Document No. ED426767)

Ladson-Billings, Gloria, & Tate, William F., IV. (1995). Toward a critical race theory of education. *Teachers College Record, 97*(1), 47-68. (ERIC Journal No. EJ519126)

Lakey, Jennifer. (1997). Teachers and parents define diversity in an Oregon preschool cooperative—Democracy at work. *Young Children, 52*(4), 20-28. (ERIC Journal No. EJ544914)

Lamb-Parker, Faith; Piotrkowski, Chaya S.; Baker, Amy J. L.; Kessler-Sklar, Susan; Clark, Beryl; & Peay, Lenore. (2001). Understanding barriers to parent involvement in Head Start: A research-community partnership. *Early Childhood Research Quarterly, 16*(1), 35-51. (ERIC Journal No. EJ635670)

Lareau, Annette. (1996). Assessing parent involvement in schooling: A critical analysis. In Alan Booth & Judith F. Dunn (Eds.), *Family-school links: How do they affect educational outcomes?* (pp. 57-64). Mahwah, NJ: Erlbaum. (ERIC Document No. ED411048)

Lareau, Annette. (2000). *Home advantage: Social class and parental intervention in elementary education* (2nd ed.). Lanham, MD: Rowan & Littlefield.

Lashley, Myrna; Talley, William; Lands, Larry; & Keyserlingk, Edward W. (2000). Informed proxy consent: Communication between pediatric surgeons and surrogates about surgery. *Pediatrics, 105*, 591-597.

Lazarus, Wendy, & Mora, Francisco. (2000). *Online content for low-income and underserved Americans: The digital divide's new frontier* [Online]. Available: http://www.childrenspartnership.org/pub/low_income/ and http://www.childrenspartnership.org/pub/low_income/low_income.pdf [2003, October 1].

Lee, Hwa; Ostrosky, Michaelene M.; Bennett, Tess; & Fowler, Susan A. (2003). Perspectives of early intervention professionals about culturally appropriate practices. *Journal of Early Intervention, 25*(4), 281-295.

Lewit, Eugene M., & Baker, Linda Schuurmann. (1995). School readiness. *Future of Children* [Online], *5*(2), 128-139. Available: http://www.futureofchildren.org/usr_doc/vol5no2ART9.pdf [2003, October 6]. (ERIC Journal No. EJ522415)

Lightfoot, Sara Lawrence. (1978). *Worlds apart: Relationships between families and schools.* New York: Basic Books.

Lombard, Avima D. (1994). *Success begins at home: The past, present, and future of the Home Instruction Program for Preschool Youngsters.* Guilford, CT: Dushkin Publishing. (ERIC Document No. ED368491)

Lonigan, Christopher J., & Whitehurst, Grover J. (1998). Relative efficacy of parent and teacher involvement in a shared-reading intervention for pre-school children from low-income backgrounds. *Early Childhood Research Quarterly, 13*(2), 263-290. (ERIC Journal No. EJ574139)

Lopez, Gerardo R.; Scribner, Jay D.; & Mahitivanichcha, Kanya. (2001). Redefining parental involvement: Lessons from high-performing migrant-impacted schools. *American Educational Research Journal, 38*(2), 253-288. (ERIC Journal No. EJ636338)

Lott, Bernice. (2002). Cognitive and behavioral distancing from the poor. *American Psychologist, 57*(2), 100-110.

Love, John M.; Kiskar, Ellen Eliason; Ross, Christine M.; Schochet, Peter Z; Brooks-Gunn, Jeanne; Boller, Kimberly; Paulsell, Diane; Fuligini, Alison Sidle; & Berlin, Lisa J. (2001, June) *Building their futures: How Early Head Start programs are enhancing the lives of infants and toddlers in low-income families: Vol. I: Technical report* [Online]. Princeton, NJ: Mathematica Policy Research. Available: http://www.mathematica-mpr.com/PDFs/buildingvol1.pdf [2003, October 29] (ERIC Document No. ED454952)

Love, John M.; Kiskar, Ellen Eliason; Ross, Christine M.; Schochet, Peter Z; Brooks-Gunn, Jeanne; Paulsell, Diane; Boller, Kimberly; Constantine, Jill; Vogel, Cheri; Fuligini, Alison Sidle; & Brady-Smith, Christy. (2002, June). *Making a difference in the lives of infants and toddlers and their families: The impacts of Early Head Start. Executive summary* [Online]. Princeton, NJ: Mathematica Policy Research. Available: http://www.mathematica-mpr.com/PDFs/ehsfinalsumm.pdf [2003, October 29].

Lubeck, Sally, & deVries, Mary. (2000). The social construction of parent involvement in Head Start. *Early Education and Development, 11*(5), 633-658. (ERIC Journal No. EJ618578)

Lubeck, Sally; Jessup, Patricia; deVries, Mary; & Post, Jackie. (2001) . The role of culture in program improvement. *Early Childhood Research Quarterly, 16*(4), 499-523. (ERIC Journal No. EJ647669)

Lucas, M.-A. (2001). Reports from the field: The military child care connection. *Future of Children, 11*(1), 130-133.

Machida, Sandra; Taylor, Angela R.; & Kim, Juhu. (2002). The role of maternal beliefs in predicting home learning activities in Head Start families. *Family Relations, 51*(2), 176-184. (ERIC Journal No. EJ644565)

MacPhee, David; Fritz, Janet; & Miller-Heyl, Jan. (1993, March). *Ethnic variations in social support networks and child rearing.* Paper presented at the biennial meeting of the Society for Research in Child Development, New Orleans, LA. (ERIC Document No. ED356088)

Mahoney, Gerald, & Wheeden, C. Abigail. (1997). Parent-child interaction: The foundation for family-centered early intervention practice: A response to Baird and Peterson. *Topics in Early Childhood Special Education, 17*(2), 165-184. (ERIC Journal No. EJ550597)

Marden, Mary, & Nicholas, David. (1997). The information needs of parents. *Aslib Proceedings, 49*(1), 5-7.

Marfo, Kofi; Dinero, Thomas; Browne, Noel; Gallant, Don; Smyth, Rosalind; & Corbett, Allan. (1992). Child, program, and family ecological variables in early intervention. *Early Education and Development, 3*(1), 27-44. (ERIC Journal No. EJ441920)

Masten, Ann S. (1997). Resilience in children at-risk. *Research/Practice* [Online], *5*(1). Available: http://education.umn.edu/CAREI/Reports/Rpractice/Spring97/resilience.htm [2003, March 11].

Mattingly, Doreen J.; Prislin, Radmila; McKenzie, Thomas L.; Rodriguez, James L.; & Kayzar, Brenda. (2002). Evaluating evaluations: The case of parent involvement programs. *Review of Educational Research, 72*(4), 549-576.

McBride, Brent A.; Rane, Thomas R.; & Bae, Ji-Hi. (2001). Intervening with teachers to encourage father/male involvement in early childhood programs. *Early Childhood Research Quarterly, 16*(1), 77-93. (ERIC Journal No. EJ635673)

McClelland, Jerry. (1996, April). *Knowing and being known: Parents' experiences with rural schools.* Paper presented at the annual meeting of the American Educational Research Association, New York. (ERIC Document No. ED396887)

McCubbin, Hamilton I.; McCubbin, Marilyn A.; & Thompson, Anne I. (1993). Resiliency in families: The role of family schema and appraisal in family adaptation to crises. In Timothy H. Brubaker (Ed.), *Family relations: Challenges for the future* (pp. 153-177). Newbury Park, CA: Sage.

McDowell, Teresa. (1999). Systems consultation and Head Start: An alternative to traditional family therapy. *Journal of Marital and Family Therapy, 25*(2), 155-168. (ERIC Journal No. EJ600946)

McInnis-Dittrich, Kathleen. (1996). Violence prevention: An ecological adaptation of Systematic Training for Effective Parenting. *Families in Society, 77*(7), 414-422.

McKenzie, Pamela J. (2002). Communication barriers and information-seeking counterstrategies in accounts of practitioner-patient encounters. *Library and Information Science Research, 24*(1), 31-47.

McQuail, Denis, & Windahl, Sven. (1993). *Communication models for the study of mass communication.* New York: Longman.

Meehan, Merrill; Walsh, Sandra; Swisher, Angie; Spring, Janet; & Lewis, Harry. (1999, April). *Process and outcomes evaluation of an Even Start program.* Paper presented at the annual meeting of the American Educational Research Association. (ERIC Document No. ED436333)

Meier, Deborah. (2002). *In schools we trust: Creating communities of learning in an era of testing and standardization.* Boston: Beacon Press. (ERIC Document No. ED468057)

Melaville, Atelia I.; Blank, Martin J.; & Asayesh, Gelareh. (1993). *Together we can: A guide for crafting a profamily system of education and human services.* Washington, DC: U.S. Department of Education. (ERIC Document No. ED357856)

Moore, Evelyn, & Barbarin, Oscar A. (2003). Respecting the voices of parents: How the Spirit of Excellence Parent Empowerment Project connects with African American Parents. In Jean Mendoza, Lilian G. Katz, Anne

S. Robertson, & Dianne Rothenberg, *Connecting with parents in the early years*. Champaign: University of Illinois at Urbana-Champaign, College of Education, Early Childhood and Parenting Collaborative.

Morisaki, Seiichi, & Gudykunst, William B. (1994). Face in Japan and the United States. In Stella Ting-Toomey (Ed.), *The challenge of facework: Cross-cultural and interpersonal issues* (pp. 47-93). Albany: State University of New York Press.

Morisset, Colleen E. (1994). *School readiness: Parents, and professionals speak on social and emotional needs of young children. Report 26.* Baltimore, MD: Center on Families, Communities, Schools, and Children's Development, Johns Hopkins University. (ERIC Document No. ED380233)

Mulholland, Lori; Heffernon, Rick; & Shaw, Kathleen. (1998). *Head Start goes to school. Head Start-Public School Transition Project. 1992-1997. Final evaluation report.* Tempe: Arizona State University. (ERIC Document No. ED427863)

Nation, Maury; Crusto, Cindy; Wandersman, Abraham; Kumpfer, Karol L.; Seybolt, Diana; Morrissey-Kane, Erin; & Davino, Katrina. (2003). What works in prevention: Principles of effective prevention programs. *American Psychologist, 58*(6/7), 449-456.

National Association for the Education of Young Children (NAEYC). (1995). *Responding to linguistic and cultural diversity: Recommendations for effective early childhood education* [Online]. Available: http://www.naeyc. org/resources/position_statements/psdiv98.pdf [2003, October 29].

National Association for the Education of Young Children (NAEYC). (1998). *Guide to accreditation by the National Association for the Education of Young Children.* Washington, DC: Author. (ERIC Document No. ED438932)

National Education Goals Panel. (n.d.). *Reconsidering children's early development and learning: Toward common views and vocabulary* [Online]. Available: http://www.negp.gov/Reports/child-ea.htm [2003, October 1].

National Parent Teacher Association (NPTA). (2000). *Building successful partnerships: A guide for developing parent and family involvement programs.* Bloomington, IN: National Educational Service. (ERIC Document No. ED442910)

Newman, Rebecca. (1999). *Educating homeless children: Witness to a cataclysm.* New York: Garland.

Nicholas, David, & Marden, Mary. (1998). Parents and their information needs. A case study: Parents of children under the age of 5. *Journal of Librarianship and Information Science, 30*(1), 35-58.

North Carolina School Improvement Panel. (2000). *School readiness in North Carolina: Strategies for defining, measuring, and promoting success for all children. Report of the Ready for School Goal Team* [Online]. Available http://www.serve.org/publications/NCFull%20Report.pdf [2003, October 1].

O'Neil, Dara V. (1999). *Ubiquitous access to telecommunications technologies: Is access a positive freedom?* [Online]. Available: http://infoeagle.bc.edu/bc_org/avp/law/st_org/iptf/commentary/content/1999060402.html [2003, October 6].

Owen, Margaret Tresch; Ware, Anne M.; & Barfoot, Bill. (2000). Caregiver-mother partnership behavior and the quality of caregiver-child and mother-child interactions. *Early Childhood Research Quarterly, 15*(3), 413-428. (ERIC Journal No. EJ633377)

Pillow, Wanda S. (2000). Exposed methodology: The body as a deconstructive process. In Elizabeth A. St. Pierre & Wanda S. Pillow (Eds.), *Working the ruins: Feminist poststructural theory and methods in education* (pp. 199-219). New York: Routledge.

Pizzo, Peggy Daly. (1998). *Does Head Start help parents? A critical review of longitudinal studies of Head Start children and families.* Unpublished manuscript, Harvard Medical School, Cambridge, MA. (ERIC Document No. ED425868)

Powell, Douglas R. (1989). *Families and early childhood programs.* Washington, DC: National Association for the Education of Young Children. (ERIC Document No. ED309872)

Powell, Douglas R., & Diamond, Karen E. (1996). Approaches to parent-teacher relationships in U.S. early childhood programs during the twentieth century. *Journal of Education, 177*(3), 71-94. (ERIC Journal No. EJ538653)

Public Law 107-110, 2001, Sec. 1235.10 [Online]. Available: http://www.ed.gov/policy/elsec/leg/esea02/107-110.pdf [2003, October 6].

Public Law 107-110, 2001, Sec. 1241 [Online]. Available: http://www.ed.gov/policy/elsec/leg/esea02/107-110.pdf [2003, October 6].

Quine, Lyn, & Rutter, D. R. (1994). First diagnosis of severe mental and physical disability: A study of doctor:parent communication. *Journal of Child Psychology and Psychiatry, 35*(7), 1273-1287.

Quintero, Elizabeth. (1998). Family literacy informing Head Start: Lessons from Hmong and Latino families. In Jeanne Ellsworth & Lynda J. Ames (Eds.), *Critical perspectives on Project Head Start: Revisioning the hope and challenge* (pp. 200-218). Albany: State University of New York Press. (ERIC Document No. ED426767)

Raver, C. Cybele. (2002). Emotions matter: Making the case for the role of young children's emotional development for early school readiness. *Social Policy Report, 16*(3), 3-10, 12-18.

Raver, C. Cybele, & Knitzer, Jane. (2002). *Ready to enter: What research tells policymakers about strategies to promote social and emotional school readiness among three- and four-year-olds* [Online]. New York: National Center for Children in Poverty. Available: http://cpmcnet.columbia.edu/dept/nccp/ProEmoPP3.pdf [2003, October 1]. (ERIC Document No. ED467045)

Ray, Nancy K.; Rubenstein, Harriet; & Russo, Natalie J. (1994). Understanding the parents who are mentally retarded: Guidelines for family preservation programs. *Child Welfare, 73*(6), 725-743. (ERIC Journal No. EJ495280)

Reid, M. Jamila; Webster-Stratton, Carolyn; & Beauchaine, Theodore. (2001). Parent training in Head Start: A comparison of program response among African American, Asian American, Caucasian, and Hispanic mothers. *Prevention Science, 2*(4), 209-227.

Reinelt, Claire, & Fried, Mindy. (1993). "I am this child's mother": A feminist perspective on mothering with a disability. In Mark Nagler (Ed.), *Perspectives on disability* (2nd ed., pp. 195-202). Palo Alto, CA: Health Markets Research.

Reynolds, Arthur J. (2000). *Success in early intervention: The Chicago Child-Parent Centers.* Lincoln: University of Nebraska Press. (ERIC Document No. ED443532)

Roggman, Lori A.; Boyce, Lisa K.; Cook, Gina A.; & Jump, Vonda K. (2001). Inside home visits: A collaborative look at process and quality. *Early Childhood Research Quarterly, 16*(1), 53-71. (ERIC Journal No. EJ635671)

Romer, Eileen F., & Umbreit, John. (1998). The effects of family-centered service coordination: A social validity study. *Journal of Early Intervention, 21*(2), 95-110.

Romero, Mary Eunice. (in press). Cultural literacy in the world of Pueblo children. In Eve Gregory, Susi Long, & Dinah Volk (Eds.), *Many pathways to literacy.* New York: Routledge Falmer.

Rubin, Kenneth H.; Bukowski, William; & Parker, Jeffrey G. (1998). Peer interactions, relationships, and groups. In William Damon (Series Ed.) & Nancy Eisenberg (Vol. Ed.), *Handbook of child psychology: Vol. 3. Social, emotional, and personality development* (5th ed., pp. 619-700). New York: Wiley.

Ryan, Bruce A., & Adams, Gerald R. (1995). The family-school relationships model. In Bruce A. Ryan, Gerald R. Adams, Thomas P. Gullotta, Roger P. Weissberg, & Robert L. Hampton (Eds.), *The family-school connection: Theory, research, and practice* (pp. 3-28). Thousand Oaks, CA: Sage. (ERIC Document No. ED387226)

Salovey, Peter; Mowad, Linda Z.; Pizarro, Judith; Edlund, Denielle; & Moret, Marta E. (2002). Developing computer proficiency among Head Start parents: An in-progress case study of a New England CIS Digital Divide Project. *Electronic Journal of Communication* [Online], *11*(3,4). Available: http://www.cios.org/getfile\salovey_v11n3 [2003, October 1].

Saluja, Gitanjali; Early, Diane M.; & Clifford, Richard M. (2002). Demographic characteristics of early childhood teachers and structural elements of early care and education in the United States. *Early Childhood Research and Practice* [Online], *4*(1). Available: http://ecrp.uiuc.edu/v4n1/saluja.html [2002, July 31]. (ERIC Document No. ED464765)

Savolainen, Reijo. (1995). Everyday life information seeking: Approaching information seeking in the context of "way of life." *Library and Information Science Research, 17*(3), 259-294. (ERIC Journal No. EJ513754)

Scher, Paula Januzzi. (1998). Practitioner's perspective: Shared-reading intervention. *Early Childhood Research Quarterly, 13*(2), 291-292.

Schorr, Lisbeth B. (1997). *Common purpose: Strengthening families and neighborhoods to rebuild America.* New York: Anchor Books.

Schwandt, Thomas A. (2001). *Dictionary of qualitative inquiry* (2nd ed.). Thousand Oaks, CA: Sage.

Seefeldt, Carol; Denton, Kristin; Galper, Alice; & Younoszai, Tina. (1999). The relation between Head Start parents' participation in a transition demonstration, education, efficacy, and their children's academic abilities. *Early Childhood Research Quarterly, 14*(1), 99-109. (ERIC Journal No. EJ586528)

Serpell, Robert; Baker, Linda; Sonnenschein, Susan; Gorham, Linda; & Hill, Susan. (1996). *Cooperative communication among parents and teachers about children's emergent literacy. Final project report to the National Reading Research Center.* Baltimore, MD: National Reading Research Center. (ERIC Document No. ED414566)

Shimanoff, Susan B. (1994). Gender perspectives on facework: Simplistic stereotypes vs. complex realities. In Stella Ting-Toomey (Ed.), *The challenge of facework: Cross-cultural and interpersonal issues* (pp. 159-207). Albany: State University of New York Press.

Shirley, Dennis. (2002). *Valley Interfaith and school reform: Organizing for power in South Texas.* Austin: University of Texas Press. (ERIC Document No. ED463932)

Shonkoff, Jack P., & Phillips, Deborah A. (Eds.). (2000). *From neurons to neighborhoods. The science of early childhood development.* Washington, DC: National Academy Press. (ERIC Document No. ED446866)

Shore, Rima. (1997). *Rethinking the brain: New insights into early development.* New York: Families and Work Institute. (ERIC Document No. ED418770)

Shore, Rima. (1998). *Ready schools* [Online]. Washington, DC: National Education Goals Panel. Available: http://www.negp.gov/Reports/readysch.pdf [2003, October 6].

Shores, Elizabeth F. (1998). *A call to action: Family involvement as a critical component of teacher education programs.* Tallahassee, FL: SERVE Publications Department. (ERIC Document No. ED421229)

Skilton-Sylvester, Ellen. (2002). Should I stay or should I go? Investigating Cambodian women's participation and investment in adult ESL programs. *Adult Education Quarterly, 53*(1), 9-26. (ERIC Journal No. EJ654913)

Sleeter, Christine. (1993). How white teachers construct race. In Cameron McCarthy & Warren Crichlow (Eds.), *Race, identity, and representation in education* (pp. 157-171). New York: Routledge. (ERIC Document No. ED372158)

Sligo, Frank, & Williams, Jocelyn. (2001). *Investigating information poverty and its implications for community development* [Online]. Available: http://www.sprc1.sprc.unsw.edu.au/nspc2001/abstract.asp?PaperID=196 [2003, October 1].

Smrekar, Claire. (1996). The Kentucky Family Resources Centers: The challenges of remaking family-school interactions. In James G. Cibulka & William J. Kritek (Eds.), *Coordination among schools, families, and communities: Prospects for educational reform* (pp. 3-25). Albany: State University of New York Press. (ERIC Document No. 395718)

Solomon, Paul. (1997). Conversation in information-seeking contexts: A test of an analytical framework. *Library and Information Science Research, 19*(3), 217-248.

Soodak, Leslie C., & Erwin, Elizabeth J. (2000). Valued member or tolerated participant: Parents' experiences in inclusive early childhood settings. *Journal of the Association for Persons with Severe Handicaps, 25*(1), 29-41. (ERIC Journal No. EJ608082)

Squires, Jane K.; Potter, LaWanda; Bricker, Diane D; & Lamorey, Suzanne. (1998). Parent-completed developmental questionnaires: Effectiveness with low and middle income parents. *Early Childhood Research Quarterly, 13*(2), 345-354. (ERIC Journal No. EJ574144)

Starkey, Prentice, & Klein, Alice. (2000). Fostering parental support for children's mathematical development: An intervention with Head Start families. *Early Education and Development, 11*(5), 659-680. (ERIC Journal No. EJ618579)

St. Pierre, Robert; Gamse, Beth; Alamprese, Judith; Rimdzius, Tracy; & Tao, Fumiyo. (1998). *The national evaluation of the Even Start Family Literacy Program: Evidence from the past and a look to the future* [Online]. Washington, DC: U.S. Department of Education, Planning and Evaluation

Service. Available: http://www.ed.gov/pubs/EvenStart/index.html [2003, December 5]. (ERIC Document No. ED427890)

St. Pierre, Robert; Ricciuti, Anne; Tao, Fumiyo; Creps, Cindy; Swartz, Janet; Lee, Wang; Parsad, Amanda; & Rimdzius, Tracy. (2003). *Third national Even Start evaluation: Program impacts and implications for improvement* [Online]. Washington, DC: U.S. Department of Education. Available: http://www.ed.gov/rschstat/eval/disadv/evenstartthird/toc.html [2003, December 5].

St. Pierre, Robert; Swartz, Janet; Gamse, Beth; Murray, Stephen; Deck, Dennis; & Nickel, Phil. (1995). *National evaluation of the Even Start Family Literacy Program. Final report.* Washington, DC: Department of Education. (ERIC Document No. ED386328)

Strauss, Ronald P.; Sharp, Michael C.; Lorch, S. Claire; & Kachalia, Beejal. (1995). Physicians and the communication of "bad news": Parent experiences of being informed of their child's cleft lip and/or palate. *Pediatrics, 96*, 82-89.

Strong, Marlene F. (1999). Serving mothers with disabilities in early childhood programs. *Young Children, 54*(3), 10-17. (ERIC Journal No. EJ586487)

Swap, Susan McAllister. (1993). *Developing home-school partnerships: From concepts to practice.* New York: Teachers College Press. (ERIC Document No. ED358220)

Tamis-LeMonda, Catherine S., & Cabrera, Natasha (Eds.). (2002). *Handbook of father involvement: Multidisciplinary perspectives.* Mahwah, NJ: Erlbaum. (ERIC Document No. ED465459)

Tannen, Deborah. (1994). *Gender and discourse.* New York: Oxford University Press.

Thomas, Volker; McCollum, Eric E.; & Snyder, Wendy. (1999). Beyond the clinic: In-home therapy with Head Start families. *Journal of Marital and Family Therapy, 25*(2), 177-189. (ERIC Journal No. EJ600948)

Ting-Toomey, Stella. (1994). Face and facework: An introduction. In Stella Ting-Toomey (Ed.), *The challenge of facework: Cross-cultural and interpersonal issues* (pp. 1-14). Albany: State University of New York Press.

Ting-Toomey, Stella. (1999). *Communicating across cultures.* New York: Guilford Press.

Treichel, Christa J. (1995). *The MELD for Young Moms program: A national study of demographics and program outcomes.* Minneapolis, MN: MELD. (ERIC Document No. ED396847)

Trivette, Carol M.; Dunst, Carl J.; & Hamby, Deborah. (1996). Characteristics and consequences of help-giving practices in contrasting human services programs. *American Journal of Community Psychology, 24*(2), 273-293.

Wagner, Mary; Spiker, Donna; Gerlach-Downie, Suzanne; & Hernandez, Frances. (2000). *Parental engagement in home visiting programs: Findings from the Parents As Teachers multisite evaluation.* Menlo Park, CA: SRI International. (ERIC Document No. ED455957)

Webster-Stratton, Carolyn. (1997). From parent training to community building. *Families in Society, 78*(2), 156-171.

Webster-Stratton, Carolyn. (2000, June). *The Incredible Years training series. OJJDP Juvenile Justice Bulletin* [Online]. Available: http://www.ncjrs.org/html/ojjdp/2000_6_3/contents.html [2003, October 29].

Wegner, Mark V., & Girasek, Deborah C. (2003). How readable are child safety seat installation instructions? *Pediatrics, 111*(3), 588-591.

Wendland-Carro, Jacqueline; Piccinini, Cesar A.; & Millar, W. Stuart. (1999). The role of an early intervention on enhancing the quality of mother-infant interaction. *Child Development, 70*(3), 713-721. (ERIC Journal No. EJ595703)

Werner, Emmy E. (1993). Risk, resilience, and recovery: Perspectives from the Kauai longitudinal study. *Development and Psychopathology, 5*(4), 503-515.

Werner, Emmy E., & Smith, Ruth S. (1992). *Overcoming the odds: High risk children from birth to adulthood.* Ithaca, NY: Cornell University Press. (ERIC Document No. ED344979)

What Works Clearinghouse Web Site. (2003, July). *Introduction to the What Works Clearinghouse evidence report process and the role of scientific standards* [Online]. Available: http://w-w-c.org/july2003.html [2003, November 1].

Wheeler, J. Gary; Fair, Melinda; Simpson, Pippa M.; Rowlands, Leigh Ann; Aitken, Mary E.; & Jacobs, Richard F. (2001). Impact of a waiting room videotape message on parent attitudes toward pediatric antibiotic use. *Pediatrics, 108*(3), 591-596.

White, Karl R.; Taylor, Matthew J.; & Moss, Vanessa D. (1992). Does research support claims about the benefits of involving parents in early intervention programs? *Review of Educational Research, 62*(1), 91-125. (ERIC Journal No. EJ445315)

Whitehurst, Grover J. (n.d.). *Evidence-based education (EBE)* [Online]. Available: http://www.ed.gov/admins/tchrqual/evidence/whitehurst.html [2003, October 29].

Williams, Jocelyn; Comrie, Margie; & Sligo, Frank X. (2001). *Walking the path with new parents.* Paper presented at National Social Policy Conference 2001, University of New South Wales, Sydney. Available: http://

www.sprc.unsw.edu.au/nspc2001/NSPC%202001Papers/
Williams_Comrie_Silgo.pdf [2003, October 1].

Winton, Pam. (1998). Socially valid but difficult to implement: Creative solutions needed. *Journal of Early Intervention, 21*(2), 114-116. (ERIC Journal No. EJ568614)

W.K. Kellogg Foundation. (2002). *Youth and education: What is "vulnerable?"* [Online]. Available: http://www.wkkf.org/Programming/ RenderRes.aspx?CID=3&ID=3359 [2003, October 1].

Worchel, Frances F.; Prevatt, Bruce C.; Miner, Jennifer; Allen, Melissa; Wagner, Linda; & Nation, Pat. (1995). Pediatrician's communication style: Relationship to parent's perceptions and behaviors. *Journal of Pediatric Psychology, 20*(5), 633-644.

Yeung, W. Jean; Linver, Miriam R.; & Brooks-Gunn, Jeanne. (2002). How money matters for young children's development: Parental investment and family processes. *Child Development, 73*(6), 1861-1879. (ERIC Journal No. EJ668465)

Zigler, Edward, & Anderson, Karen. (1979). An idea whose time had come. In Edward Zigler & Jeanette Valentine (Eds.), *Project Head Start. A legacy of the War on Poverty* (pp. 3-20). New York: Free Press. (ERIC Document No. ED183266)

Zill, Nicholas; Resnick, Gary; Kim, Kwang; O'Donnell, Kevin; Sorongon, Alberto; McKey, Ruth Hubbell; Pai-Samant, Shefali; Clark, Cheryl; O'Brien, Robert; & D'Elio, Mary Ann. (2003). *Head Start FACES 2000: A whole-child perspective on program performance. Fourth progress report* [Online]. Washington, DC: Administration on Children, Youth, and Families, Department of Health and Human Services. Available: http:// www.acf.hhs.gov/programs/core/ongoing_research/faces/ faces2000_final.pdf [2003, October 6].

Zuckerman, Barry, & Parker, Steven. (1995). Preventive pediatrics: New models of providing needed health services. *Pediatrics, 95*(5), 758-762.

Appendix

Symposium Papers and Responses

Relations between Families and Early Childhood Programs   Page 141
    Douglas R. Powell
Symposium Response

Respecting the Voices of Parents: How the Spirit of Excellence Parent   Page 157
Empowerment Project Connects with African American Parents
    Evelyn K. Moore and Oscar A. Barbarin
Symposium Response

Connecting with Parents: The AVANCE Experience   Page 171
    Gloria G. Rodriguez
Symposium Response

Parent Panel   Page 191

Closing Panel: Key Issues for Early Childhood Programs   Page 199

Comments on Search Strategies Used   Page 203

Tentative Topics for Proposed Educational Materials   Page 205

Symposium Participants   Page 207

Relations between Families and Early Childhood Programs

Douglas R. Powell

Introduction

Relations between families and early childhood programs represent a mixed picture in the United States. At one level, the field has a long and distinguished record of working with families. It has consistently promoted a view of parents as valuable partners in educating young children and has generated more innovative program designs for engaging families than any other level of education. At a deeper level, there is considerable variation between and within different types of early childhood programs in the quality of connections with parents. Head Start program standards and resources for forming partnerships with families typically are not found in child care programs, for example, and most of the field's innovations in working with families have not been widely adopted. Importantly, approaches to partnerships with parents differ in major ways, particularly in viewing parents as limited versus full partners with program staff.

Recent developments offer promise of improving this state of affairs. Increasingly it is expected that high-quality early childhood programs engage in family-centered practices with children and with parents that result in mutually supportive environments for children's learning and development. This paper examines the concept of family-centered early education by describing long-standing and recent ideas influencing relations between programs and families, the concept of family-centered early education, approaches to fostering connections between programs and families, and needed directions in broadening the use of family-centered practices in early education.

Influential Ideas

The early childhood field's interest in parents is grounded in several powerful ideas about parental influences and responsibilities. Clearly the most influential idea shaping relations between early childhood programs and families is that early childhood programs need the active support of parents to maximize program impacts on children. This idea has been consistently bolstered by theories and scientific evidence pointing to the lasting impact of families on

Noting that there is considerable variation between and within different types of early childhood programs in the quality of connections with parents, this paper examines the concept of family-centered early education by describing (1) long-standing and recent ideas influencing relations between programs and families, (2) images of "connectedness," (3) practice standards, (4) parent-staff communication, (5) supporting family child rearing, and (6) needed directions in broadening the use of family-centered practices in early education. The paper concludes that advances in program efforts to form responsive connections with families require a systematic understanding of what works, including the conditions under which family-centered practices enable programs and families to jointly support the optimal development of children.

children's development, and by research demonstrating the formative quality of the early years. It has led to program efforts to encourage parental understanding and appreciation of program goals and curriculum, and to initiatives aimed at supporting family capacity to promote the healthy development of children, often through parenting education strategies.

A second powerful idea is that parents should contribute to decisions about the nature of their child's early education and care experiences. This idea emanates from our country's long-standing tradition of endorsing religious, ideological, and cultural diversity in child-rearing matters and the rights of parents in decisions affecting the child. The U.S. propensity for child care policies to emphasize parental choice in an open market of early childhood options reflects this orientation. Also connected to this idea is concern that early childhood programs, especially full-day child care, may be disruptive to parents' child-rearing values and interests. Provisions for helping parents in this decision-making role include informational supports for selecting a program, ongoing communication with program staff about goals for a child and the child's experiences, classroom volunteering for the purpose of monitoring and reinforcing program operations, and voice or vote regarding program governance decisions.

Two other important ideas are gaining influence in the early childhood field and are contributing to a rethinking of relations between programs and families. One is that children's development is embedded in an interconnected system of families and communities. This idea reflects growing interest in how children's development interacts with different social contexts and is enriched by the work of developmental scientists examining the ecology of human development and parenting. The influence of this idea has been advanced by societal interest in a rapidly changing social landscape characterized by increases in single-parent households; mothers working outside the home; and the racial, ethnic, and linguistic diversity of families.

The other idea gaining influence is that family strengths should be marshaled toward the optimal development of children and parents. This concept is supported by scholarly work on the flow of social support in natural helping systems, the resilience of families in difficult circumstances, and the benefits of building on strengths in efforts to promote individual and family well-being.

The latter two ideas are a basis of an emerging set of expectations of early childhood programs: to be culturally and socially relevant to the families they serve, to foster mutually respectful and reciprocal relations between staff and families, to empower parents with information and social support that promotes optimal engagement of the child-rearing role, and to function as a bridge between families and other services in the community (Larner, 1997).

Images of Connectedness: Key Dimensions

The concept of family-centered early education calls for early childhood programs to broaden the boundaries of their work to be more inclusive of families and their social contexts as a basis of supporting children's learning and development. The program lens widens considerably. Consider the following description from a *Wall Street Journal* article on how some child care centers are now taking care of stressed parents as well as children (Shellenbarger, 2000):

> Marley Couchon, director of a … child care center, was greeting parents arriving for their children when one parent's demeanor touched off an alarm in her mind. The mother, her eyes downcast and her step unusually rushed, was hurrying past when Ms. Couchon caught her eye. "Would you like to talk?" the director asked. As they stepped into Ms. Couchon's office, the mother, a nurse, burst into tears. Her husband, a software engineer, had just lost his job, she explained, leaving the family strapped. "I gave her a hug and let her cry," Ms. Couchon says. (This director) also refused the mother's request to drop her two preschoolers from the center's roster, telling her she would cut their tuition until her husband got a new job.

The article goes on to report that at the center where Ms. Couchon is director, "soothing classical music greets parents in the reception area, where they are encouraged to take a moment to relax. Ms. Couchon also takes up to 25 calls during lunch hour from parents checking on their kids. And teachers avoid talking to parents about their kids' problems when they arrive, tired and rushed, to pick them up, saving discussions for meetings at parents' convenience."

Family-centered approaches to early education and care also emphasize assessments of family and program resourcefulness: How resourceful are families in meeting their children's developmental needs? Do programs have sufficient resources to support families in this task? What resources might families contribute to the support of programs?

Responses to these types of questions generally suggest that resources for appropriately supporting child and family development are in short supply. Urie Bronfenbrenner and colleagues concluded from an analysis of demographic trends in the United States that there is

> growing chaos in the lives of families, in child care settings, schools, peer groups, youth programs, neighborhoods, workplaces, and other everyday environments in which human beings live their lives. Such chaos, in turn, interrupts and undermines the formation and stability of relationships and activities that are essential for psychological growth. Moreover, many of the conditions leading to that chaos are the often unforeseen products of policy decisions made both in the private and the public sector. Today, in both of these arenas, we are considering profound economic and social changes, some of which threaten to raise the degree of chaos to even higher and less psychologically (and biologically) tolerable levels. (Bronfenbrenner & Morris, 1999, p. 1022)

Findings from the Commonwealth Fund's national survey of parents with young children highlight parents' views of their child-rearing situations. For instance, the survey found that only 37% of parents felt that they were spending about the right amount of time with their children; 57% reported that

Connecting with Parents

they would like to spend more time with their children. Thirty-nine percent reported reading or looking at a book with their child on a daily basis (Halfon & McLearn, 2002).

Early childhood program policies and practices regarding parents have historically focused on family resourcefulness, reflecting the assumption that programs can help families meet their needs. However, the attention to reciprocity in family-centered principles implies that families have resources that can benefit the early childhood program. The flow of influence in the family-program connection, then, is two-way.

Practice Standards

Family-centered principles are well articulated in the National Association for the Education of Young Children's (NAEYC's) revised statement of developmentally appropriate practice. The revised statement, issued in 1997 (Bredekamp & Copple, 1997), offers greater clarity than its earlier 1986 version (Bredekamp, 1986) on the importance of viewing children in the context of family, culture, and society, and the need for programs to support close ties between child and family (Powell, 2001). The clearer language in NAEYC's descriptions of recommended program relations with families contrasts with the field's long-standing use of fuzzy terminology (e.g., parent involvement) and represents a major conceptual shift from the conventional approach to parent-teacher relationships as a task of parents serving as helpmates in implementing program-determined agendas (Powell, 2001; Powell & Diamond, 1995).

The current NAEYC statement calls for program goals to be developed in collaboration with families and for program staff to learn about each child through relationships with the child's family. The practice guidelines (Bredekamp & Copple, 1997) promote

- the development of reciprocal and collaborative relationships between teachers and families;
- parents participating in decisions about their child's care and education, including involvement in assessing and planning for individual children;
- teacher sensitivity to and respect for parents' preferences and concerns without abdicating professional responsibility to children;
- teachers and parents frequently sharing their knowledge of the child and understanding of children's development and learning;
- programs facilitating family linkages with a range of appropriate services; and
- teachers, parents, and other professionals with educational responsibility for a child sharing developmental information about children as they move to a new program or setting.

In similar fashion, the NAEYC position paper on responding to linguistic and cultural diversity recommends that teachers become familiar with the child's community (NAEYC, 1996a), and the NAEYC code of ethical conduct emphasizes ideals and principles that focus on mutual trust as well as respect for family child-rearing values and decision-making rights (NAEYC, 1996b). Clear language also is found in the Division for Early Childhood of the Council for Exceptional Children practice standards, which specify that families are to be equal to professionals in formulating decisions about a child's program of care and education (Sandall, McLean, & Smith, 2000).

Head Start's performance standards on program relations with families have long emphasized responsiveness to families. Scholars often point to Head Start's approach to parent involvement as a cornerstone of the program's success (e.g., Zigler & Muenchow, 1992). Other early proponents of family-centered principles include the National Black Child Development Institute's safeguards for public school involvement in early childhood education (National Black Child Development Institute, 1987), and the anti-bias curriculum (Derman-Sparks and the A.B.C. Task Force, 1989).

The early childhood field's current expectations of program relations with families are consistent with standards for parent/family involvement programs issued by the National PTA in 1997. These standards specify that (1) communication between home and school is regular, two-way, and meaningful; (2) parenting skills are promoted and supported; (3) parents play an integral role in assisting student learning; (4) parents are welcome in the school, and their support and assistance are sought; (5) parents are full partners in the decisions that affect children and families; and (6) community resources are used to strengthen schools, families, and student learning (National PTA, 1997).

The NAEYC standards also are compatible with guidelines for family support practice issued by Family Support America (formerly Family Resource Coalition). The latter guidelines embrace relationships between staff and families that are based on equality and respect, and call for programs to mobilize formal and informal resources to support family development, among other guidelines (Family Resource Coalition, 1996).

The expectations of reciprocal and collaborative parent-staff relationships, and for program responsiveness to family interests and circumstances, have major implications for the two main domains of early childhood program relations with parents: parent-staff communication and supports for parenting. What do we know about current status of these two areas?

Parent-Staff Communication

Recommendations for close communication between parents and early childhood staff are on strong theoretical grounds. Bronfenbrenner (1979, 1986) has offered the most detailed set of propositions about the developmental benefits of frequent and personal communication between teachers and parents. Surprisingly little research has been conducted on this topic. However, one recent study found that more communication between mother and child care provider was significantly related to more sensitive and supportive interactions between the caregiver and child, and between mother and child, even after controlling for child-rearing beliefs. The more frequent communication involved mother and child care provider seeking and sharing information about the child and the child's experiences. The study did not involve attempts to alter the frequency or content of communication between mother and child care provider (Owen, Ware, & Barfoot, 2000).

Communication between parent and child care provider was identified as a key feature of high-quality care by both parents and providers in a major study of family child care (Kontos, Howes, Shinn, & Galinsky, 1995) and in a smaller study of centers (Ghazvini & Readdick, 1994). Parents have been found to express higher levels of satisfaction than program staff with the quantity and quality of communication (for a review, see Powell, 1989).

Studies indicate that most communication between parent and staff occurs at child drop-off and pick-up points. This transition time typically is not conducive to meaningful exchanges; parents can be rushed, staff are understandably focused on children's transitions, and in the case of full-day programs, staff members who spend the largest amount of time with a child may not be on duty at the point parents are present. Anecdotal evidence suggests that some centers seeking to be more family centered are accommodating these circumstances by arranging for staff to participate in lunch-hour telephone calls with parents checking on their child's day and to talk about children's problems only at meetings scheduled at parents' convenience rather than at the point parents arrive, reportedly tired and rushed, to retrieve their child at the end of the day (Shellenbarger, 2000).

Teacher judgmentalness about parents' child-rearing abilities is an obvious barrier to establishing and maintaining respectful relations between parents and program staff. Findings of a recent descriptive study of 11 family-focused early childhood programs indicate that, in some cases, staff believed parents were not giving their children proper attention and care, and staff found it difficult to avoid being judgmental and to identify family strengths (Lopez & Dorros, 1999). Other studies point to a pattern of negative teacher attitudes regarding parents' child-rearing abilities (Kontos, Raikes, & Woods, 1983; Galinsky, Shinn, Phillips, Howes, & Whitebook, 1990). In one study, mothers held in low esteem by center staff had significantly fewer daily communications with staff than parents held in high esteem (Kontos & Dunn, 1989). Another consequence of negative teacher views of parents' child-rearing abilities may be staff adoption of a "child savior" orientation wherein staff view themselves as surrogate parents and try to assume more responsibility for the child than is appropriate or desired by the parent. A lack of clarity in the roles of parents and program staff has been found to be associated with tensions in the parent-staff relationship (Lopez & Dorros, 1999).

A primary purpose of frequent communication between parent and program staff is to establish and implement shared goals for a child. Research on the nature and consequences of this process is nonexistent. This issue is particularly salient for the growing number of children from linguistic and cultural backgrounds that are not represented in their early childhood program. Early education is likely to be most beneficial if program activities are made meaningful for children through the incorporation of activities that parents value and in which the children engage at home (Fitzgerald & Goncu, 1993).

Supporting Family Child Rearing

The evidence is mixed on whether children's outcomes are significantly improved when early childhood programs provide information and other types of supports to families aimed at enhancing their child-rearing functions. Methodologically, this area is complicated to investigate. A recent analysis of studies of parent involvement programs in K-12 education, for example, identified numerous flaws in evaluation design and methods that seriously limit conclusions about the effects of parent involvement initiatives on children's learning (Mattingly, Prislin, McKenzie, Rodriguez, & Kayzar, 2002).

Some research findings point to improved benefits for children when programs provide focused educational supports for parents. For example, a recent investigation of an interactive shared-reading program with 3- to 4-year-old children from low-income families who attended a child care center found that effects of the reading program were largest for children in program conditions involving home reading. In this study, children were randomly assigned to 1 of 4 conditions: (1) a no treatment control group, (2) an early childhood program condition in which children were read to by their teachers in small groups, (3) a home condition in which children were read to by their parents, and (4) a combined early childhood program plus home condition. Parents and teachers received videotaped instruction on how to read interactively with young children. Children in the third and fourth conditions demonstrated the largest gains in language outcomes (Lonigan & Whitehurst, 1998).

The above findings are consistent with results of earlier investigations of the effects of early childhood intervention programs, typically aimed at low-income populations. Previous studies indicate that programs are more effective if they involve parents (for reviews, see Benasich, Brooks-Gunn, & Clewell, 1992; Gray & Wandersman, 1980; Seitz, 1990). This general pattern of findings does not hold across all early intervention programs, however (Brooks-Gunn, Berlin, & Fuligni, 2000; White, Taylor, & Moss, 1992), and some studies of early childhood intervention programs have not found that increased educational work with parents boosts child outcomes (e.g., Wasik, Ramey, Bryant, & Sparling, 1990). Most likely the quality and quantity of work with parents are key determinants here. Factors that appear necessary for early intervention programs to have an impact on parenting effectiveness and the home environment include sufficient intensity and duration; appropriate timing; direct engagement of parents, children, and the larger family context; diverse supports and services; and responsive and individualized programming (Ramey & Ramey, 1998). Family support of children's learning during the school years also has been found to be an important contributor to sustained positive effects of early childhood programs for children from low-income families (Reynolds, 2000; Reynolds, Temple, Robertson, & Mann, 2001).

The dominant approach to providing information and support to parents is for professionals to determine the content and method of work with parents. An alternative approach is for parents to take control of decisions about the topics and resources they would like to explore. Discussion groups, outings, and other activities that foster mutually supportive linkages among parents in an early childhood program, with or without involvement of professionals, are examples of strategies aimed at enhancing family life without professional direction. More research is needed on the processes and effects of these approaches.

Similarly, research is needed on early childhood program provisions aimed at reducing stress and increasing the quality of family time. Some full-day programs, for example, seek to provide meals-to-go, pick/up and drop/off for dry cleaning, and even calm music in the center's waiting room, in the hope of reducing stress and increasing efficiency in parents' efforts to balance work and family (Shellenbarger, 2000). These provisions may be viewed as creative program adaptations to a growing population of stressed, single- or dual-worker families with young children. Programs serving low-income parents affected by welfare reform also need research attention. There is some indication that Head Start parents are increasingly less available for traditional program participation opportunities because of participation in job training or work (Parker et al., 1997).

Needed Directions

The mixed picture offered at the outset of this paper emphasized the considerable variation across early childhood programs in engaging families. Steps to improve this situation require significant investments in staff through personnel preparation and the development of effective tools for staff to form and sustain supportive ties with families. Advances in family-centered early education also require additional program resources and additional research knowledge on effective practices.

Probably few early childhood professionals enter the field with a strong interest in working with families, and their professional preparation is unlikely to have included much, if any, serious attention to the knowledge and skills necessary for effective work with families. This domain is not central to licensing or certification standards and professional preparation programs in higher education, although early childhood teacher preparation programs have been found to require more courses on this topic than programs preparing teachers to work with older children (Shartrand, Weiss, Kreider, & Lopez, 1997). Some of the more interesting personnel preparation models are in the field of early childhood special education where, for example, parents have served as co-instructors of college-level courses on working with families (McBride, Sharp, Hains, & Whitehead, 1995). Inservice training resources also are available (e.g., Cornell Empowerment Project). Areas to emphasize in training and in the development of tools for staff to use in engaging families are identified below.

- **Understanding Relationship Development.** A view of relations with parents as a series of discrete events (e.g., parent-teacher conferences, open houses) is unlikely to yield shared goals for a child or mutual exchange of information. Staff and program policies need to approach parent-teacher relationships as relationship systems that evolve over time.

  Research suggests that parents and teachers are likely to approach their connection with one another through different relationship emphases. For example, confidence has been found to be a strong factor in both parent and child care staff views of what is important in the parent-staff relationship, but confidence meant somewhat different things to each party. Parents emphasized staff competence, while staff emphasized open communication and agreement about caregiving issues. Parents and staff also emphasized slightly different matters regarding the concept of collaboration, and parents valued affiliative ties with staff while staff valued the caring capacities of the parent as important qualities of the parent-staff relationship (Elicker, Noppe, Noppe, & Fortner-Wood, 1997).

- **Developing Shared Goals for Child.** Early childhood teachers need strategies for developing shared goals with parents. Parental responsiveness to a parenting education program has been found to be more positive when the parent and program worker share similar goals for the child (Segal, 1985). More generally, children's academic performance has been found to be positively associated with mother-teacher congruence regarding perceptions of child competence (Peet, Powell, & O'Donnel, 1997). For many parents, it appears that a useful point for initial engagement may be parents' concerns about their preschool child's readiness for school success. National survey data suggest that a majority of parents of young children want specific information on how to encourage their child's learning (Young, Davis, Schoen, & Parker, 1998) and generally feel less able to positively impact their child's intellectual development than any other area of childhood development (Melmed, 1997). These patterns may partly explain the positive parental response to programs like Parents As Teachers and the Early Childhood Family Education program in Minnesota that focus on parents' educational roles.

- **Working with Children in Family Contexts.** The field needs more work in the development of strategies for helping early childhood professionals build on children's home cultures. One of the key features of culturally responsive education is continuity between the child's experiences in the home and in the early childhood program (Neuman & Roskos, 1994). Although tools and activities for facilitating the flow of information from home to program have been developed in areas such children's literacy experiences (Neuman, 1999), much more programmatic effort is needed to deal with potential conflicts when parents and teachers do not share the same template for ideal educational practices (Okagaki & Diamond, 2000).

- **Integrating Work with Parents and Children.** There is a tendency for efforts to support parents to be disconnected from work with young children, particularly when the work with parents is viewed as a separate program component staffed by professionals who have minimal contact with classroom teachers (Powell & D'Angelo, 2000). Because the ultimate goal is to support parent-child relationships and the child's continuity between program and home, family-centered programs strive toward a coherent, integrated entity, not separate spheres of activities.

- **Working with High-Stress Circumstances.** Even in early childhood programs deemed to be family centered, staff members express major concerns about working with highly stressed families, especially families characterized by poverty, substance abuse, or child neglect, and also adolescent parents and parents having extreme difficulty balancing work and family commitments (Lopez & Dorros, 1999). Clearly, this area is in need of training attention as well as program resources for careful referral work with community agencies.

This paper notes a number of key questions and issues about which we have a paucity of research. For more than three decades, the pressing research questions in the early childhood field have pertained to program quality and outcomes and, to a lesser extent, family access to early childhood programs. More generally, relations with families have not been viewed as a component of quality in studies of early childhood programs. For example, the instruments most commonly used to assess program quality give minimal attention to family support practices (Raab & Dunst, 1997). Advances in program efforts to form truly responsive connections with families require a systematic understanding of what works, including the conditions under which family-centered practices enable programs and families to jointly support the development of successful children.

Acknowledgments

An earlier version of this paper was presented at the Kauffman Early Education Exchange, February 5, 2003.

References

Benasich, April A.; Brooks-Gunn, Jeanne; & Clewell, Beatriz C. (1992). How do mothers benefit from early intervention programs? *Journal of Applied Developmental Psychology, 13*(3), 311-362.

Bredekamp, Sue (Ed.). (1986). *Developmentally appropriate practice in early childhood programs serving children from birth through age 8*. Washington, DC: National Association for the Education of Young Children. (ERIC Document No. ED283587)

Bredekamp, Sue, & Copple, Carol. (1997). *Developmentally appropriate practice in early childhood programs* (Rev. ed.). Washington, DC: National Association for the Education of Young Children. (ERIC Document No. ED403023)

Bronfenbrenner, Urie. (1979). *The ecology of human development.* Cambridge, MA: Harvard University Press.

Bronfenbrenner, Urie. (1986). Ecology of the family as a context for human development: Research perspectives. *Developmental Psychology, 22*(6), 723-742. (ERIC Journal No. EJ347778)

Bronfenbrenner, Urie, & Morris, P. A. (1999). The ecology of developmental processes. In William Damon & R. M. Lerner (Eds.), *Handbook of child psychology: Vol. 1* (5th ed., pp. 939-1028). New York: John Wiley.

Brooks-Gunn, Jeanne; Berlin, Lisa J.; & Fuligni, Allison S. (2000). Early childhood intervention programs: What about the family? In Jack P. Shonkoff & Samuel J. Meisels (Eds.), *Handbook of early childhood intervention* (2nd ed., pp. 549-588). New York: Cambridge University Press.

Derman-Sparks, Louise, & the A.B.C. Task Force. (1989). *Anti-bias curriculum: Tools for empowering young children.* Washington, DC: National Association for the Education of Young Children. (ERIC Document No. ED305135)

Elicker, James; Noppe, Illene C.; Noppe, Lloyd D.; & Fortner-Wood, Cheryl. (1997). The parent-caregiver relationship scale: Rounding out the relationship system in infant child care. *Early Education and Development, 8*(1), 83-100. (ERIC Journal No. EJ538110)

Family Resource Coalition. (1996). *Guidelines for family support practice.* Chicago: Author. (ERIC Document No. ED401020)

Fitzgerald, Linda M.; & Goncu, Artin. (1993). Parent involvement in urban early childhood education: A Vygotskian approach. In Stuart Reifel (Ed.), *Advances in early education and day care, Vol. 5: Perspectives on developmentally appropriate practices* (pp. 197-212). Greenwich, CT: JAI Press.

Galinsky, Ellen; Shinn, Marybeth; Phillips, Deborah; Howes, Carollee; & Whitebook, Marcy. (1990). *Parent/teacher relationships.* New York: Families and Work Institute.

Ghazvini, Alisa S., & Readdick, Christine A. (1994). Parent-caregiver communication and quality of care in diverse child care settings. *Early Childhood Research Quarterly, 9*(2), 207-222. (ERIC Journal No. EJ493682)

Gray, Susan W., & Wandersman, Lois P. (1980). The methodology of home-based intervention studies: Problems and promising strategies. *Child Development, 51*(4), 993-1009. (ERIC Journal No. EJ246075)

Halfon, Neal, & McLearn, Kathryn Taaffe. (2002). Families with children under 3: What we know and implications for results and policy. In Neal Halfon, Kathryn Taaffe McLearn, & Mark A. Schuster (Eds.), *Child rearing in America: Challenges facing parents with young children* (pp. 367-412). New York: Cambridge University Press.

Kontos, Susan, & Dunn, Loraine. (1989). Attitudes of caregivers, maternal experiences with day care, and children's development. *Journal of Applied Developmental Psychology, 10*(1), 37-51.

Kontos, Susan; Howes, Carollee; Shinn, Marybeth; & Galinsky, Ellen. (1995). *Quality in family child care and relative care.* New York: Teachers College Press. (ERIC Document No. ED390536)

Kontos, Susan; Raikes, Helen; & Woods, Alice. (1983). Early childhood staff attitudes toward their parent clientele. *Child Care Quarterly, 12*(1), 45-58.

Larner, Mary. (1997). Creative tension: Applying family support principles to early childhood programs. In Stuart Reifel (Series Ed.) & Carl J. Dunst & Mark Wolery (Vol. Eds.), *Advances in early education and day care: Vol. 9. Family policy and practice in early child care* (pp. 41-60). Greenwich, CT: JAI Press. (ERIC Document No. ED416974)

Lonigan, Christopher J., & Whitehurst, Grover J. (1998). Relative efficacy of parent and teacher involvement in a shared-reading intervention for preschool children from low-income backgrounds. *Early Childhood Research Quarterly, 13*(2), 263-290. (ERIC Journal No. EJ574139)

Lopez, M. Elena, & Dorros, Sybilla. (1999). *Family-centered child care*. Cambridge, MA: Harvard Family Research Project. (ERIC Document No. ED434745)

Mattingly, Doreen J.; Prislin, Radmilla; McKenzie, Thomas L.; Rodriguez, James L.; & Kayzar, Brenda. (2002). Evaluating evaluations: The case of parent involvement programs. *Review of Educational Research, 72*(4), 549-576.

McBride, Susan L.; Sharp, Lisa; Hains, Ann H.; & Whitehead, Amy. (1995). Parents as co-instructors in preservice training: A pathway to family-centered practice. *Journal of Early Intervention, 19*(4), 343-389. (ERIC Journal No. EJ527681)

Melmed, Matthew. (1997). Parents speak: Zero to Three's findings from research on parents' view of early childhood development. *Young Children, 52*(5), 46-49. (ERIC Journal No. EJ547963)

National Association for the Education of Young Children. (1996a). NAEYC position statement: Responding to linguistic and cultural diversity—Recommendations for effective early childhood education. *Young Children, 51*(2), 4-12. (ERIC Journal No. EJ516723)

National Association for the Education of Young Children. (1996b). NAEYC's code of ethical conduct: Guidelines for responsible behavior in early childhood education. *Young Children, 51*(3), 57-60.

National Black Child Development Institute. (1987). *Safeguards: Guidelines for establishing programs for four-year-olds in the public schools*. Washington, DC: Author. (ERIC Document No. ED321891)

National Parent Teacher Association. (1997). *National standards for parent/family involvement programs*. Chicago: Author. (ERIC Document No. ED405405)

Neuman, Susan B. (1999). Creating continuity in early literacy: Linking home and school with a culturally responsive approach. In Linda B. Gambrell, Lesley M. Morrow, Susan B. Neuman, & Michael Pressley (Eds.), *Best practices in literacy instruction* (pp. 258-270). New York: Guilford Press.

Neuman, Susan B., & Roskos, Kathy. (1994). Bridging home and school with a culturally responsive approach. *Childhood Education, 70*(4), 210-214. (ERIC Journal No. EJ483959)

Okagaki, Lynn, & Diamond, Karen E. (2000). Responding to cultural and linguistic differences in the beliefs and practices of families with young children. *Young Children, 55*(3), 74-80. (ERIC Journal No. EJ610247)

Owen, Margaret T.; Ware, Anne M.; & Barfoot, Bill. (2000). Caregiver-mother partnership behavior and the quality of caregiver-child and mother-child interactions. *Early Childhood Research Quarterly, 15*(3), 413-428. (ERIC Journal No. EJ633377)

Parker, Faith L.; Piotrkowski, Chaya S.; Kessler-Sklar, Susan; Baker, Amy J. L.; Peay, Lenore; & Clark, Beryl. (1997). *Parent involvement in Head Start*. New York: National Council of Jewish Women, Center for the Child. (ERIC Document No. ED425796)

Peet, Susan H.; Powell, Douglas R.; & O'Donnel, Barbara K. (1997). Mother-teacher congruence in perceptions of the child's competence and school engagement: Links to academic achievement. *Journal of Applied Developmental Psychology, 18*(3), 373-393.

Powell, Douglas R. (1989). *Families and early childhood programs. Research monographs of the National Association for the Education of Young Children #3*. Washington, DC: National Association for the Education of Young Children. (ERIC Document No. ED309872)

Powell, Douglas R. (2001). Visions and realities of achieving partnership: Parent-school relationships at the turn of the century. In Artin Goncu & Elisa L. Klein (Eds.), *Children in play, story, and school* (pp. 333-357). New York: Guilford Press. (ERIC Document No. ED456935)

Powell, Douglas R., & D'Angelo, Diane. (2000). *Guide to improving parenting education in Even Start family literacy programs*. Washington, DC: U.S. Department of Education. (ERIC Document No. ED445331)

Powell, Douglas R., & Diamond, Karen E. (1995). Approaches to parent-teacher relationships in U.S. early childhood programs during the twentieth century. *Journal of Education, 177*(3), 71-94. (ERIC Journal No. EJ538653)

Raab, Melinda M., & Dunst, Carl J. (1997). Early childhood program assessment scales and family support practices. In Stuart Reifel (Series Ed.) & Carl J. Dunst & Mark Wolery (Vol. Eds.), *Advances in early education and day care: Vol. 9. Family policy and practice in early child care* (pp. 105-131). Greenwich, CT: JAI Press. (ERIC Document No. ED416974)

Ramey, Craig T., & Ramey, Sharon L. (1998). Early intervention and early experience. *American Psychologist, 53*(2), 109-120.

Reynolds, Arthur J. (2000). *Success in early intervention: The Chicago Child-Parent Centers*. Lincoln: University of Nebraska Press. (ERIC Document No. ED443532)

Reynolds, Arthur J.; Temple, Judy A.; Robertson, Dylan L.; & Mann, Emily A. (2001). Long-term effects of an early childhood intervention on educational achievement and juvenile arrest. *Journal of the American Medical Association, 285*(18), 2339-2346. (ERIC Journal No. EJ637869)

Sandall, Susan; McLean, Mary E.; & Smith, Barbara J. (Eds.). (2000). *DEC recommended practices in early intervention/early childhood special education*. Denver, CO: Division for Early Childhood of the Council for Exceptional Children. (ERIC Document No. ED451662)

Segal, Marilyn. (1985). A study of maternal beliefs and values within the context of an intervention program. In Irving E. Sigel (Ed.), *Parental belief systems: The psychological consequences for children* (pp. 271-286). New York: Plenum.

Seitz, Victoria. (1990). Intervention programs for improverished children: A comparison of educational and family support models. *Annals of Child Development, 7*, 73-103.

Shartrand, Angela M.; Weiss, Heather B.; Kreider, Holly M.; & Lopez, M. Elena. (1997). *New skills for schools: Preparing teachers in family involvement.* Cambridge, MA: Harvard Family Research Project. (ERIC Document No. ED414254)

Shellenbarger, S. (2000, April 19). Now, day-care centers have started helping stressed parents, too. *Wall Street Journal,* p. B1.

Wasik, Barbara H.; Ramey, Craig T.; Bryant, Donna M.; & Sparling, Joseph J. (1990). A longitudinal study of two early intervention strategies: Project CARE. *Child Development, 61*(6), 1682-1696. (ERIC Journal No. EJ426160)

White, Karl R.; Taylor, Matthew J.; & Moss, Vanessa T. (1992). Does research support claims about the benefits of involving parents in early intervention programs? *Review of Educational Research, 62*(1), 91-125. (ERIC Journal No. EJ445315)

Young, Kathryn T.; Davis, Karen; Schoen, Cathy; & Parker, Steven. (1998). Listening to parents: A national survey of parents with young children. *Archives of Pediatric Adolescent Medicine, 152*(3), 255-262.

Zigler, Edward, & Muenchow, Susan. (1992). *Head Start: The inside story of America's most successful educational experiment.* New York: Basic Books. (ERIC Document No. ED357887)

Responses to Douglas Powell's Presentation

After presenting his paper, Professor Powell answered questions from symposium participants. A panel then convened to respond to his presentation.

Questions and Comments from Participants Responding to Douglas Powell's Paper

Participant: What are some of the professional development programs?

Doug Powell: There is the purchase of service model and the PSP (Parent Services Project) model. The Reggio model is different from the purchase of service model. We just don't have enough data on the benefits of a community-building strategy with early learning and parents.

There was also information about Bright Horizons focused on individual families, not on connecting families with community or other parents.

Participant: I'm uncomfortable with the professional development problem. Seems to me that the bulk of training goes on where there are faculties stuck in what they were doing 20 years ago. It's not just the kids—we have issues with change, too. Inservice training, especially with supervisors and teacher-providers modeling what they want the students to do, is also extremely important.

Teacher sensitivity and respect for parents and families are essential.

Panel Session—Responding to "Relations between Families and Early Childhood Programs"

Moderator: Professor Jerlean Daniel, University of Pittsburgh.

Low audio quality prevented full transcription of the panel session. The themes that were addressed during the discussion are summarized below.

1. The importance of preservice training for teachers so they understand the value of parent participation.

When various systems—education, child welfare, and social services—are integrated, educators have more knowledge and experience in learning how to access systems in ways that benefit children and families. Educators often feel that they have inadequate knowledge about ways to link families to other resources in the community. Using other teacher mentors—even if it is done electronically—may be one method of helping bridge some of the preservice training gaps along with more classroom experience.

2. The need for schools to be ready for kids.

There is too much attention placed on getting kids ready for school rather than focusing on getting schools ready for children. The idea that parents and early childhood educators should teach their children more during the early years so that rigorous academics can be implemented in earlier years is fundamentally flawed. Focusing on social-emotional development is critical to a young child's development and should be given a high priority in early childhood programs and in the materials that are shared with parents about their child's development.

3. The need to build the capacity of parent leaders.

Understanding the parent culture is important, along with developing appropriate interventions that are respectful of the family's culture. Also, clarifying what type of communication is important between parents and teachers may be most helpful in building the parent-teacher relationship and the advocacy role for parents. Keep in mind that parents and educators are allies and that educators have a role in increasing parents' self-confidence. That role might include clarifying the educational infrastructure and educational terminology for parents so that they begin to feel comfortable advocating for their child in a variety of contexts. Expand on models such as Head Start and AVANCE, which have a priority of moving parents from the participant's role into the leadership role.

4. The need to develop communities of practice.

Educators need to focus on exploring their work through a variety of different frameworks and using an integrated approach. By working with parents, and with other professionals in allied fields such as social services and child welfare, educators will be more equipped to effectively solve a variety of problems. Understanding the social influences that affect children and families should also be incorporated into educators' professional development. Ongoing preservice training and teacher education will encourage communities of practice between faculty, students, schools, and parents that will encourage systemic change and a breaking away from entrenched issues.

Respecting the Voices of Parents:
How the Spirit of Excellence Parent Empowerment Project Connects with African American Parents

Evelyn K. Moore and Oscar A. Barbarin

Introduction

Over the course of 10 years, the National Black Child Development Institute (NBCDI) has reached at-risk parents in urban and rural areas across the country through a curriculum that respects and affirms the voices of African American parents. This program is called the Parent Empowerment Project (PEP) curriculum. As a result of widespread implementation of PEP, we have learned important lessons about enhancing the role that low-income African American families play in their children's early learning.

In this paper, we hope to broaden the conversation on providing meaningful support to low-income African American parents as well as contribute findings from PEP to the growing body of knowledge on parent involvement in early learning. Our reflections are arranged in five parts. The first section provides an overview of the PEP curriculum describing the lessons NBCDI has learned about developing and providing a curriculum that responds to the wants and needs of low-income African American parents. The second section describes the need for high-quality parent education programs. The third section reviews the literature on early learning and parent education with a focus on school readiness for African American children. The fourth section provides insights from parents regarding attitudes, beliefs, and behaviors concerning parental involvement in early learning. In the final section, we consider the implications of our practical experience and research.

PEP Overview

In 1990, education reform became a national priority as then-President Bush and America's governors announced six national education goals. The first goal inspired a national movement with its call for all children in America to start school ready to learn. NBCDI responded to the urgent need for school readiness support by launching PEP in 1992 as a community-based demonstration project. PEP is an outgrowth of NBCDI's long-standing activism in the fields of child advocacy, parent training, and early education. The national policy shift to improve education created a welcome opportunity for NBCDI to continue to address the needs of African American parents. At the time of

The National Black Child Development Institute (NBCDI) has reached at-risk parents in urban and rural areas across the country through a curriculum called the Parent Empowerment Project (PEP) curriculum. The first section of this paper provides an overview of the PEP curriculum, describing the lessons NBCDI has learned about developing and providing a curriculum that responds to the wants and needs of low-income African American parents. The second section describes the need for high-quality parent education programs. The third section reviews the literature on early learning and parent education with a focus on school readiness for African American children. The fourth section provides insights from parents regarding attitudes, beliefs, and behaviors concerning parental involvement in early learning. The final section considers the implications of NBCDI's experience and research.

rollout, we had already amassed 20 years of experience with developing and distributing parent education and child development models that our affiliate network used in communities nationwide.

We formed PEP from our core value that *effective training begins with respecting the voices of parents*. In their own words, parents had something to say about their vision for their children and themselves. But who was listening? According to our early research, low-income African American parents complained that traditional capacity-building programs attempted to transplant aspirations and ideals into their lives as if to fill a void. However, most parents want to obtain or maintain a high standard of living regardless of race or income. Poor mothers and fathers are no different from affluent parents in having ambitions for their children and themselves (Hyson & DeCSipkes, 1993). Therefore, the tendency of traditional programs to ignore intrinsic family and personal goals can stand in the way of connecting with parents. Not surprisingly, we found that deficit-oriented models offended and alienated target audiences and overlooked opportunities to build on existing strengths.

In keeping with our core belief in the value of genuine parent involvement, we collaborated with a group of low-income African American parents living in Washington, DC, to research the resources and educational approaches that they would find most effective in strengthening their self-confidence and child-rearing practices. Consistent with our target demographic, the parents had young children ranging in age from birth to 3. The community-based demonstration projects produced important findings that formed the basis of the PEP curriculum.

The curriculum is composed of three units that can stand alone or be used in the sequence considered most appropriate by a parent or family facilitator. Covering fundamental self-development and child-rearing topics from an African American perspective, the units are *African American Culture*, *Successful Parenting*, and *My Vision for the Future*. Family facilitators trained by NBCDI implement the curriculum. Each unit employs a variety of educational strategies designed to engage the interest of parents and make them active participants in the teaching/learning process. These strategies include audio and visual aids, games, numerous interactive and participatory activities, formal and informal presentations by professionals, and role models from within the parents' own communities.

Throughout the educational process, parents play an important role in determining the information, resources, and experiences that will be most helpful to them. The curriculum is designed to allow parents and family facilitators to structure the choice and sequence of units, topics, and activities. The result is an experience that is active rather than passive and flexible as opposed to linear.

The Need

Raising children is not an exact science. There is no precise formula for helping children to develop their full potential. As a result, parents get on-the-job training through which they experience the successes and foibles that accompany the learning process. They experiment with parenting methods that fit their values. Some replicate the parenting styles of their parents. Others modify the parent-child relationship they had growing up. Others depart completely from their parents' behavior. Through trial and error, many parents discover ways to give their children the support that they need to grow. However, many parents need assistance with developing effective parenting skills. Parent education aims to address this need. Ideally, parent education programs serve the purpose of taking some of the guesswork out of parenting while demonstrating to parents that they have what it takes to be successful.

High-quality parent education programs should provide access to information on best parenting practices and make the information meaningful through project-based learning. Head Start, HIPPY, and Even Start, for example, uphold those quality standards. But while the early childhood profession is teeming with research on best parenting practices, the literature seldom reaches low-income populations, including poor African Americans. Therefore, effective parent education programs can decode the literature and teach low-income mothers and fathers best practices for nurturing the cognitive, emotional, and physical development of their young children. In the following sections, we explore the need and describe what has been learned about the benefits and limits of parent education. In addition, we share our experience with PEP and use that experience to form recommendations for connecting with low-income African American parents.

Parental Involvement and School Readiness

Multiple factors shape parent involvement in early learning. As with any behavior, the way in which parents interact with their young children develops in a multidimensional realm as opposed to in a vacuum. Cultural norms, educational attainment, income, and the demands of work life are among the leading factors that influence parenting styles and patterns of involvement with their children. The 1997 *National Study of the Changing Workforce* presents groundbreaking research on how work, family, and personal life interrelate and affect parenting (Bond, Galinsky, & Swanberg, 1997). The study reports that most members of America's workforce live in households with family and have responsibilities associated with raising children. Against this backdrop of family responsibilities, the amount of time devoted to work outside of the home is increasing. As a result, a growing number of working parents struggle to manage the competing priorities of work and family. They race through weekdays and weekends at the command of demanding schedules. Pushing multitasking to the limits, they try to align their parenting duties—including arranging child care, participating in school life, assisting with homework, and organizing enrichment activities—with their numerous career obligations. Concurrent imperatives to earn a living and raise children present an enormous challenge that requires commitment, stamina, resources, time-management skills, and a support network. Tragic events such as those of September 11, 2002, coupled with a fluctuating national economy, heighten anxiety and deepen concerns parents have over the safety, quality of care, and effectiveness of education for their children. This tumultuous beginning to the 21st century has given rise to a beleaguered generation of parents who are increasingly turning to self-help books, peer groups, school systems, faith-based organizations, public policy makers, and advocacy organizations for relief.

For at-risk parents, the rigors of everyday life produce additional challenges. Hardships such as unemployment, low educational attainment, and lack of access to high-quality health care, child care, and housing can threaten their ability to manage parenting responsibilities (Lerman, 2002). Current U.S. Census data show that African American parents are disproportionately at risk. Poverty rates, for example, indicate a gap in well-being along racial lines. Distressingly, the poverty rate for African Americans is nearly quadruple the poverty rate for non-Hispanic Whites (23% and 6%, respectively). Likewise, African Americans have attained less education than their White counterparts. Only 77% of African Americans 25 years and older have a high school diploma or more compared with 88% for non-Hispanic Whites. In addition, the unemployment rate for African Americans is more than twice that for non-Hispanic Whites, 9% and 4%, respectively.

Within this disparate socioeconomic context, 4.8 million African American families are raising 11.8 million children, according to the 2000 U.S. Census. The impact of poverty and related factors reverberates in home, school, and community life. Volumes of research since the 1960s underscore the fact that experiences that take place at home before a child enters school significantly affect his or her school readiness (Slaughter-Defoe, 2000). Noted consequences of poverty on school readiness include an increase in emotional, physical, and behavioral problems for poor children as compared to children who are not poor (Emig, 2000). As a result, low-income children are more likely than their counterparts to arrive at school hungry, tired, physically ill, or troubled. In the 1993 *Kindergarten Teacher Survey on Student Readiness*, kindergarten teachers posit that being physically healthy, rested, and well nourished are the most important parts of school readiness (West, 1993).

Language and cognitive development also suffer under poverty. Studies find that low-income parents are less likely than higher-income parents to perform activities that support early literacy and cognition, such as reading to their preschoolers frequently, modeling reading at home, and engaging their young children in conversation (Marcon, 1999). The literature presents copious evidence that poor children disproportionately start school without having developed emergent literacy skills. Based on kindergarten assessments, poor children are less likely to recognize letters, assign sounds to letter combinations, represent ideas through writing or drawing, and understand the sequence of stories. In addition to being associated with the child's basic understanding of letters, words, and their combinations, literacy development is also related to the number and complexity of words the child has available for speech and discourse (Beals, DeTemple, & Dickinson, 1994; Jordan, Snow, & Porche, 2000). This relationship means that vocabulary and oral language skills are especially important in promoting reading development. Parents who promote these skills help their children to (1) grasp a deeper understanding of the meaning and function of words, ideas, stories, and the world around them (Beals, DeTemple, & Dickinson, 1994; Rush, 1999); (2) recognize the link between spoken words and print (Rush, 1999); and (3) become familiar with sophisticated vocabulary (Jordan, Snow, & Porche, 2000; Dickinson & Tabors, 1991). Building the vocabulary and discourse skills that are crucial to literacy development happens when parents routinely read books to their young children, discuss opinions, explain events, and share experiences (Beals, DeTemple, & Dickinson, 1994).

In conjunction with the need for parents to actively promote language development, the literature suggests that a child's home environment is also an important aspect of early literacy. A literacy-rich environment is characterized by the ready availability of print materials, writing utensils, and space to read and write. Literacy-rich environments also feature adults who promote literacy development in a number of ways, including reading and writing as part of their daily routine, encouraging children to ask and answer questions during reading and writing activities, and guiding and monitoring television viewing for content and frequency (Marvin & Mirenda, 1993; Jordan, Snow, & Porche, 2000; Senechal & LeFevre, 2001). Children with early exposure to literacy experiences are especially likely to have positive early reading outcomes (Marvin & Mirenda, 1993; Senechal & LeFevre, 2001). As mentioned above, economically disadvantaged children are least likely to have exposure and access to literacy materials and experiences at home that promote language development and reading acquisition (Neuman, 1999).

Although only a modest amount of research has been done on the ways in which home environments and parental behavior relate to early numeracy skills, the National Institute on Early Childhood Development and Education published a report (Fromboluti, Magarity, & Rinck, 1999) outlining activities that parents can engage in to encourage the learning and development of the "whole child," including children's early learning in mathematics. The suggestions highlight important concepts in early math learning and recommend everyday activities that parents can carry out in order to promote their children's understanding of those concepts. The reports proposes, for example, that parents read rhyming books to their children, use words such as "near," "approximately," and "in between," when estimating time or distance, create graphs and charts that contain information about the child or events, play with puzzles, ask their children to look for numbers in their environment, and allow their children to measure and divide objects. Essentially, those activities can build mathematics skills such as problem solving, reasoning, number sense, numeration, geometry, spatial skills, estimation, fractions, statistics, and probability. Moreover, the proposals can be incorporated easily into everyday routines (see also Anderson, 1997).

In summary, parent involvement in the lives of young children produces remarkably positive outcomes related to school readiness. This axiom holds true across cultural, racial, and population lines (Grolnick, Benjet, Kurowski, & Apostoleris, 1997; Fantuzzo, Tighe, & Childs, 2000). Most certainly, when parents take part in their children's early learning, children do better in school

(Little, 1998). For a number of reasons, parent education and parent involvement add extraordinary value to the learning process. Among the benefits, *parental involvement* allows children to maintain continuity between the learning that takes place at home and school. In addition, learning gains appear to be longer lasting when parental involvement begins at an early age (Christenson, Rounds, & Franklin, 1992). However, for low-income African American parents, a myriad of factors interfere with the relationship between parent involvement and school readiness. The challenge for parents, educators, and advocates is to develop and implement strategies for addressing and ameliorating the negative impact that poverty, low educational attainment, and other hardships pose on parent involvement.

In Their Own Voices

As part of our research on attitudes, beliefs, and behaviors concerning parental involvement in early learning, NBCDI conducted six focus groups in the fall of 2002 in Richmond, Virginia; Chicago, Illinois; and Oakland, California. The groups in Richmond consisted of African American mothers with children under 6 years old and African American fathers of children under 6 living in low-income households. The mothers were single, between the ages of 18 and 24 years old, living in low-income households up to 200% of the federal poverty guideline. The groups in Chicago consisted of low-income, African American mothers with children under 6 and grandparents with grandchildren under 6 years old living in low-income households. The mothers were between the ages of 25 and 35 years old, married or unmarried with partners. The groups in Oakland consisted of low-income, young African American mothers who were married or unmarried with partners and older low-income single African American mothers. We recognize that the following findings must be considered in a qualitative frame of reference because of the limited number of respondents and the restrictions of recruiting, but, nevertheless, these findings provide invaluable insight into what parents view as their role in early learning.

Our findings reveal a wide divergence between what the literature recommends for parental involvement and what our focus group participants view as their role in promoting early learning. In contrast to conventional theory that parents are their children's primary teachers, the parents we convened view schools as primarily responsible for educating their children. They cast themselves in a supporting role in the education process. When probed about the hierarchy they espoused, parents expressed doubt in their ability to nurture their children's early learning. However, the groups believed that low-income parents, including themselves, could increase their involvement in their young children's education both at home and in school.

As an extension of their belief about the primacy of schools, most participants opined that the nation's schools are not doing a good job of educating African American children and providing safe havens for learning. Participants related school safety to high-quality education, voicing a belief that violence is prevalent in their children's schools. However, the groups suggested that turbulent home and community environments contribute to poor educational outcomes and that parents should take more responsibility for improving their children's readiness for school.

Another salient finding is that participants did not see a relationship between poverty and poor school readiness until the facilitator substantiated the relationship with data. However, the focus groups emphasized that poverty does not necessarily predict school readiness.

Regarding language development, parents' beliefs were consistent with research regarding the value of some practices but not others. For example, few parents recognized the value of encouraging curiosity about the world and using exploratory questioning. However, they did recognize the importance of conversations, actively listening to children, and creating predictable environments in the home. Nevertheless, the facilitators observed a dichotomy between values and behavior between acknowledging the importance of practices that contribute to early literacy and the actual use of those practices. Moreover, parents in the focus groups viewed reading as a life skill necessary for survival. A majority acknowledged that reading for pleasure or to expand knowledge, or to model reading for their young children, was not part of their day-to-day routine.

Despite the focus groups' alternative viewpoints and behaviors regarding parent involvement in early learning, the participants' attitudes about the value of education were consistent with mainstream ideology. Like most parents, they want their children to receive a high-quality education across the continuum, from kindergarten to college or other higher learning experiences. They associate educational attainment with employability, reasoning that higher education will prepare their children to gain rewarding careers. Education is seen as a mechanism for breaking their families' cycle of poverty. They aspire to place their children on a positive trajectory that leads to economic stability and overall well-being.

Our preliminary focus groups revealed implications for programs serving low-income African American parents. We plan to expand our research to include a wider sampling of low-income African American parents and, accordingly, report on our findings.

Implications of the Success of PEP for Other Parent-Focused Programs

Today, many different programs have been developed for connecting with parents and involving them in their children's education. A cursory review of the evaluations of some of these programs suggests that they are very good at working with a self-selected and narrow range of families. Unfortunately, few have been very successful in enlisting and retaining families where the risks of poor outcomes for children appear greatest. The experience and success of the PEP program in successfully engaging such families hold out lessons for all who seek to work with parents. These experiences demonstrate clearly that success in working with difficult-to-reach families will be dependent on whether the program possesses several very specific features. They begin with a focus on men and women, persons with individual histories and needs who are important in their own right not just because they are parents. The program, irrespective of the content, must reflect the goals and needs of its participants at least as it must reflect the goals of the program developer or parent educator. It must therefore be flexible enough and provide room to individualize goals. Most importantly, it must affirm parental competence and knowledge and reflect a sensitive understanding of participants' culture and history.

Accordingly, we have synthesized lessons from our experience into recommendations for developing and implementing successful parenting programs. The recommendations are a guideline for respecting the voices of African American parents. Simultaneously, they have broader applicability. The recommendations that follow underscore qualities to be included in any program of outreach and collaboration with all families—rich or poor, Black or White, English speaking or not:

- Build programs on a foundation of respect for the opinions and experiences of parents. **Respect is the cornerstone of PEP. Our curriculum is based on our belief that *all* parents aspire to be successful parents and are capable of transforming their aspirations into reality. Anchored by this principle, PEP identifies and builds on the strengths of parents. We let them know that their opinions, attitudes, and behaviors matter to us and to their development.**

- **Affirm the value of parents.** From Maslow's seminal research on humanistic psychology to anecdotal findings, a body of evidence confirms that self-esteem is a basic human need. As part of human nature, people want to achieve, be competent, and gain approval and recognition. PEP, therefore, is committed to affirming the value of parents.

- **Ask questions and listen to the answers.** Communicating effectively is an interactive process that involves asking questions and listening to the answers. PEP establishes an open line of communication with parents in order to encourage candid dialogue, impart information, and gather information that will strengthen our connection with parents. We explore attitudes and beliefs and encourage parents to seek information from us, too. In promoting linear conversation, PEP validates that learning is an ongoing and reciprocal process. Parents realize that they help us expand our knowledge of their needs while we broaden their understanding of successful parenting.

- **Integrate cultural traditions into the program.** The African American Culture unit provides the cultural context for working with parents. Its purpose is to inform and to reinforce in parents a sense of pride in themselves, their community, and their history. Within the context of exploring cultural art forms and historical influences, parents gain inspiration and self-esteem and are given a framework for using literature, art, music, entertainment, and community life to enhance the development of their children.

Conclusion

Since 1970, NBCDI has worked to promote a high-quality life for African American children and their families. Serving African American children and families has been our sole mission for more than 30 years. Our experiences prior and subsequent to the inception of PEP in 1992 have taught us important lessons about connecting with African American parents. African American parents who are poor want what is best for their children. Poverty, despite its deleterious effects on life quality, has not weakened the fundamental aspiration of parents to provide their children with a safe, loving, and nurturing home life nor diminished their optimism about the prospects of their children's success at school. They understand that most, if not all, parents yearn to foster their children's full potential. Successful programs also know that if they take hold of and internalize the aspirations of parents, they have a powerful means of motivating parents toward positive action. Most of all, effective parenting programs acknowledge, respect, and build on these aspirations and give parents additional tools to make those dreams reality.

References

Anderson, Ann. (1997). Families and mathematics: A study of parent-child interactions. *Journal for Research in Mathematics Education, 28*(4), 484-511. (ERIC Journal No. EJ549752)

Beals, Diane E.; DeTemple, Jeanne M.; & Dickinson, David K. (1994). Talking and listening that support early literacy development of children from low-income families. In David K. Dickinson (Ed.), *Bridges to literacy: Children, families, and schools* (pp. 19-40). Malden, MA: Blackwell.

Bond, James T.; Galinsky, Ellen; & Swanberg, Jennifer E. (1997). *The national study of the changing workforce, 1997. No. 2.* New York: Families and Work Institute. (ERIC Document No. ED425871)

Christenson, Sandra L.; Rounds, T.; & Franklin M. (1992). Home-school collaboration: Effects, issues, and opportunities. In Sandra L. Christenson & Jane C. Conoley (Eds.), *Home-school collaboration enhancing children's academic and social competence* (pp. 19-51). Bethesda, MD: National Association of School Psychologists.

Dickinson, David K., & Tabors, Patton O. (1991). Early literacy: Linkages between home, school, and literacy achievement at age five. *Journal of Research in Childhood Education, 6*(1), 30-46. (ERIC Journal No. EJ460123)

Emig, Carol (Ed.). (2000). *School readiness: Helping communities get children ready for school and schools ready for children.* Washington, DC: Child Trends. (ERIC Document No. ED444712)

Fantuzzo, John; Tighe, Erin; & Childs, Stephanie. (2000). Family involvement questionnaire: A multivariate assessment of family participation in early childhood education. *Journal of Education Psychology, 92*(2), 367-376. (ERIC Journal No. EJ619382)

Fromboluti, Carol Sue; Magarity, Diane; & Rinck, Natalie. (1999). *Early childhood: Where learning begins. Mathematics: Mathematical activities for parents and their 2- to 5-year old children.* (Report No. ECI-1999-9002). Washington, DC: National Institute on Early Childhood Development and Education. (ERIC Document No. ED430734)

Grolnick, Wendy S.; Benjet, Corina; Kurowski, Carolyn O.; & Apostoleris, Nicholas H. (1997). Predictors of parent involvement in children's schooling. *Journal of Educational Psychology, 89*(3), 538-548. (ERIC Journal No. EJ553145)

Hyson, Marion C., & DeCsipkes, Candace. (1993, March). *Educational and developmental belief systems among African-American parents of kindergarten children.* Paper presented at the Biennial Meeting of the Society for Research in Child Development, New Orleans, LA. (ERIC Document No. ED364336)

Jordan, Gail E.; Snow, Catherine E.; & Porche, Michelle V. (2000). Project EASE: The effect of a family literacy project on kindergarten students' early literacy skills. *Reading Research Quarterly, 35*(4), 524-546. (ERIC Journal No. EJ616175)

Lerman, Robert, I. (2002). *Impact of marital status and parental presence on the material hardship of families with children.* Washington, DC: Urban Institute and American University.

Little, Priscilla. (1998). *Family involvement in early childhood programs: How to choose the right program for your child. Early Childhood Digest.* Cambridge, MA: Harvard Family Research Project. (ERIC Document No. ED419612)

Marcon, Rebecca A. (1999). Differential impact of preschool models on development and early learning of inner-city children: A three-cohort study. *Developmental Psychology, 35*(2), 358-375. (ERIC Journal No. EJ582451)

Marvin, Christine, & Mirenda, Pat. (1993). Home literacy of preschoolers enrolled in Head Start and special education programs. *Journal of Early Intervention, 17*(4), 351-367. (ERIC Journal No. EJ483489)

Neuman, Susan B. (1999). Books make a difference: A study of access to literacy. *Reading Research Quarterly, 34*(3), 286-311. (ERIC Journal No. EJ587549)

Rush, Karen L. (1999). Caregiver-child interactions and early literacy development of preschool children from low-income environments. *Topics in Early Childhood Special Education, 19*(1), 3-14. (ERIC Journal No. EJ583793)

Senechal, Monique, & LeFevre, Jo-Anne. (2001). Storybook reading and parent teaching: Links to language and literacy development. In Pia Rebello Britto & Jeanne Brooks-Gunn (Eds.), *New directions in child development: No. 92. The role of family literacy environments in promoting young children's emerging literacy skills* (pp. 39-52). San Francisco: Jossey-Bass.

Slaughter-Defoe, Diana T. (2000, September). *Early childhood development and school readiness: Some observations about "homework" for new century working parents.* Paper presented at the Annual Meeting of the Voices for Illinois Conference, Chicago, IL. (ERIC Document No. ED447952)

West, Jerry. (1993, September). *Readiness for kindergarten: Parent and teacher beliefs.* Statistics in Brief. (NCES 93-257). Washington, DC: U.S. Department of Education, National Center for Education Statistics. (ERIC Document No. ED363429)

Responses to the Presentation by Representatives of the National Black Child Development Institute

Wanda Roundtree Henderson and Rozita La Gorcé Green represented NBCDI at the symposium because Evelyn Moore and Oscar Barbarin could not present. After their presentation, Wanda Roundtree Henderson and Rozita La Gorcé Green answered questions from symposium participants. A panel then convened to respond to their presentation.

Questions and comments after the presentation by NBCDI

Participant: Do parents view schools as not doing a good job?

NBCDI response: Parents view the teacher as the primary educator, and focus groups were concerned about safety because parents felt that schools were not the best place for their children to learn. On the one hand, parents viewed the teacher and school as problematic, but focus groups also felt that parents had the primary job to teach their children prior to school (during the preschool years) but not after school begins.

Participant: Regarding the focus group data—how did that inform the refining of the curriculum?

NBCDI response: We are still new with using the focus group process and realize that we need more "flags" that help the parents understand specific issues. The focus group pilot sites were selected to include rural and urban settings. NBCDI provides facilitators to train the focus group leaders and will also work with schools and organizations. Clearly, we need to develop ways to get parents more information about particular issues and topics that are of interest to them, such as the African American cultural unit. We also need to be more receptive to school readiness and loop it into parent training. Another area where we need more attention is on quantitative research to confirm success of the program, and then we need to interweave the cultural components.

Participant: With the second version of the model—how does it really clarify African American culture?

NBCDI response: Participants learned about African American history and culture, and this experience helped open discussion up a lot about how their culture is different or the same. It helped to open up discussion about culture and traditions, beliefs, and practices.

Participant: Do parents know what they need to do to become better parents?

NBCDI response: Parents may or may not know strategies, but they will often know that there is something that they might need, or they may have the idea that they can be doing something better—sort of an intuitive situation. Their issues might be about relationships and people. They may want some help about these or a different issue.

For example, if we looked more deeply into the socialization of children, parents often recognize that they have a responsibility to perpetuate their social world, understand children's ways of knowing and doing. Lily Wong Fillmore found that children were not "ready for school" but that parents were doing a very good job of letting the children know what they needed to know for success in their community. Children knew all they needed to know to help them survive in their cultural world. Perhaps we need to focus more on schools being ready for children?

Participant: How do we research these parenting concepts with quantitative testing and NCLB?

NBCDI response: Not sure—but one way to think about it is to focus on "Funds of Knowledge" or knowledge about what parents need. We have found that parents do reveal what they are confident about and what they are not confident about once we have built a trusting relationship. Those trusting relationships overflow into the school environment, and often a parent's view of the school is to identify with the teacher as opposed to identifying with the school. Also, parents related better to older teachers or guidance counselors; they related better to the older staff person rather than the younger teacher. Younger teachers seemed to have less respect for parents.

Panel Session: Responding to NBCDI's presentation

Moderator: Professor Susan Matoba Adler, University of Illinois at Urbana-Champaign

Low audio quality prevented full transcription of the panel session. The themes that were addressed during the discussion are summarized below.

1. The importance of duplicating programs that are successful in providing comprehensive support for parents.

Every attempt should be made to identify successful programs and duplicate characteristics in other areas. Successful programs provide a model of community-based interventions for young children. They also support parent leadership from the community by building a cadre of specially trained local people to work in the field and provide sustainable growth for the community.

2. *The importance of building relationships of trust and respect.*

Because we understand that culture plays such an important role in getting information to parents, we should make every effort to first build relationships of trust and respect. This process begins with the planning stages of the program and understanding the values of the parents in the community so that those values can be incorporated into the program. For example, if being multilingual is important, then the maternal language should be incorporated into the parenting and early childhood program. Key parenting and early childhood principles or concepts can be adapted to the cultural context so that it is more respectful of the way the community learns.

Working to build relationships may mean stepping outside of traditional divisions or roles between professionals and parents. For example, in AVANCE, staff members are often invited to parties or other events at a parent's home, and it is appropriate for staff to attend. Hiring people who are either from the community or who represent the community's culture is important and resolves many universal issues or concerns. Home visitors should be from the same cultural background or community. Programs need to be creative about reaching and building relationships with parents from the community who are most vulnerable.

3. *The need for high-quality preservice training.*

Once every effort has been made to provide high-quality preservice training, it is important to provide ongoing incentives to continue training and advancement. Cross-training, or integrating other systems with education such as social services, mental health, substance abuse, and health care, so that staff and parent leaders have diverse opportunities to learn more is important. Cross-training also helps to bring the right resources to the program or parent at the time it is really needed.

4. *The importance of understanding economics in early child care settings and with parents.*

Any program designed to reach vulnerable parents and families that does not recognize the importance of economics will fall short. Although raising the salaries of family care providers and family support professionals is important, the problems are deeper than an increase in wages. An integrated program will help provide opportunities for parents to learn, get jobs, get adequate housing, and advance their status. The program recognizes that for children to be secure and ready to learn, parents and families need to be stable and secure. Program policies will need to reflect the time that parents need to work, get further education, or search for jobs. The community services available, such as affordable health care that covers both basic needs and catastrophic issues, will be available so that families are not severely set back financially by a crisis.

Connecting with Parents:
The AVANCE Experience

Gloria G. Rodriguez

The mission of AVANCE: *To build the confidence and competence of low-income parents and children in high-risk communities within a community context.*

Introduction

In preparation for the "Connecting with Parents in the Early Years" Symposium, a lengthy historical document was developed that described the agency's goals, organizational structure, target population, funding, services, outcomes, characteristics of a successful program, and lessons learned in our replication effort. In 1985, AVANCE submitted to ERIC a similar document describing AVANCE's 12-year evolution (Rodriguez, 1985). It was extremely interesting to see how much AVANCE has remained true to its mission these past 30 years and how much it has grown. The timing could not have been better for this paper, as AVANCE has been trying to take its proven model to cities throughout Texas and California without losing its quality. Replicating a successful, proven model to other cities without affecting AVANCE's integrity and viability has not been easy. The most critical element of taking a program to scale is to truly understand what the mission, principles, and philosophy are, and to develop the infrastructure, policies, and procedures to safeguard them. Documenting where AVANCE was at 12 years—and again at 30—was extremely interesting and beneficial for the author. It was critical as AVANCE was trying to formulate what produced the positive outcomes in the early years and what needed to be safeguarded as AVANCE attempted to replicate AVANCE. While any program needs to adapt and respond to the needs of the community, there are those critical elements that are unique and critical to AVANCE, while also producing the successful outcomes of getting poor Latino children ready for school, of transforming lives, and strengthening families and communities in very poor communities.

The purpose of this paper is to describe AVANCE's unique experience, including its proven model, outcomes, principles, and lessons learned in connecting with poor Latino parents. AVANCE has remained true to its original mission, philosophy, and target population.

AVANCE grew from a small community-based organization serving 30 low-income Latino individuals annually in the Mirasol Housing Project in San Antonio, Texas, in 1973, to a large service organization serving over 15,000 individuals annually in 11 cities and over 100 service sites in 2003. This paper describes AVANCE's history, structure, target population, philosophy, services, model, evaluations, funding, and program modifications during the past 30 years.

Structure and History

AVANCE is a Spanish word meaning "advancement, progress." AVANCE grew from a small grassroots community-based organization serving 30 individuals annually in the Mirasol Housing Project in San Antonio, Texas, in 1973, to a large service organization serving over 15,000 individuals annually in 11 cities and over 100 service sites in 2003. It has grown from a staff of 3 to a staff of over 600 and from an annual budget of $100,000 to a budget of over $26,000,000.

AVANCE operates as one organization under one 501(c)3, with unincorporated chapters adhering to the original mission, philosophy, and standards of AVANCE. It has a national headquarters that ensures that programmatic, fiscal, fund development, and human resource standards are met. The National Office is also responsible for training, research and development, program and curriculum development, and the coordination of all fund development. The growth and development of the agency, as well as significant factors that have contributed to its success, are provided as part of this historical perspective.

Dr. Gloria G. Rodriguez became involved in the field of parent education/family support in a desperate attempt to find a solution to the academic problems that many Hispanic children faced throughout the nation in 1970, and which today are still prevalent in many Hispanic communities. She became concerned about issues affecting low-income Hispanic families when she attended Our Lady of the Lake University from 1967-1970 with the assistance of a federally subsidized program entitled *Project Teacher Excellence*. The purpose of this program was to find low-income students graduating from high school in various San Antonio *barrios* and to offer them an opportunity to enter college and become bilingual teachers, with the understanding that they would return to the *barrio* to teach.

Upon graduation from college in December of 1970, Dr. Rodriguez became a bilingual teacher of a group of 35 first-grade children who came from four classrooms and were considered to be so far behind the other children that their retention in first grade had already been determined. According to the principal, the children had been labeled by their teachers as "retarded," "slow learners," and "uneducable." Initially, Dr. Rodriguez strongly believed that the problem stemmed from monolingual Spanish-speaking children and monolingual English-speaking teachers. However, it was soon evident that the children were not proficient in either Spanish or English. They lacked the necessary foundation in either language to help them achieve academic success. Dr. Rodriguez worked extensively with this group of children for one and a half years, and with another similar group the subsequent year.

All but five of the children from the first group were promoted. Even though they did learn to read and write in both languages, it appeared that they would never catch up to the academic level of the children who entered school more prepared. While the children who entered school less well prepared were learning concepts and readiness skills that they should have learned in their formative years, the children who had a stronger foundation were already learning more advanced skills and knowledge, and they continued to be ahead of the group of children who were not as well prepared to start school. The children may have progressed to the subsequent grade, but some would still be classified in the lower group, the labeling would continue, and they would never be able to catch up to the other children. Dr. Rodriguez felt frustrated as a teacher because she did not have control over the children's environment before and after they were in her class.

It was in a graduate research class that Dr. Rodriguez stumbled onto the new (at that time) concept of "parenting education." The concept was so logical: Education begins at birth (and even before), and the first and most important teacher is the parent, especially during the child's critical formative years from birth through age 4. Effective parenting is learned, and parents need assistance in carrying out this function and support to alleviate any obstacles that impede effective parenting.

Dr. Rodriguez conducted an attitudinal survey with the parents of the first group of children she taught to determine their attitudes on child rearing and their desire for parenting education. The parents' responses reflected a strong need and desire for a parenting program. Contrary to teachers' expectations, the responses showed that parents believed that learning begins at school; that the child's most important teacher is the first professional teacher the child will come in contact with, whether the child is in Head Start, kindergarten, or first grade; and that the basic role of the parent is to care for the children's physical needs. In addition, the parents held low academic aspirations for their children. When they were asked, "How far do you think your child will go in school?" most parents replied, "Probably the seventh grade." Most of the parents had only attained a seventh-grade education, and they did not think their children would go any further in formal education.

Research indicates that the child's formative years from birth through age 3 are critical in the development of a strong learning foundation, as well as in the development of important values and personality formation. Recent research findings in brain research, however, suggest that what the child experiences in the first three years of life sets the basic foundation for later learning and social relationships. Many parents, including those surveyed, did not realize the importance of their role as teachers of their children. Although all parents desire a better life for their children than they had, many feel that achieving such an outcome is beyond their control. In addition, many Hispanic parents have to deal with other difficulties, including a language and culture different from the mainstream, isolation, and immigration issues. Effective parenting in any situation is not easy, but it can be especially difficult for high-risk parents who often cope with social and economic stress.

Parents need training just as any other professional needs training. How parents choose to parent has largely been left to chance or to how they were parented as children. The school system needs to reform and take aggressive action to restructure and assist parents of children under 3 so that children will enter school prepared to be successful. When the home and school work together, the high illiteracy rate and the disproportionately high dropout rate among Hispanics (up to 50% in some communities) can be reduced.

If we will have the home neglecting to carry out certain readiness activities, and the school assuming that the parents did their role in preparing the child for school, then in the end, the child will suffer. The child will be labeled, teased, and ignored until he can tolerate it no longer, and at about the seventh or eighth grade, he will drop out of school. In today's world, an education is critical in order to be part of the mainstream of society. Rather than having competent, independent, productive, contributing members of society, the home and school will have produced a group of children who will become isolated, dependent individuals who are at risk for such social problems as mental illness, family violence, crime, delinquency, teenage pregnancy, dropping out of school, and another generation of poverty.

Dr. Rodriguez felt then, as she feels now, that all parents need and desire support in their parenting role. Parents, especially poor, high-risk Hispanic parents, want and need assistance in strengthening the family unit and in helping their children realize their fullest potential.

In 1973, when Dr. Rodriguez was strongly committed to the philosophy of parenting education, the second AVANCE program was initiated in San Antonio, Texas, and she became the director. The first AVANCE program had been implemented in 1972 in Dallas, Texas, with a grant from the Zale Foundation that was submitted by two doctoral students of Dr. Urie Bronfenbrenner from Cornell University: Bonnie Parks and Ann Willig.

Mission

The mission of AVANCE is to build the confidence and competence of poor parents and children in high-risk communities. AVANCE uses its Intervention Model for Hard-to-Reach Families and its Circular Model as a road map for providing preventive, comprehensive, continuous services for both parents and children within a community context. The AVANCE 0-3 Parent Child Education Program is the core of the intervention model.

In 1991, the AVANCE National Office was created to support the expansion of AVANCE to cities outside of San Antonio, Texas. AVANCE went through a long, arduous journey in attempting to develop an organizational structure whereby the National Office, its chapters, and its affiliates have the capacity to survive and flourish; its mission, philosophy, curriculum, programs, reputation, and assets are protected; its positive outcomes and quality standards are maintained; it can expand into new communities; and it can remain a premiere organization in providing early childhood, parenting, and family support services to low-income families, especially in Latino communities. AVANCE is one of the oldest and largest national parenting education and family support models in the country. It has been evaluated; proven to work; and recognized widely by local, state, and national media, the philanthropic community, numerous documents and textbooks, and the White House (and is mentioned in three First Ladies' books).

Target Population

AVANCE serves predominantly low-income, Hispanic/Latino families throughout Texas (San Antonio; Houston; Rio Grande Valley; Dallas; Austin; Laredo; and Middle Rio Grande, which includes Eagle Pass and Del Rio; El Paso; Corpus Christi; and Waco) and in Los Angeles, California. AVANCE currently has a 5-year plan to expand to five sites in California. The primary participants and the starting point of intervention are the mother and her children under the age of 3, although some family centers also serve fathers. Services are provided in family centers located in schools, churches, houses, community centers, storefronts, and federally funded housing projects.

To qualify for the AVANCE core parenting program, families must have a child under 3 years of age and reside in the community, and the mother and/ or father and child must participate. To be enrolled in the literacy and eco- nomic development components, parents must have completed the Parent Child Education Program. Although no fees are charged, families can contrib- ute volunteer hours in clerical, craft, fund-raising, or child care assistance. Potential participants are introduced to the program by word of mouth and by a biannual door-to-door outreach effort. AVANCE accepts referrals from other service providers, such as from Child Protective and Regulatory Services.

2002 Demographic Data for the Core AVANCE Parent Child Education Program

Mexican American (third generation)	99%
Immigrant/first generation	69%
Spoke Spanish at home	67%
Dropped out of school	83%
Married or living with partner	70%
Annual incomes less than $6,000	37%
Annual income less than $15,000	73%
Median annual income	$7,700
Mean age	28.9
Mean family size/people in household	4.5

AVANCE, Inc. Demographic Survey, 2002.

Since 1980, the populations served by AVANCE have been similar in their demographic characteristics. They are mostly poor Hispanics or Latinos. However in 1980, 93% of the population living in San Antonio was predomi- nantly Mexican American, with the majority being third-generation Latinos.

As AVANCE expanded into other cities, the communities that it served and the people that attended the program became mainly first-generation Hispanics from Mexico, Central America, and South America (69%). A 1980 survey of the AVANCE catchment area indicated that 53.8% of the women were separated, widowed, divorced, or single. In 2002, the population that was surveyed was predominantly first-generation Latinos, reflecting a more stable family situation, with 70% reporting that they were married or living with a partner. Eighty-five percent of the respondents in 1980 reported having no occupation, and the remaining 15% held unskilled or semiskilled positions.

In 1980, the mean monthly income for the families surveyed was $473.00, or $5,676 annually. By 2002, 82% had incomes of less than $15,000, with a median income of $7,700. This change can be attributed to national policies regarding Welfare or TANF, or to the fact that first-generation Latinos, who cannot benefit from TANF, have multiple low-paying unskilled jobs. In 1980, the high school dropout rate was 77% among the parents, and in 2002, the rate of parents who had dropped out or never completed high school was 82%. The program serves two-parent families, single parents, teen parents, formerly AFDC (Aid to Families with Dependent Children) recipients, and high-risk and abused/neglected children. The family size, or participants living in the home, decreased from 6.1 members to 4.5 members over the last two decades. In 1980, the age of participants ranged from 15 to 69 with a mean age of 32; in 2002, the population got younger, with a mean age of 28.9 years.

Many of the parents surveyed were abused as children, lacked knowledge and skills related to child growth and development, had few support systems, and experienced continuous economic and social pressures. First-generation immigrants seemed more hopeful toward the future than third-generation Hispanics. They come to this country with hopes and dreams, but by the third generation, many lose their family strengths and their hopefulness toward the future.

Organizational Structure

AVANCE is a nonprofit organization. It is made up of a National Board, the national headquarters, and incorporated affiliates and unincorporated chapters, who are governed by their own local boards of directors. The AVANCE chapters and affiliates are perpetually linked to the National Office by an affiliation agreement, and all chapters and affiliates operate under one 501(c)3 designation. The National Board sets policy, direction, and guidance and is ultimately responsible for the preservation and protection of AVANCE's mission, philosophy, interests, and assets, as well as maintaining its favorable reputation and its unique commitment to strengthening and supporting low-income families and communities, especially in predominantly poor Latino communities. The National Board is the holder and protector of AVANCE's 501(c)3 IRS tax-exempt designation.

The National Office is the entity responsible for carrying out the policies, direction, and guidance of the board. It is also responsible for

- designing and developing programs, curriculum, products, and services in the name of AVANCE, Inc.;
- establishing and ensuring quality standards and developing the organization's operations manuals;
- providing training, technical assistance, and support to AVANCE chapters and affiliates;
- conducting research and evaluation;
- coordinating and conducting joint fund-development efforts and raising funds at the state, regional, and national levels;
- promoting and marketing AVANCE's mission, programs, and philosophy at the state, regional, and national levels;
- ensuring the operational integrity, viability, and growth of AVANCE, Inc.; and
- expanding AVANCE into new communities.

The AVANCE chapters and affiliates are the service arm for AVANCE, Inc., and serve as living laboratories for the National Office. The chapters and affiliates are responsible for providing high-quality AVANCE programs, beginning with the core birth to 3 parenting education program. When an AVANCE chapter increases its financial and organizational capacity and is able to meet certain criteria for incorporation, it can become an affiliate. The chapters and affiliates raise their funds locally and through joint efforts with the National Office. Affiliation fees are paid to the National Office for the use of the name, curriculum, programs, training and technical assistance, evaluation, research, marketing, and monitoring.

Services and the AVANCE Model

AVANCE chapters and affiliates are responsible for providing high-quality AVANCE programs, beginning with the core 0-3 parenting education program and following the AVANCE philosophy using the AVANCE Intervention Model for Hard-to-Reach Families, also known as the "Circular Model," as a road map. The AVANCE model outlines a path for both parents and children that is intended to be preventive, comprehensive, community-based, and sequential, and that requires partnerships and collaborative initiatives. For AVANCE parents, the model may include opportunities to increase their educational level and/or improve their literacy and language skills, job training, parent leadership development, housing, and community development. For AVANCE children, the model may include opportunities to participate in preschool programs in the public schools, Head Start, or HIPPY; recreational, mentoring, and educational activities in math, science, and computer training; and career development and scholarships.

Once the core AVANCE Parent Child Education Program is firmly established, local chapters can add AVANCE programs or services, such as the

Guiding Principles of AVANCE Family Support and Education Programs

1. Believe that people need support and that people can and want to change.
2. Begin with the strengths that parents bring and the love parents have for their child(ren).
3. Be responsive to the needs of the community.
4. Stay family focused: serve all family members (AVANCE child, mother, father, siblings).
5. Focus on prevention: have AVANCE child under the age of 3 as the entry point for family participation in AVANCE and non-AVANCE programs and services and the foundation for all services.
6. Focus on predominantly low-income Latino communities.
7. Focus on communities/neighborhoods: Each AVANCE affiliate has a designated geographic service area (GSA) in which to provide AVANCE and non-AVANCE services. Each community/neighborhood within the GSA must include an AVANCE Parent Child Education Program as the core and foundation of all services.
8. Focus on strengthening the social support network of neighbor helping neighbor.
9. Conduct extensive outreach/door-to-door recruiting.
10. Transform lives—by rekindling the spirit of hope and motivation by getting to the soul and treating participants with dignity and respect, providing encouragement and support.
11. Hire people that graduate from the program as role models.
12. Provide supportive services: child care and transportation.
13. Use culturally relevant curriculum and activities.
14. Engage in public/private partnerships.
15. Be consistent with AVANCE's mission, standards, and philosophy, yet adaptable to the community.
16. Follow the AVANCE Intervention Model for Hard-to-Reach Families, also known as the "Circular Model." The AVANCE model outlines a road map for both parents and children, beginning with the core AVANCE Parent Child Education Program. Services are comprehensive, developmental, and sequential, and all programs complement the AVANCE Parent Child Education Program and are linked to public/private community agencies.
17. Services in the Circular Model include:
    a. Core AVANCE Parent Child Education Program (parenting classes, toy making, community resources, home visits, child care, transportation, field trips, etc.).
    b. Path for Children: AVANCE child care; Head Start; preschool; education with emphasis in math, science, computer skills, and reading; after school; tutoring; mentoring; and scholarships.
    c. Path for Parents: Parenting (0-3 years–Adolescent); Literacy (English, GED, college), Personal Development, Leadership and Advocacy Skills, Career Awareness and Job Training, Employment, Housing, and Community Development.
    d. Other AVANCE programs: Fatherhood, Marriage/Couple Program, Health Education, Family Child Care Training Program, Families Building Communities (Parents as Leaders and Advocates in the School and Society).
    e. Examples of non-AVANCE programs and supplementary curriculum: I Am Your Child videos, Head Start, HIPPY, educational literacy programs.

Families Building Communities, the Health Education Program, and the Family Day Home Provider Training Program.

AVANCE has the following separate programs/curriculum available for use by the affiliates for 2001-2003: (1) the core Parent Child Education Program (2) the Fatherhood Program, (3) Families Building Communities: Parents as Leaders and Advocates in the Schools and Society, (4) the Family Child Care Provider Training Program, (5) the Promotora Health Education Program, and (6) the child abuse prevention Homebound Program. In addition, AVANCE parents can attend literacy classes (English classes, GED, college) by partnering with local community resources. Some of the chapters operate Even Start Family Literacy Programs, Early Head Start, and Head Start.

Non-AVANCE programs, such as Head Start and Even Start, meet local community needs and complement AVANCE programs. They also contribute to the comprehensive developmental and sequential process for parents and children, as described in the AVANCE Intervention Model for Hard-to-Reach Families, so long as they do not duplicate or compete with AVANCE programs. Each affiliate operates in a designated geographic area. As the AVANCE chapters or affiliates expand services to a specific geographic community within the geographic service area, they include the AVANCE Parent Child Education Program as the core program and the entry point for family participation in other AVANCE programs and services. A fuller description of AVANCE's programs is provided below.

The Core AVANCE Parent Child Education Program for Parents and Children (0-3)

The Parent Child Education Program, AVANCE's core program, seeks to familiarize parents with the basic social, emotional, physical, and cognitive needs of young children in a practical and supportive manner. It also provides assistance, information, and support to parents for the purpose of alleviating problems and obstacles that may impede the improvement of effective parenting skills. The parents form their own social support network that provides sanctions for desirable behaviors. Parents attend weekly 3-hour center-based activities for 9 months. Classes are held between 10:00 a.m. and 1:00 p.m. daily, with each class consisting of approximately 15 mothers and 45 children.

The weekly classes include 27 bilingual lessons in child growth and development, and toy-making classes that emphasize learning through play. Special group field trips, picnics, and parties are planned for parents and children. For example, Halloween might be celebrated with a parade through the community in which mothers and children wear costumes and receive treats. At Thanksgiving, parents bring food items to have a turkey dinner to celebrate and give thanks together. At Christmas, Santa distributes presents to all the children, and Easter includes Easter egg hunts for the children and the breaking of *cascarones* for the adults. These activities strengthen the parent-child relationship, build the social support network, improve parents' self-esteem, and teach parents how to enjoy life with their children while creating pleasant family memories. These activities also give the parents a sense of belonging and a desire to participate and complete the program. Group activities also include field trips to the public library.

Transportation is provided to and from the center for families residing within assigned geographic tracts, and the preschool children are cared for in an early childhood educational setting. Each parent is asked to volunteer at least 12 times for day care as a required child care practicum. Third-hour activities include speakers from different community organizations that serve as resources and support for the parents. In some family centers, the day is extended by having the parents interact with their children before the parents go to the parenting class.

While participating in the Parent Child Education Program, the parents are visited in their homes once a month for 30 minutes for an observation or videotaping of parent-child play interactions. The tapes are first viewed by the parent in the home and later shown to the class during the parent group. Parents learn from each other and reinforce best "teaching strategies through play." Parents also receive one-to-one support during this time, and social service needs of parents are referred to community agencies with staff follow-up to assure that services were received.

The educational opportunities and economic development program available to graduates of the parenting program is designed to foster self-sufficiency among low-income minority women. AVANCE promotes economic stability and personal growth by providing on-site literacy and educational services. Students are assisted in preparing for college and in college admittance. Parents are encouraged to attend English classes, GED classes, and college classes on-site at the family center. AVANCE works with the local adult education provider to obtain the instructors, while AVANCE offers child care, transportation, and classroom space. As the students acquire the knowledge of how the system works, they gain confidence and enroll on their own, but many continue to need child care provided through AVANCE.

AVANCE Families Building Communities Program: Parents as Leaders and Advocates in the School and Society

Begun with a grant from the Annenberg Foundation, this 3-year program consists of the following three components:

Families Building Community (FBC I): Parenting information for school-age children: This 9-month program consisting of personal development, leadership, and education for parents with children 5 to 17 years is provided for AVANCE parents as a follow-up to the core AVANCE Parent Child Education Program. Some selected topics include "Introduction to How the School and Community Government Works" and "Parents as Decision Makers in School and Civic Engagement."

Connecting with Parents

Parents in School Reform (FBC II): This component provides a project-based learning phase where parents select topics to work on, such as curriculum selection, review of school education and quality standards, and site-based management. FBC II also involves understanding how the system works, including school budgets, teacher selection, school board, and parent or staff roles and responsibilities.

Parent Networking/Advocacy Program (FBC III): This component is organized as the application-based phase, including developing parent councils, a Web site for parents, attending an annual meeting for parents participating in the program, school and community projects, advocacy, and public policy.

Promotora Health Education Program

Begun with a grant from the Hasbro Children's Foundation, this program enhances AVANCE's Core Parenting Education curriculum in the area of health education. The curriculum is formatted in different pamphlets addressing various aspects of health promotion and wellness. Lay parents are also trained to go into the community to educate their neighbors about health promotion and safety. AVANCE is extremely effective in reaching low-income parents and enrolling their children in a health insurance program.

Family Child Care Provider Training Program

This program began with a grant from the Annie E. Casey Foundation. AVANCE developed a curriculum to train parents who desired to become family child care providers. The program consists of a 12-week training course that includes child growth and development, how to begin a business, and specific information about providing high-quality child care in the home. In addition, parents are provided support in financing and getting their home licensed to provide services.

The AVANCE Homebound Child Abuse Program

Begun with a grant from the Texas Department of Human Resources, this support program is for the most at-risk families, those parents who have been referred to AVANCE for child abuse and neglect. Its goals are (1) to provide additional support for families confirmed as child abuse and neglect cases through an individual program in the home and (2) to prevent the reoccurrence of abuse and neglect by developing more effective parenting practices and positive parental role attitudes. Services include weekly visits, individualized parenting education classes in the home, social activities to break isolation, and a comprehensive program for meeting needs through service integration. The parents are mainstreamed to the center-based program when the family situation is stabilized and when the parent is ready for group interactions.

The programs that AVANCE sponsors under its umbrella are those that best respond to the needs of the low-income Hispanic family. Although the needs are probably similar in any disadvantaged group regardless of race or ethnicity, the methodology is unique to this particular population, taking into consideration dialects and cultural characteristics.

Evaluation Outcomes

There have been several evaluations of the AVANCE programs. Summaries of the research findings are included below.

Project CAN PREVENT

The research findings of Project CAN PREVENT demonstrated that AVANCE was effective in changing the factors and conditions that were contributing to child abuse and neglect, such as increased knowledge of child growth and development, the development of a social support network that had an effect on isolation, and the improvement of self-esteem and hopeful-ness. Parents attending the AVANCE core program had a change in attitude regarding discipline and how they would handle infractions.

Carnegie Study of Core Parent Child Education Program

In 1987, the agency reached a major milestone in its development with the advent of a Research and Evaluation Study of the AVANCE Parent Child Education Program (1987-91) funded by the Carnegie Corporation of New York. This scientific evaluation has provided strong evidence supporting the effectiveness of the core Parent Child Education Program. AVANCE participants were compared to a control group that did not receive any services. The evaluation found that the program had a substantial effect on the ability of mothers to provide a cognitively stimulating and emotionally nurturing environment for their children. It had strong effects on child-rearing attitudes, knowledge of parenting behavior, and an awareness of community resources. Behavioral observations revealed that AVANCE participants were more responsive to their children, talked more frequently with them, and used play opportunities to teach educational concepts. The mothers understood, accepted, and actively pursued their role as the first teacher of their children. In addition, many more program than control mothers enrolled in classes to obtain a high school equivalency certificate or to acquire college credits. The evaluation concludes that AVANCE parents have the necessary skills to provide an educationally stimulating environment and provide emotional support, they value education for themselves and their children, and they have a knowledge base for effective rearing of children (Johnson & Walker, 1996).

In 1990, an informal 17-year follow-up survey of the first AVANCE class was conducted. Information gathered from the survey revealed that although 91% of the parents had dropped out of school in 1973, 57% had subsequently returned to complete their GED. In addition, 94% of their children had either completed high school, received their GED, or were still in school, and 43% of the children were attending college.

Long-Term Impact on Family Economics—St. Mary's University

A survey conducted by students at St. Mary's University included 100 parents who participated and graduated from the AVANCE programs in San Antonio between 1994 and 2001. An important finding was that 60% of families reported an annual income of under $9,000 before attending AVANCE, and at the time of the interview, 62% reported an annual income of over $9,000.

Funding

It is not easy keeping a nonprofit grassroots organization in operation. Funds are limited or categorical, and getting ongoing funds is difficult because funders tend to want to support new demonstration projects—and at the most for 3 years. One needs to be entrepreneurial, resourceful, and creative in pooling funds and ensuring that new funds come in before the previous funds run out. In addition, most government funds are provided on a cost-reimbursement basis, and the organization must have at least 3 months' worth of working capital in order to secure needed funds.

AVANCE began with a 3-year $100,000-a-year grant from the Zale Foundation to fund the Parenting Program and a Tutoring Program. The Zale Foundation was AVANCE's sole funder from 1973-75 and continued to support AVANCE with 30% matching funds for 3 additional years. The primary funder from 1975-78 was the Texas State Department of Human Services; by 1979, the City of San Antonio had replaced the Zale Foundation in providing the 30% match. In 1979, the AVANCE programs were funded by a variety of organizations, including the City of San Antonio's Human Services Department, United Way, and the National Center on Child Abuse and Neglect. The Project CAN PREVENT grant was the first federal grant prepared and submitted by AVANCE to a federal funding source. It was one of 300 submitted nationally and one of nine selected for funding. Through the grant, the organization gained credibility from a formal needs assessment of the community and the first evaluation of the AVANCE Parent Child Education Program.

Throughout its 30 years, AVANCE has been able to thrive with many different funding partners at a time when many social programs have been affected by massive federal budget cuts. Some funds have been received to support or enhance the core parenting program or to address a community need with services that are connected to the core parenting program. It has not been easy—especially as AVANCE has stayed committed to its original mission. In times of funding crises, it has been the parents and children who have become AVANCE's greatest advocates.

In 1984, the AVANCE annual budget was $420,000, with 47% of funds coming from the City of San Antonio Human Services Department, 20% from United Way, 12% from the Texas Department of Human Services (TDHS), 19%

from the federal government, and 2% from the Zale Foundation. The annual budget for the National Office and chapters at the end of June 2002 was $26,631,898, which consisted of $20,640,423 from government (86% federal, 8% state, 6% local); $2,747,677 from foundations; $110,100 from corporations; $351,085 from fund-raising; $1,143,462 from in-kind support; and $1,639,151 from other sources (United Way, individuals, chapter fees, interest, etc.). In 2000, the Los Angeles County Government awarded AVANCE $250,000 to incorporate AVANCE in Los Angeles and to serve the first group of parents in that community. The Hilton Foundation provided $250,000 in California as seed funds for 5 years.

The AVANCE National Office was established with the support of a consortium of the largest foundations, including Carnegie, Ford, Kellogg, Rockefeller, Mott, and Hilton. In 2002, AVANCE received grants from Kellogg and other major foundations to increase its working capital fund, to begin a sustained leadership endowment, and to expand AVANCE to California. AVANCE will be completing a $4.5 million capital campaign this year for a new headquarters building. Its first annual appeal was held in 2003 as a challenge to a Kresge grant for the capital campaign. In 2001, AVANCE received the Annie E. Casey Families Count Award, which also carries a $500,000 unrestricted gift.

Program Modifications over the Past 30 Years and Lessons Learned

While still staying centered on its original mission, AVANCE has continued to grow and change over the years to improve on the original program or to accommodate the changing needs of families in the community. For example,

- Changing the supervised baby-sitting program that was provided for parents while they attended their classes to a developmental day care, called the Day Care Lab. Parents are required to volunteer for 12 hours in the Lab to receive a practicum certificate to graduate from the program.

- Condensing the program curriculum from 2 years to 1 year while expanding from 2 hours daily to 3 hours in order to provide as much of the curriculum as possible to a highly transient population located in the housing projects. Adding the third hour gave an unforeseen benefit of providing parents with more information and links to community-based services.

- Adjusting to include more activities when funding for a stipend provided to parents for participating in the program was stopped. AVANCE staff developed a variety of activities for parents to encourage the parents to feel more engaged in the program.

- Adding new topics and new toys to fit the needs and interests of the parents and children.

- Continuing to become more comprehensive, and developmental, providing continuous support to the parents and children.

- Developing resources for fathers when staff realized that they were inadvertently negatively affecting the family by only working with the mothers and the target child under the age of 3.
- Providing more intensive support in the home and in partnership with other social and mental health service providers for at-risk families. For these parents and for the referrals from protective services, AVANCE began a program for parents to prevent child abuse and neglect.
- Developing a Promotora Health Education Program to work with parents in rural areas needing health education services and to encourage enrollment in a health insurance program.
- Adding developmental services to the core program for the children, ensuring that AVANCE children entered early childhood preschool programs or Head Start.
- Collaborating with other early learning programs.
- Creating a curriculum to provide parents with more information about transitioning their child to elementary school and into adolescence as well as becoming advocates in the community.
- Finding ways to address the economic conditions of the parents, including hiring parents from the program and from the community, encouraging parents to continue their high school education and to be aware of various careers, and assisting them with college attendance.
- Creating a Family Child Care Training Program for those parents wanting to work out of their home and provide care for other children.
- Establishing a formal graduation ceremony for children and parents to highlight their accomplishments and build self-confidence.

AVANCE sites have become one of the best employers for the parents and their growing children, especially along the border cities and in poor communities. Staff members strongly believe that AVANCE must be responsive to the needs of the family, and the Circular Intervention Model was developed as a road map for providing services.

Community Development Impact

AVANCE is an active participant and advocate of community development. As a result of leadership emerging from within the community, a group of parents, assisted by AVANCE, obtained a $100,000 Community Development Block Grant to construct a playground in the Mirasol Housing Project. Parents educated their state representatives about the importance of supporting and sustaining AVANCE in their community and helped secure a $1.7 million grant from the Texas Education Agency. Also, parents become more active and involved in the schools and in their community as leaders in the PTA and Resident Association, and in initiating community projects such as building a playground for their children or starting a community crime watch program.

Other programs are added to the existing organization to be responsive to the needs of the community. AVANCE changed from a focus of getting the child ready for school to a more comprehensive and continuous support of the entire family to simultaneously strengthening the family and the community. Slogans that were used were "the strength of the community lies in the strength of the family" and "from the cradle to the job." Dr. Rodriguez and AVANCE staff came to the realization that social and economic problems are interrelated; for example, if one finds a dropout problem, one may also find child abuse, crime, poverty, spouse abuse, etc. The root cause of most of these problems lies in a dysfunctional family in great need of assistance and support. Parents rekindle their spirit of hope when they receive culturally relevant and effective services.

AVANCE felt that there needed to be a developmental sequential service approach for both parents and children. The child needed to continue to grow developmentally; the parents needed continued support in their role as parents (especially during the critical period of preadolescence and adolescence); and the whole family needed to grow educationally, personally, and economically.

Expansion of Facilities, Locations, and Clients

Initially, AVANCE was housed in two 3-bedroom apartments in the Mirasol Housing Project. Then it replicated to three San Antonio communities in six 3-bedroom apartments in the Mirasol Housing Project, in a house located adjacent to a low-income housing complex, and in a large wing in a city-owned building called the West End Multi-Service Center. Today, AVANCE chapters and affiliates can be found in schools, housing projects, churches, storefronts, houses, and in their leased/own buildings. In Houston, AVANCE has six sites. Individuals served have increased from 58 in 1973 to 15,000 in 2002; staff increased from 4 in 1973 to over 600 by 2002.

Name Change

The organization's name changed from AVANCE Neighborhood Intervention Program to AVANCE, Inc., in 1990. AVANCE, Inc., is now AVANCE's legal name. Today, it is more commonly known as AVANCE Family Support and Education Programs, which include the Parent Child Education Program (the core program) and all AVANCE programs.

References

AVANCE, Inc. (2002). *AVANCE, Inc., demographic survey.* San Antonio, TX: Author.

Johnson, Dale L., & Walker, Todd B. (1996). *Final report of an evaluation of the AVANCE Parent Education and Family Support Program.* San Antonio, TX: AVANCE.

Rodriguez, Gloria. (1985). *AVANCE educational program for parents and children: A historical perspective of its twelve year evolvement.* San Antonio, TX: AVANCE, Inc.

Responses to the Presentation by Gloria Rodriguez

After presenting her paper, Gloria Rodriguez answered questions from symposium participants. A panel then convened to respond to her presentation.

Questions and Comments from Participants Responding to Gloria Rodriguez's Presentation

Participant: Could you explain a little more about the chapter system of AVANCE?

Gloria Rodriguez: We have a national headquarters and then individual chapters in other locations. Each chapter has a local board of directors, but each chapter must meet the standards—a checklist including finance and other programmatic standards—of AVANCE. They are allowed some flexibility to adjust the program to their community, but within our guidelines and standards.

Participant: I understand that AVANCE uses a structured curriculum. Could you explain a little more about your curriculum and why you have chosen a structured approach?

Gloria Rodriguez: Yes, we do use a structured approach that we have worked to build over many years and, after reviewing research, with our parents. We don't ask parents to come and then say, "Learn what you want," because many of the families come to us not knowing where they should start. Our approach includes working in the parent group on predesigned activities, in the classroom settings, and also in the home.

People come to the program knowing what we expect—there are desks, they raise their hands to ask questions, they can't smoke or bring firearms. Once the parent goes through the program, then he or she is ready to move on to another level, such as community college. That is partly because although the program is structured, it is also nurturing. We believe that with the right support, you can make progress.

Panel Session—Responding to the AVANCE Experience and the Question "What Should Be Done to Help Hard-to-Reach Parents Get Ready for School?"

Moderator: Jean Paine Mendoza, University of Illinois

Low audio quality prevented full transcription of the panel session. The themes that were addressed during the discussion are summarized below.

1. *The need to acknowledge that perhaps the right question is "How do we get schools ready for hard-to-reach parents?"*

Understanding how schools should prepare for parents and students seems to be the more respectful way of looking at this issue. Then we can ask, "How do we change infrastructures and bureaucracies that are not conducive to providing parent support?"

One way is to bring people—parents and teachers—together to build formal and informal relationships in a variety of settings. Parents often interpret school-related terminology as a personal attack on them. If school personnel begin early by forming groups of parents and school staff who have regular conversations about a variety of topics, then parents won't view school personnel as potentially threatening and will be more receptive to, for example, early literacy-related concepts.

School personnel should also be creative in developing ways to engage parents and eventually develop a "parent-driven" model. For example, in one school, a regular Saturday morning play day and cookout was most effective with involving fathers.

2. *The need to clarify effective methods of communication.*

It is important to understand the actual goals of the communication and then take the information to where it is accessible to the parents such as the church, the grocery store, clinics and hospitals, or other places that parents frequent. In communities where neighbor-to-neighbor conversation is a primary source of information, it is helpful to develop verbal ways of sharing information. Programs could provide a multidimensional platform where folks have a variety of ways and opportunities to share information and work together. Television is a medium that reaches most parents, and even though it is expensive, it should not be ruled out as a possibility.

3. *The need to identify what are sustainable models for programs and how to create them.*

Sometimes program guidelines get in the way of really serving families and maintaining the program. Programs should have a set of principles, a leadership base, and structure (for example, a business model) that will ensure its continuity in the community for as long as the program is needed. Establishing trust and long-term relationships with the families in the community is critical. One of the reasons that the Reggio model is so successful is because children and families are approached respectfully with an understanding that there will be long-term relationships.

If the program guidelines are flexible enough to adjust to the changing needs of parents and families, participation is more likely to be sustainable. Although it is obvious that we want to look at programs that are working, it is also important to look critically at the ones that are not working, even if it sets a negative frame. Understanding the barriers to a program's successful implementation will help improve outcomes over the long run.

4. *The need to define what is meant by "vulnerable" without being disrespectful of families but still acknowledging that there are inequalities.*

All too frequently, politicians and educators are making decisions about who is "vulnerable" or "at risk." Parents should be included in the conversation about what is meant by vulnerable children and families. Including parents in the conversation will help reduce the possibility of seeing vulnerable parents as "those" parents, or of seeing the problems or issues of vulnerable families as so separate from the problems of others. Individuals who are given the responsibility as educators to prepare parents may not know the intricacies and protocol that are important within the culture that they are serving. Sometimes there are dual goals in terms of the skills that the parents and their community expect for their children and what the educator may expect. When educators understand the goals of the parents and larger community, it may then be possible to integrate expectations, thereby reducing vulnerability.

Parent Panel

This panel consisted of parents who had participated at some time in programs serving vulnerable parents with young children. They were invited to attend the symposium with representatives of their organizations. One panel discussion was set aside for them to tell their stories. Lisa Lee of the Parent Services Project facilitated.

AVANCE: Rita San Miguel, speaker

I just wanted to share my adventure with AVANCE and how it changed my life. Gloria was only 25 years old when she came to my door. I was young and had dropped out of school after I married and had my son. I stayed with my mother, but she said, "Do not open the door to anyone or they will hike up the rent." So, Gloria knocked on the door, and being a teenager, I opened the door. Gloria said, "I am looking for people just like you." She told me that she had a program to help me and my son. I called my husband to tell him about it, and then I called my sister to see if she wanted to come. We walked to the school, and Gloria was there with the children in the school. I learned about being a parent and about what children needed. At that point, I was good with my child's basic needs. I bathed him, fed him—attended to his needs—but I wasn't talking to him and didn't know that he needed other things to help with his growth.

However, to make a long story a little shorter, my husband and I got divorced because he couldn't accept the changes that he saw in me as a result of the AVANCE program. When he began to accept it, we got remarried, and this year we would have been married 27 years if we had stayed married. While going to school, I had all the support for my son, and for me, to do well in school. I even learned how to drive. Gloria helped me study and lent me her car to learn. Because AVANCE believes in hiring from within, I eventually took over the day care and continued to grow until I begin to work at the national office. I have had adventures that, prior to participating in AVANCE, would have been unbelievable to me.

I started [when] AVANCE had a staff of three people. They combined all their duties and were willing to help with anything. I really thought that it was

191

impossible to get out of the [welfare] system that I was in, but my son who is not 30 years old has a better life. My daughter is attending community college to obtain her associate's degree, and my son is a very loving father and good provider. With the core AVANCE staff, the door is open all the time. Incentives were provided to families to continue, and there was a lot of encouragement. Staff welcomed us from the very beginning without judging. They became like a family. They were trusting and not negative. We were guided but in a disciplined way. We could socialize during class and bring soft drinks or fruit and become "comrades." Various professionals came to teach us different things, like doctors about health care, and nutritionists about food, and what to look for when purchasing food. For me, all of this had to be learned—it was not part of my life.

HIPPY USA: *Merle Greene and Stacy Blais, speakers*

Merle Greene (Early Childhood Education Director of HIPPY USA): HIPPY is a home-based school readiness home involvement program. It is designed to meet individual needs of parents who have low-income and low socioeconomic levels with the philosophy that all children do learn and all parents need support. Some parents may need more support to learn how to be their child's first teacher. There are four essential features:

- Home-based curriculum—30 weeks of activities in activity packets are included.
- Professional coordinator and home visitors—Trained staff including a coordinator oversee the program and recruit and train the home visitors.
- Role play—Role play is the instructional method of training between the coordinator and the home visitor.
- Group meetings—Home visits are interspersed with group meetings on alternate weeks, although many HIPPY programs reserve the right to have home visits 3 weeks a month. There is tremendous flexibility for HIPPY programs to structure them based on what the community needs.

There is often training going on at the local and national levels to help parents and staff to continue to grow. We offer our families a lot of enrichment and extension materials, including a lot of outreach. The curriculum is in English, Spanish, and Chinese.

Stacy Blais (former HIPPY parent and home visitor): I started HIPPY 4 years ago with my son. I heard about it from the public schools, with my kids bringing home handouts about the program. The HIPPY home visitor came over to my house and showed me some of the skills that I could teach my child. Somehow, the idea that I should be teaching my 4-year-old was new to me, because with my older children I didn't get that message. It was my first exposure to the type of skills my child needed before he started kindergarten. My older children started school, and they really weren't ready, but when I started working with my younger child, it was easy to work with him and play the games and the activities. The HIPPY program was fun. There were games and a lot of movement. When my son started school, the teacher

asked which nursery school he went to, and I said that he wasn't in a school—
he was just home with me. He could take directions, he could think logically.
Also, because I was involved with HIPPY, I had access to other services
that were also helpful for my other children. I really see the difference
between my child who did get the learning before school and those who didn't.

MELD: Kay Gudmestad and Zachary Tift, speakers

Kay Gudmestad (president and CEO of MELD): MELD's mission is to
enhance the ability of parents to raise nurturing children. We work with many
different organizations, including HIPPY and PAT. We have a variety of
publications and training, and we train many practitioners in service community. However, we're really focused on school-related issues and the ethnically diverse communities.

Zachary Tift (MELD parent and Young Dads and Hmong Parents Coordinator): I became a parent at 18 years old. Mariah was born just 2 weeks
before our high school graduation. Mariah's mother and I definitely did not do
that senior slide thing. However, when we found out that we were pregnant,
I had the support of my family, including my mother and the women in my
family. They taught me a lot of the "hands-on"—how to hold the baby and
the child development issues. My father and the other men in my family
prepared me and helped mentor me into fatherhood. There is a saying that a
woman's role is to bring a child into the world, but a father's role is to bring
the child up in the world. My father also helped with a father's resource
center (which is still going) so that young fathers could learn where to place
their priorities. Last year, we worked with 180 fathers, and 146 fathers
attended a conference. MELD gives a stable program that has helped for
over 30 years, and MELD grows and changes where needed. They have the
young fathers and young mothers program as well as programs for ethnically
diverse groups. It just keeps growing.

Parents As Teachers (PAT): Sue Stepleton and Samantha Fishman, speakers

Sue Stepleton (president and CEO of PAT): I am really struck by some of
the similarities in the programs. Our vision also changed to focus on children,
with the mission being for parents and the focus on parents' needs. We (in
our guiding principles) believe that parents are the first teachers; we emphasize the importance of the early years and that all children and families
deserve the same opportunities. Personal home visits, developmental screenings, and group meetings are all methods that we use to find problems early.
Sixty percent of the children and families served would be considered high
needs. We also thought you might be interested in some of the things that
we struggle with. For example, PAT is a universal access model. We want
the service to have both intensity and quality. We hope that the same quality
is maintained across the country. We also try not to be all things to all
people, but we understand when other groups work better with ethnically
diverse people.

Samantha Fishman (former PAT parent and PAT Coordinator): When I first heard about PAT, I was a teen parent with two children 14 months apart. I also had a 13-year-old brother living with me at the time. So, basically there were four children living in the household. I was involved in a family center that wrote a grant for PAT services. We were approved for the grant, and eventually the program hired their staff. The staff were called Developmental Specialists. I remember one of my first experiences with my specialist coming out to the house with little bags of things and seeing her pulling out scissors. I didn't understand, and I thought she was crazy. Why would anyone give a young child scissors? However, over time I realized that you could give children scissors and other things, and they could learn from that.

Eventually, we had both children assessed. My older child was tested and put into a program for academically advanced children, but it was frustrating because the younger child couldn't seem to do some basic things. My home visitor suggested that she should be tested for a learning disability. When we realized that she did have a disability, then my home visitor explained that my daughter wasn't doing these things to frustrate me but she just wasn't able to learn in the same way as my older child. However, we were able to get the help that she needed to make progress.

I became very involved with the government work that I learned about at our center, and our parents are very vocal and will come forward for things like school bills. My involvement in PAT has helped me improve my advocacy skills for special needs children. You can also see the impact with my older child. For example, my older child was with her stepmother when she had her first child. It was my daughter who explained to the stepmother what the new baby needed. So it was really clear to me that my daughter has benefited from PAT in ways that we didn't expect.

Questions from Symposium Participants to Parents on the Panel

Participant: What would you suggest as being the best practices in the program that you were involved with?

Stacy: I would like see parents get the information much sooner than, for example, when an older child starts school. In my situation, I heard about HIPPY because my older children brought home a flyer about the program. However, if the information was in clinics, doctors' offices, or other places that young parents visit, they would get the information earlier so it would be more helpful.

Samantha: The personal connection and courtesy are so important. If a parent calls an agency to get more information, and the person who answers them puts them off, then that parent may never call again. Establishing a personal bond or relationship with someone in the program is so important.

Rita: Not only the parents of the group attract us to stay involved, but there are others involved like the fathers in the fathers' classes. There are evening classes for those who are working.

Zachary: Programs need to stake their claims in the community because it shows their commitment to the community.

Participant: What should programs be covering?

Rita: We were told that we would be learning about how to prepare our child for school and also about how to be a part of that, including how we can get ready for school, too.

Stacy: I was told that I would learn more about my child. I knew my child was learning something, but I didn't know exactly what, so the program helped me realize how my child was learning. Also, there is the curriculum that explains the skills that the child is learning, and there is a standard in education and everything that you learn from your child. It really changes things at home—the way you talk to your child changes. Basically everything changes. You begin to see that everything you do is a lesson.

Samantha: I was very isolated with my children, and none of my friends had children at that time. I was pretty convinced at 18 that I knew what I was doing. For me, the community type of atmosphere was really important. I realized that there was something to this when my children didn't cut each other up with the scissors. I started doing the activities and then seeing some positive things coming out of them. So, at that point, I thought okay—maybe the specialist wasn't really as crazy as I thought that she was. It took me doing that and seeing how it worked.

Zachary: I didn't attend a group. However, MELD staff did talk with me to make sure that my needs as a young parent were being met. Through the MELD peer-modeling program, I realized that we could really relate and empathize with that experience of being a young parent.

Participant: What has the staff learned from the parents—what growth and changes did you see in the staff?

Samantha: A lot of community support and resources came from the parents. Many of the specialists that started at our center didn't live in the area. They have a lot of academic and developmental knowledge, but they didn't know where to get things in the community. The professionals had a very clear picture of how the center was going to look and when a parent group was formed. Then we essentially said, "That's a good vision, but that's not what we want." That's when we sat down with staff and explained why our community didn't need certain things that they had put into the center.

Stacy: The staff of our program is really well trained and followed the model exactly as it is, so I'm not really sure what I can say about whether or not the staff learned anything from us.

Participant: What is one thing that the program does where you know it is really helping?

Zachary: One of the things that helps is when the guys come back. You can tell that it builds confidence—and you can see it when they keep coming back.

Samantha: A large part of the current discussion at our center is about advocacy and helping parents to get their children involved before school. There is a lot of feeling from parents that they are being judged at school. Sometimes teachers send the message that you are the "token" mom. Learning advocacy skills helps parents work past that and become better advocates in their child's school.

Stacy: Relationships between parents are helpful, because by forming those relationships, you are building a repertoire that is comfortable.

Rita: In AVANCE, the parents are made a part of the system right away. By the end of the program, the parents are feeling a part of AVANCE and inviting staff over to their homes, and the relationship is reciprocal.

Zachary: Young fathers feel judged and think that others feel they won't make it—that they will run out on their family. In the schools, it can be frustrating. For example, if something happens to their child, then the teacher or principal won't call the father. Despite the fact that the father has talked with the school, they still don't call. When other young fathers first get involved, they often feel judged, but being part of a group will help them realize that everyone has difficulty and it is a process. You don't graduate from fatherhood.

Participant: Were you approached by other groups that you did not get involved in?

Samantha: Yes, I was involved in a program before PAT but stopped going, mainly because of the staff and the feeling of being judged. When I was in a literacy program, the teacher had parents write in a "confidential" journal and then she asked me about something in the journal. That was enough—if I couldn't trust her that the journals were confidential, then how could I trust her to give advice?

Rita: Yes, I was approached by the local high school and asked to attend school, since I hadn't graduated. However, I couldn't bring my son with me, so I was unwilling to leave my child with a baby-sitter to attend school.

Participant: Do you know others who would have benefited from the program but have not gotten involved?

Samantha: Yes, there are moms who are overwhelmed—too young and too tired. They tend to be the most frequent "drops" from the program because they are unable to work it all together.

Rita: Some parents have to work longer hours to maintain their benefits, and they just don't have the time to maintain the same level of involvement—they

Connecting with Parents

are just exhausted. Also, parents with children who are fussy, sick, or who just are having difficulty maintaining certain basics.

Stacy: Sometimes the home visits work out fine, but the parent doesn't make it to the center or vice versa, so they have a type of partial involvement.

Zachary: For the fathers, many of them need help just stabilizing their lives because they are low income. They have all the challenges of basic needs—housing, food—and they need to cope with that before they can come to a fathers' meeting. The guys who are incarcerated actually have better attendance because at least they have "3 hots and a cot," or have their basic needs met.

Closing Panel: Key Issues for Early Childhood Programs

On the last evening of the Kellogg symposium, a small group of participants gathered with the goal of reflecting on the discussions of the previous two days and suggesting some priorities for programs designed to connect with parents about issues related to children's school readiness.

On Sunday morning, symposium organizers presented the list of priorities to the larger group of participants, who concurred that the list represented key issues for programs. The participants agreed to break into four groups (based on their areas of expertise) to discuss how their professions would attempt to assure that the priorities were implemented in programs serving young children and their families. The four specializations identified were: (1) public policy, advocacy, or the media; (2) direct service; (3) professional education and training; and (4) early childhood research.

Participants were asked to focus their small group discussions on providing examples of potential changes in their professional approach that would align with these four priorities to improve the capacity of parents, or those in the parenting role, to prepare their children for school.

After the small group discussions, Lisa Lee facilitated a panel discussion on Key Issues for Early Childhood Programs. The following four priorities were discussed in the Sunday morning small groups, from the perspective of each group's expertise:

1. Building a culture of mutual respect among parents and staff.

2. Sharing responsibility for defining school readiness and for defining how schools can be ready for children.

3. Providing adequate resources (financial, human, socio-cultural, and environmental).

4. Strengthening the capacity of staff to engage effectively with parents.

Group #1—Policy, Advocacy, Media

If professionals involved with public policy, advocacy, and the media are focusing on the four priorities, they will:

1. Increase access to information for parents.
2. Develop a comprehensive, multidimensional, and interagency approach to prepare children for school.
3. Identify and disseminate the specific points that research indicates are important for early learning and school readiness and the knowledge base that links social-emotional development and cognitive development with readiness.
4. Reframe the public message about "readiness" so that it reflects the view that the physical, social, and emotional processes in children's development are interrelated.
5. Promote effective practices that support relationships between parents and teachers or family support professionals.
6. Coordinate conferences where researchers, educators, and parents come together and discuss important issues related to preparing children for school.
7. Identify adequate resources to support parents' participation, and specify what outcomes are expected for a successful parent involvement effort.
8. Promote adequate funding and resources for comprehensive centers with "one-stop" access to services.
9. Increase the capacity of staff to work with vulnerable families.

Group #2— Direct Service Providers

If professionals involved with direct service are focusing on the four priorities, they will:

1. Create environments that encourage relationships between staff, and between staff and parents, including home visits and providing a common room, family resource center, or a place to serve food.
2. Provide information to parents about whom to call when they have a question, as well as emergency resources for child care, transportation, and food.
3. Treat parents and staff with trust and respect.
4. Create parent councils so that parents can be involved in leadership within programs; give parents and service staff the authority to make decisions together.
5. Provide opportunities for staff and parents to work together, with parents as classroom aides, tutors, teachers of specific skills, or advocates for children.
6. Establish a culture where parents are welcome and encouraged to be involved in the program.
7. Encourage parental involvement in defining readiness.
8. Create a bridge between the early learning program and the elementary school.

9. Increase staff understanding of learning styles.
10. Provide book- and toy-lending libraries if possible, including a staff person who is accessible to parents to address their needs or questions.
11. When possible, hire staff who reflect the culture of the families in the program; at the least, encourage staff understanding of the conditions of the community and issues in the home.

Group # 3—Teacher Education and Staff Development

If professionals involved with teacher education and staff development are focusing on the four priorities, they will:

1. Use vignettes or case studies in preservice education and staff development.
2. Use examples that are complex enough that students benefit from learning to take the perspectives of social worker, educator, early intervention professional, and child care provider.
3. Clarify what mutual respect looks like when implemented in a program serving young children and their families.
4. Promote use of a strengths-based approach and focus on resilience in parents and families.
5. Focus on intentional staff development, including talking with staff both individually and as a group about their preferences for additional training and support.
6. Collaborate with universities to work with staff in research or on staff development.
7. Develop a culture of hope and resilience.
8. Create staff awareness that there is a parent's "bill of rights" and that parents have a right to expect certain things from a program.
9. Encourage innovative ways to look for solutions to problems facing families.
10. Provide information for students about how systems work—including state and national political systems and community infrastructures.

Group #4—Researchers

If professionals involved with research are focusing on the four priorities, they will:

1. Analyze whether these priorities represent "the right questions" and whether our knowledge base is solid enough to know what "the right questions" are.
2. Analyze the research base to determine how it addresses the four priorities.
3. Clarify who should have a voice in the development and dissemination of the research (Parents? Caregivers? Experts?).
4. Clarify what we, as a society, expect with regard to school readiness. Is our society so competitive that the bar is always set higher; should every child be "above average?"

5. Develop ways to research "cultures of trust."
6. Expand the research on understanding the bridge between getting children ready for school and schools being ready for children.
7. Invest in longitudinal research on activities such as home visiting.
8. Conduct rigorous experimental studies.
9. Focus on replicating studies that have shown a demonstrated relationship between parent-staff communication and child outcomes.
10. Clarify what staff characteristics are likely to improve school readiness and parent-staff interactions (e.g., is there a relationship between increased salaries and better communication with parents, or between salary and staff stability?).
11. Give parents a voice in the research process.
12. Interpret data within a cultural context.

Questions/Comments in Response to Panel Presentations

Participants offered the following comments in response to the panel presentations:

"Another piece of research is the direct tie between program quality and child welfare. Also, the role of qualitative research really helps us think about the design as well as what types of questions should be asked."

"What research has [been] shared with parents? Most of what we know about parents and contributions to school readiness comes from correlational research. When you look closely at some of the data that are shared about the developing child and the correlational research—the relationship is pretty modest."

"Programs are on the line. We want to be mindful that researchers don't know everything and that parents don't want to hear from researchers that our best guess is that if you do x then y will happen. However, if we continue to use simple answers for parents, then we are doing a great disservice."

"If the desired outcome is for children to be happy, builders of peace, and be happy as human beings, but we put pressure on parents to achieve if they don't do x, y, and z, then perhaps we are doing a disservice. Parents should not be so concerned with winning or losing when their child is so young."

(Question directed to parent participants): Oversimplifying research for parents—how do you feel about that in terms of the messages? Would you still have been interested in the program if the staff home visitor said, "Our best guess tells us this will help?"

"In my case, there weren't any specific promises made, and I probably would have been more skeptical if there had been."

"We need to say a little more about the fathers' program—programs need to be flexible to discuss what is important to parents during that day. Parent leaders need to be humble but also have the ability to get things done. Action for fathers is important."

Comments on Search Strategies Used

Searches were conducted of the following databases: Cumulative Index to Nursing and Allied Health Literature (CINAHL), ERIC, Library and Information Science Abstracts (LISA), MEDLINE, PsycINFO, Wilson Social Sciences Abstracts, and Social Work Abstracts.

None of the databases seemed to have a specific subject heading for "parent communication" *per se*. Some databases do not recognize the term "communication" and will return entries containing words such as "community" instead of "communication."

The biomedical/nursing/allied health community seems to have a number of resources related to communicating with parents about health/medical issues. CINAHL and MEDLINE are powerful databases that allow "explosions" of terms such as "professional-family relations" (to get the major term and all narrower terms) with "communication" type terms: "communication in medicine" with "parent" terms, etc.

For example, the CINAHL search proceeded as follows:

1 Professional-Family Relations/ (2877)
2 exp COMMUNICATION/ (21210)
3 1 and 2 (455)
4 limit 3 to yr=1990-2002 (413)
5 *professional-family relations/ (1475)
6 exp *communication/ (12455)
7 5 and 6 (157)
8 limit 7 to yr=1990-2002 (129).

When a database did not accept the terms "communication" or "communicating," alternative strategies were tried. Certain terms imply communication and were effective in identifying relevant resources, such as "parent education" in ERIC and Wilson Social Sciences Abstracts. For example, "parent school relationship," "family school relationship," "parent education," "parent teacher cooperation," "parent counseling," and "parent teacher conferences" all returned some potentially useful resources in searches of the ERIC database. In the LISA database, successful strategies included combining "parent or parents" and "information needs."

Most searches required a fair amount of "sifting," whether using subject headings or keyword approaches. Many returns were related to "parents communicating with their kids," for example. Still, a substantial number of returns from all databases focused on some form of connecting with parents of young children.

Tentative Topics for Proposed Educational Materials

Chapter 7 includes discussion of creating videotaped or audiotaped "vignettes" or brief case studies for programs to use in their efforts to connect with parents around issues of school readiness.

These "vignettes" could depict such situations as:

- Incidents of affective synchrony between parents and their infants—what they are and how parents can enhance them.

- Adults using a variety of strategies to support young children's ability to stay with a task in spite of distractions around them.

- Adults using a variety of strategies to help children build the "approach skills" that they will need to form relationships with peers.

- A family preparing for a visit to a child's prospective preschool or kindergarten class, including possible interactions with the teacher.

- A parent and child visiting the child's prospective class before beginning to attend, including some possible interactions with the staff.

- Parents helping children prepare for events such as having to comply with adult requests (e.g., standing in line quietly) even though the child would prefer to do something else.

- A child's experience with taking the school bus to preschool or kindergarten, with a focus on how adults might help him or her prepare for interactions with adults and peers.

Symposium Participants

Susan Matoba Adler
Assistant Professor
University of Illinois at Urbana-Champaign

Brenda Baker
Program Associate
Voices for Illinois Children
Chicago, IL

Betty Bardige
Chair
A.L. Mailman Family Foundation
Cambridge, MA

Stacy Blais
Parent Representative
HIPPY USA
Pawtucket, RI

Charlotte Brantley
Senior Director
Ready to Learn
PBS
Alexandria, VA

Jerlean Daniel
Associate Professor, Applied Developmental Psychology
University of Pittsburgh
Sewickley, PA

Patricia A. Edwards
Professor
Michigan State University
East Lansing, MI

Clare Eldredge
Early Education Director
Academic Development Institute
Lincoln, IL

*Brad Everett
Principal, Pekin Public School District 108 &
Board of Directors, National Even Start Association
Pekin, IL

Samantha Fishman
Parent Representative, Parents as Teachers, & Coordinator,
Parents Involved Network
Norristown, PA

Susan Fowler
Dean, College of Education
University of Illinois at Urbana-Champaign

Rozita La Gorce Green
Executive Vice President
National Black Child Development Institute
Washington, DC

Merle Greene
Early Childhood Education Director
HIPPY USA
New York, NY

Kay Gudmestad
President & CEO
MELD
Minneapolis, MN

*David Harris
Director of Regional Policy and Florida Philanthropy
The John D. and Catherine T. MacArthur Foundation
Jupiter, FL

*Kirk Harris
Senior Group Vice President and General Counsel
Family Support America
Chicago, IL

Harriet Heath
Director
The Parent Center, Bryn Mawr College
Haverford, PA

Kathleen M. Hebbeler
Program Manager
SRI International
Davis, CA

*Kay Henderson
Early Childhood Division Administrator
Illinois State Board of Education
Springfield, IL

Bruce Hershfield
Program Director
Child Welfare League of America
Washington, DC

Lilian Katz
Co-Director
ERIC Clearinghouse on Elementary and Early Childhood Education
University of Illinois at Urbana-Champaign

Lisa Lee
Program Director
Parent Services Project, Inc.
San Rafael, CA

Claire Lerner
Child Development Specialist
ZERO TO THREE
National Center for Infants, Toddlers & Families
Washington, DC

M. Elena Lopez
Senior Consultant
Harvard Family Research Project
Mountain View, CA

Ruth Mayden
Director, Program for Families with Young Children
Annie E. Casey Foundation
Baltimore, MD

Jean Paine Mendoza
Graduate Student
University of Illinois at Urbana-Champaign

Doug Powell
Head, Department of Child Development and Family Studies
Purdue University
West Lafayette, IN

Aisha Ray
Director
Bilingual/ESL-Multicultural Program
Erikson Institute for Graduate Study in Child Development
Chicago, IL

Anne S. Robertson
Coordinator, National Parent Information Network
University of Illinois at Urbana-Champaign

Gloria Rodriguez
Founder
AVANCE
San Antonio, TX

Mary Eunice Romero
Program Coordinator, Native Language Shift and Retention Project
University of Arizona
Tucson, AZ

Fred Rothbaum
Chair, Eliot-Pearson Department of Child Development
Tufts University
Medford, MA

Dianne Rothenberg
Co-Director
ERIC Clearinghouse on Elementary and Early Childhood Education
University of Illinois at Urbana-Champaign

Wanda J. Roundtree
Director, Parenting Programs
National Black Child Development Institute
Bronx, NY

Rita San Miguel
Parent Representative
AVANCE
San Antonio, TX

Sue Stepleton
President & CEO
Parents As Teachers
St. Louis, MO

Ellen Swengel
Public Relations Coordinator
ERIC Clearinghouse on Elementary & Early Childhood Education
University of Illinois at Urbana-Champaign

Mark Testa
Associate Professor & Director, Children & Family Research Center
University of Illinois at Urbana-Champaign

Zachary Tift
Young Dads and Hmong Parents Coordinator
MELD
Minneapolis, MN

Teresa Vasconcelos
Professor
Lisbon Polytechnic Institute
Lisbon, PORTUGAL

Pat Wesley
Director, Partnerships for Inclusion
Frank Porter Graham Child Development Institute
Chapel Hill, NC

Laura Westberg
Reading Specialist
National Center for Family Literacy
Louisville, KY

----

*Participated in the pre-symposium listserv discussions but was unable to attend
the symposium because of last-minute circumstances.